The original and the best.

ONLY £8.99 except where priced

WORD 2000 MADE SIMPLE

OFFICE 2000 MADE SIMPLE

WINDOWS 98 MADE SIMPLE

THE INTERNET MADE SIMPLE SECOND EDITION

These books explain the basics of software packages and computer topics in a clear and simple manner, providing just enough information to get started. They are ideal for users who want an insight into software packages and computers without being overwhelmed by technical jargon

- Easy to Follow
- Task Based
- Jargon Free
- Easy Steps
- Practical
- Excellent Value

Visit our website http://www.madesimple.co.uk

COMPUTING MADE SIMPLE

NEW
Access 2000
Moira Stephen
0 7506 4182 7 1999

NEW
Access 2000 in Business
Moira Stephen 1999
7506 4611 X £11.99

Access 97 for Windows
Moira Stephen
0 7506 3800 1 1997

Access for Windows 95 (V.7)
Moira Stephen
0 7506 2818 9 1996

NEW
Adobe Acrobat & PDF
Graham Douglas
0 7506 4220 3 2000

NEW
Compuserve 2000
Keith Brindley
0 7506 4524 5 2000

NEW
Designing Internet Home Pages *Second Edition*
Lilian Hobbs
0 7506 4476 1 1999

NEW
ECDL Made Simple
Jacqueline Sherman 2000
0 7506 4835 X £14.99

NEW
Excel 2000
Stephen Morris
0 7506 4180 0 1999

NEW
Excel 2000 in Business
Stephen Morris 1999
0 7506 4609 8 £11.99

Excel 97 for Windows
Stephen Morris
0 7506 3802 8 1997

Excel for Windows 95 (V.7)
Stephen Morris
0 7506 2816 2 1996

NEW
Explorer 5.0
P K McBride
0 7506 4627 6 1999

Explorer 4.0
Sam Kennington
0 7506 3796 X 1998

NEW
FrontPage 2000
Nat McBride
0 7506 4598 9 1999

FrontPage 97
Nat McBride
0 7506 3941 5 1998

NEW
Internet In Colour *2nd Edition*
P K McBride 1999
0 7506 4576 8 £14.99

NEW
Internet for Windows 98
P K McBride
0 7506 4563 6 1999

Internet for Windows 95
P K McBride
0 7506 3846 X 1997

NEW
The iMac Made Simple
Keith Brindley
0 7506 4608 X 2000

NEW
Microsoft Money 99
Moira Stephen
0 7506 4305 6 1999

MS-DOS
Ian Sinclair
0 7506 2069 2 1994

Netscape Communicator 4.0
Sam Kennington
0 7506 4040 5 1998

NEW
Office 2000
P K McBride
0 7506 4179 7 1999

Office 97
P K McBride
0 7506 3798 6 1997

NEW
Outlook 2000
P K McBride
0 7506 4414 1 2000

NEW
Photoshop
Rod Wynne-Powell
0 7506 4334 X 1999

NEW
Powerpoint 2000
Moira Stephen
0 7506 4177 0 1999

Powerpoint 97 for Windows
Moira Stephen
0 7506 3799 4 1997

Powerpoint for Windows 95 (V.7)
Moira Stephen
0 7506 2817 0 1996

NEW
Publisher 2000
Moira Stephen
0 7506 4597 0 1999

Publisher 97
Moira Stephen
0 7506 3943 1 1998

NEW
Sage Accounts
P K McBride
0 7506 4413 3 1999

Searching the Internet
P K McBride
0 7506 3794 3 1998

Windows 98
P K McBride
0 7506 4039 1 1998

Windows 95
P K McBride
0 7506 2306 3 1995

Windows 3.1
P K McBride
0 7506 2072 2 1994

NEW
Windows CE
Craig Peacock
0 7506 4335 8 1999

Windows NT (V4)
Lilian Hobbs
0 7506 3511 8 1997

NEW
Word 2000
Keith Brindley
0 7506 4181 9 1999

NEW
Word 2000 in Business
Keith Brindley 2000
0 7506 4610 1 £11.99

Word 97 for Windows
Keith Brindley
0 7506 3801 X 1997

Word for Windows 95 (V.7)
Keith Brindley
0 7506 2815 4 1996

Works for Windows 95 (V.4)
P K McBride
0 7506 3396 4 1996

Outlook 2000 Made Simple

P. K. McBride

Made Simple
An imprint of Butterworth-Heinemann
Linacre House, Jordan Hill, Oxford OX2 8DP
A division of Reed Educational and Professional Publishing Ltd

A member of the Reed Elsevier plc group

OXFORD BOSTON JOHANNESBURG
MELBOURNE NEW DELHI SINGAPORE

First published 2000

British Library Cataloguing in Publication Data
A catalogue record for this book is available from the British Library

ISBN 0 7506 4414 1

Typeset by P.K.McBride, Southampton
Icons designed by Sarah Ward © 1994
Printed and bound in Great Britain

Contents

Preface

Outlook 2000 is the latest version of Microsoft's personal (and workgroup) organiser, and big brother to Outlook Express, the e-mail software that accompanies Internet Explorer. It has six modules: Contacts, Inbox, Calendar, Tasks, Journal and Notes.

Many features and methods of working are identical, or very similar across all the modules. The most central of these, including the Help system, are covered in the first two chapters.

Inbox, the e-mail application, will be the most important of these for most people, and it takes a substantial chunk of this book, occupying Chapters 4 and 5. But to send e-mail, you need someone to write to, so Contacts, the address book application, is covered earlier, in Chapter 3.

Calendar, Chapter 6, can help you to organise your time more efficiently, and to arrange meetings – especially with people within your networked group. Tasks, Chapter 7, will help you to keep track of current jobs; while Journal, Chapter 8, is useful for recording the work you have done. Notes, also in Chapter 8, can save a bit of paper and a lot of clutter!

This book one of a set covering the Office 2000 applications. The others are:

Access 2000 Made Simple by Moira Stephen

Excel 2000 Made Simple by Stephen Morris

FrontPage 2000 Made Simple by Nat McBride

Internet Explorer 5 Made Simple by P.K. McBride

Office 2000 Made Simple by P.K. McBride

PowerPoint 2000 Made Simple by Moira Stephen

Publisher 2000 Made Simple by Moira Stephen

Word 2000 Made Simple by Keith Brindley

1 Introducing Outlook

Outlook, the organiser

Outlook helps you to organise your office life and to work more effectively with colleagues and others. It manages this through a set of interlinked modules.

- **Inbox** is for e-mail. A cut-down version of this forms the basis of Outlook Express, the e-mail software that is packaged with Internet Explorer.
- **Calendar** is an electronic diary and meeting planner.
- **Contacts** is an address book, and a central start point for phone calls, e-mails, faxes and online meetings.
- **Tasks** helps you to log and monitor the progress of jobs.
- **Notes** are for brief, short-term reminders.
- **Journal** lets you log your activity within and beyond Outlook.

Take note

The whole is far greater than the parts! The interaction between these modules adds to their value enormously.

Menu bar

Toolbars

Outlook bar

Folder list

Main display

Inbox (Chapters 4 and 5)

When you open Inbox, Outbox or any folder in which messages are stored, the toolbar and menus display the e-mail management commands

Inbox is a part of Outlook's e-mail facilities. It is the most important part – this is where you read and manage incoming mail, and this is generally the most convenient place to write your new messages.

When you first start to use Inbox, the screen should look something like the one shown here, but Outlook allows you to customise the display in many and varied ways.

The contents of the selected folder are listed in the top pane

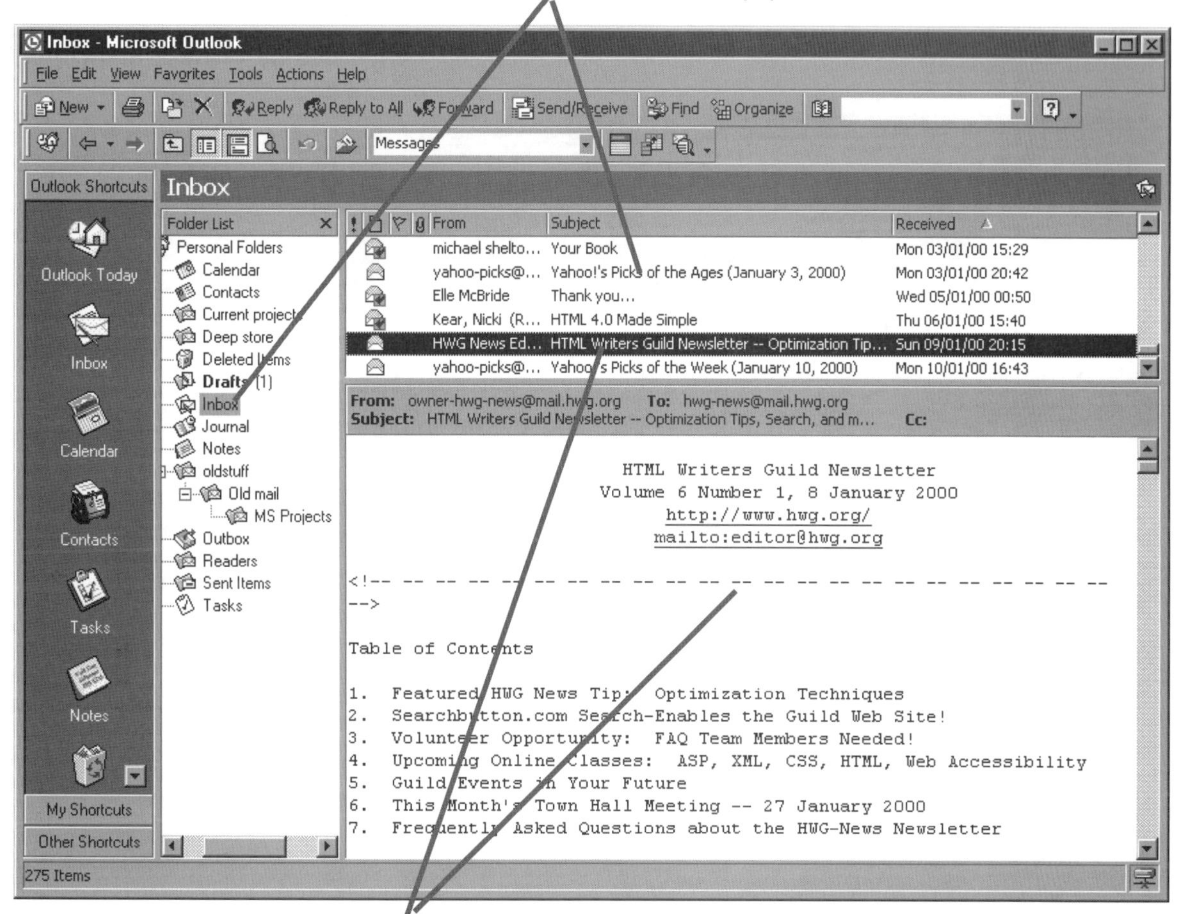

The Preview pane displays the selected message

Calendar (Chapter 6)

Calendar is an appointments diary with a few significant advantages over paper-based ones.

- Its different display modes will let you view and plan a day, week or month at a time;
- Outlook will give you reminders before your meetings;
- links to Contacts and the e-mail system make it simple to send invitations and other material to online colleagues;
- in a networked organisation, calendars can be opened online so that others can check your availability for meetings.

Calendar seen here in its 7-day week mode. Note the Taskpad in the lower right – it can be useful to be see upcoming meetings and deadlines at the same time (though it can sometimes be disheartening!)

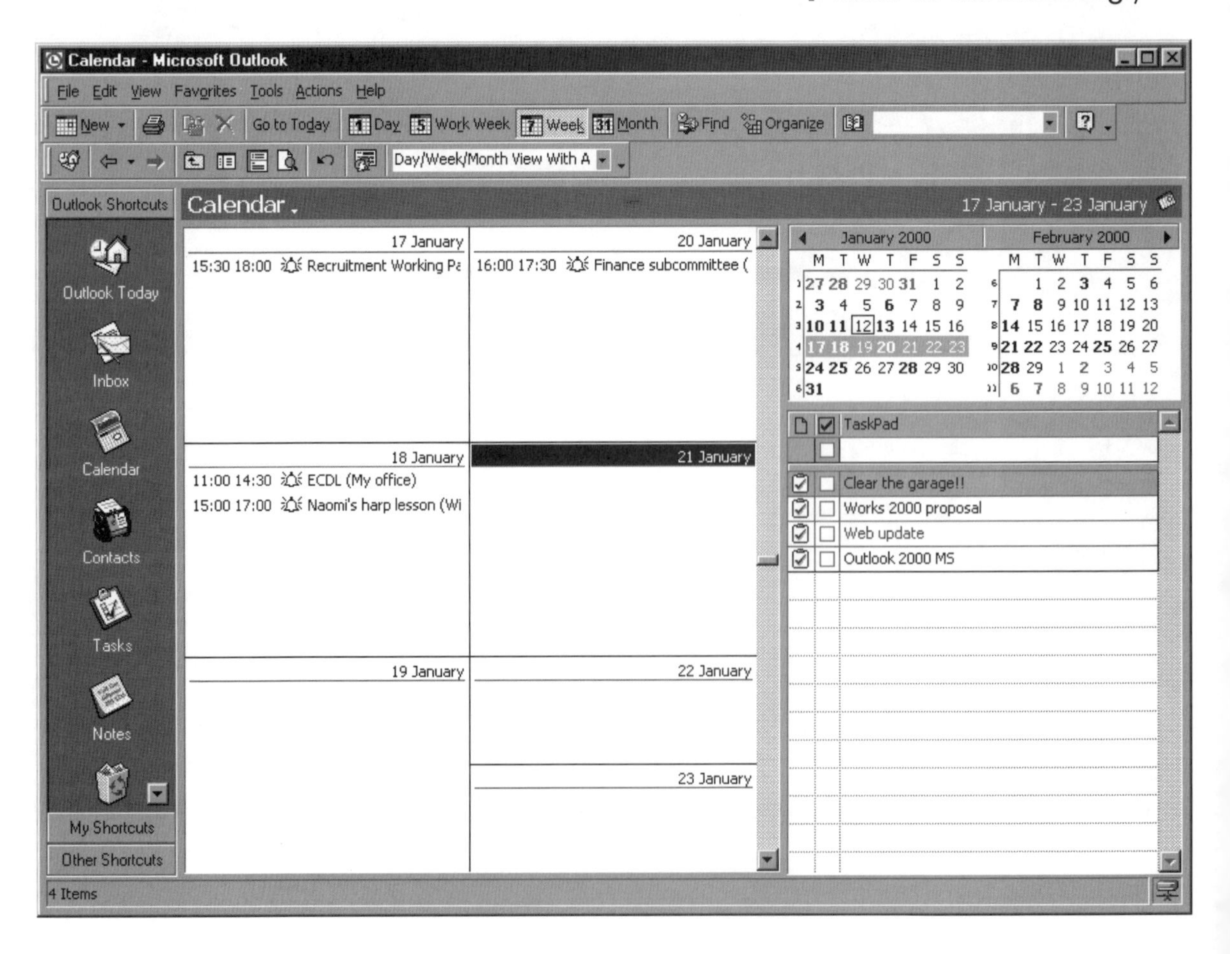

Contacts (Chapter 3)

Contacts is an interactive address book. You can write a letter, send an e-mail, set up a meeting, allocate a task or phone a contact from within this area – the system will pick up and use the relevant details in each case. It also keeps a record of e-mails received from or sent to your contacts, meetings with them and of phone calls (if required).

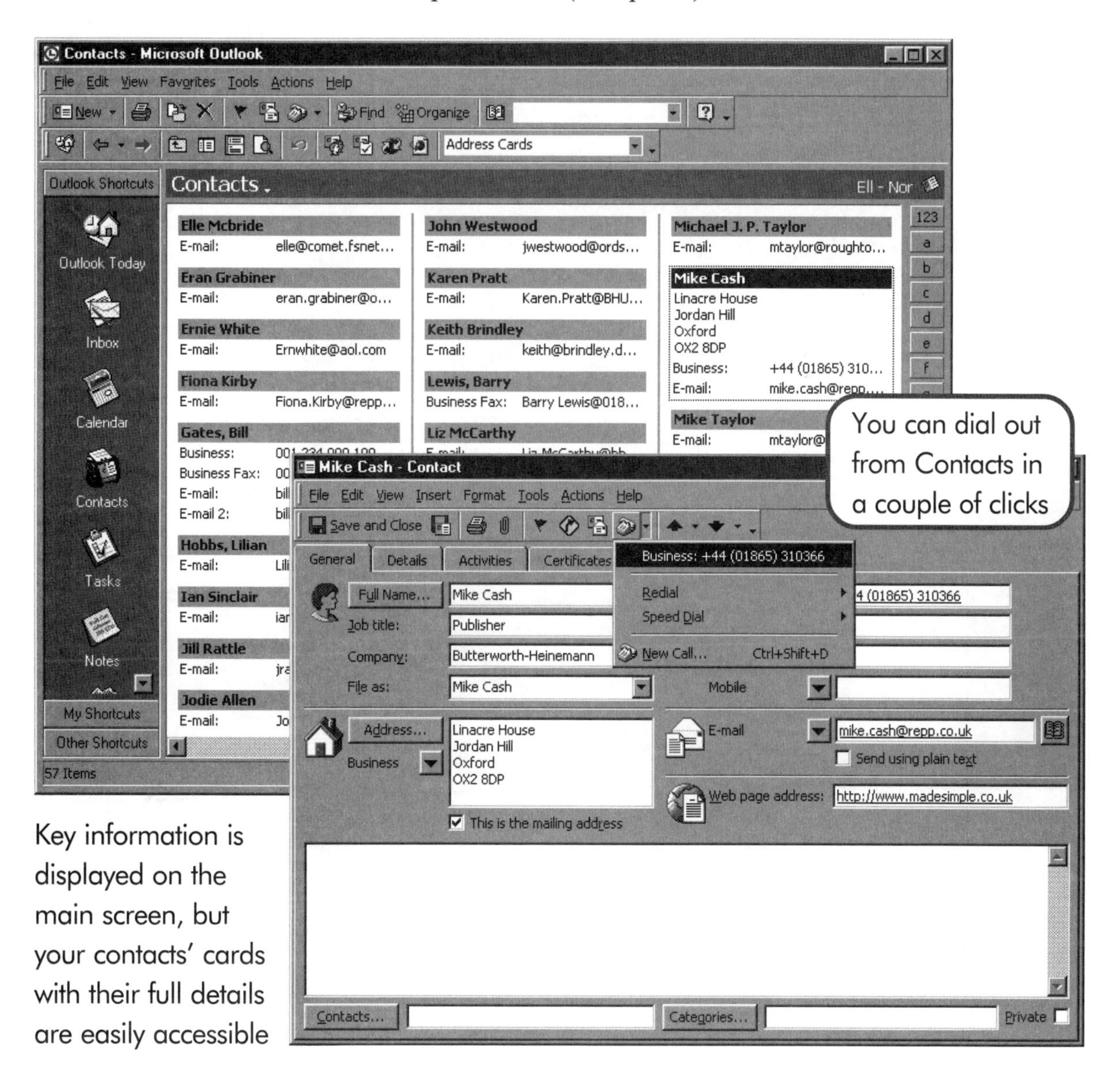

Key information is displayed on the main screen, but your contacts' cards with their full details are easily accessible

Tasks (Chapter 7)

In most of its display modes, the Calendar includes a Taskpad, where current tasks are listed and can be added to or edited. If required, you can focus on your tasks through the Task window. This gives you a better overview, showing more information about each task and offering alternative ways to organise the display to make different aspects more visible.

Take note

You may not want to use all of Outlook's facilities. Most people only use a fraction of any software's capabilities – but we all use a different fraction.

Each window has its own set of toolbars and menus, but there are many common buttons and commands

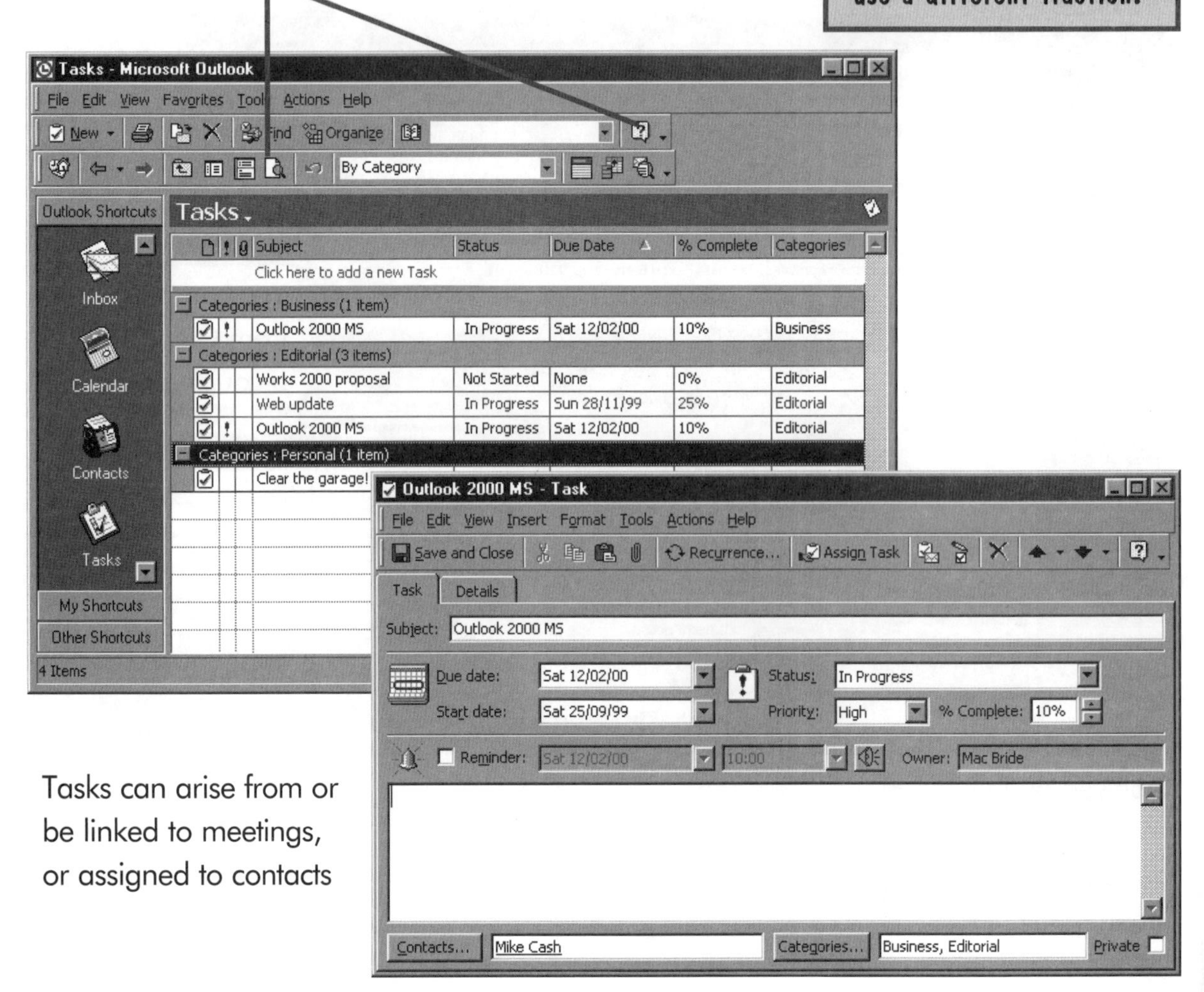

Tasks can arise from or be linked to meetings, or assigned to contacts

Notes and Journal (Chapter 8)

These two small applications should not be overlooked.

Notes are computerised Post-It™ notes – and just as handy for those of us who have to leave messages for ourselves! The notes can be 'stuck' anywhere on the screen, but are stored in the Notes area – and it's there that you need to go to manage them.

The **Journal** can be used to record the time spent on phone calls and on jobs within Outlook and elsewhere on your computer. Where the work is related to any of your Contacts, the records can also be seen on their Activities panels (see page 127).

In this Notes display mode, the top three lines of all notes can be viewed

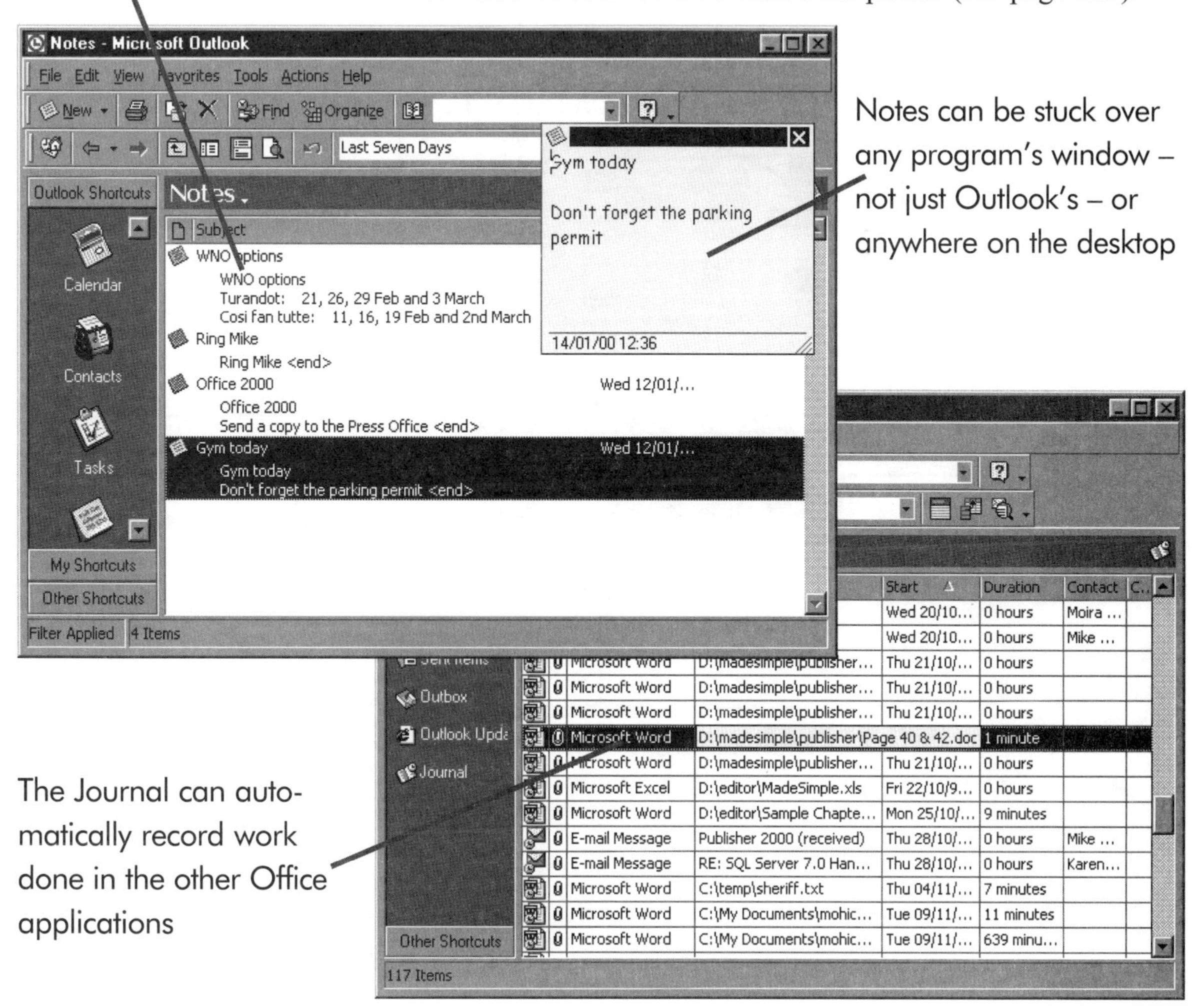

Notes can be stuck over any program's window – not just Outlook's – or anywhere on the desktop

The Journal can automatically record work done in the other Office applications

Setting up

Basic steps

If you haven't already installed Outlook 2000, do so now! And if it is installed, you may want to check – and adjust – which components are present. The routines are almost identical, and need your Office 2000 (or Outlook 2000) CD in the drive.

1 If the Setup/Update does not run automatically, use Windows Explorer to run Setup.exe on the CD.

2 Click ⊞ to open the Outlook folder.

3 For each feature:

To install, select Run from My Computer

If short of disk space, select Run from CD

If it may not be needed, select Installed on First Use.

4 Click Install/Update Now.

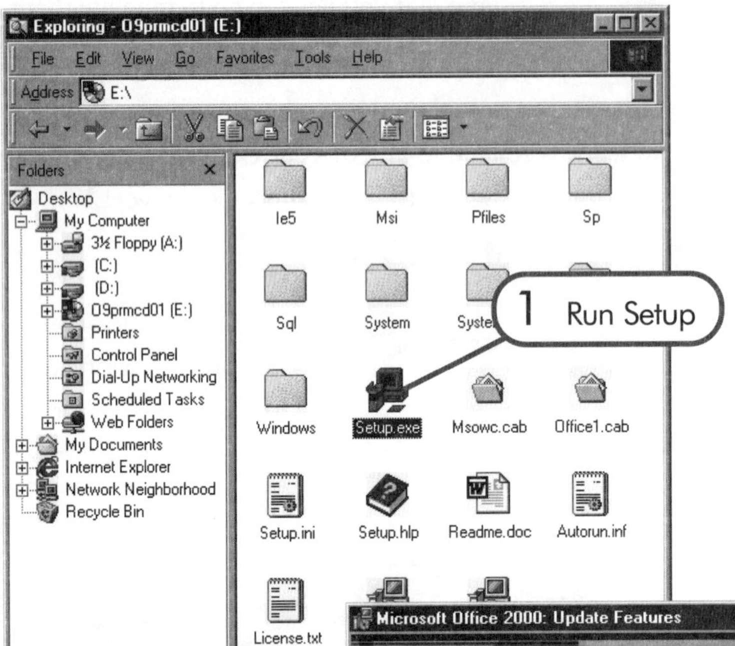

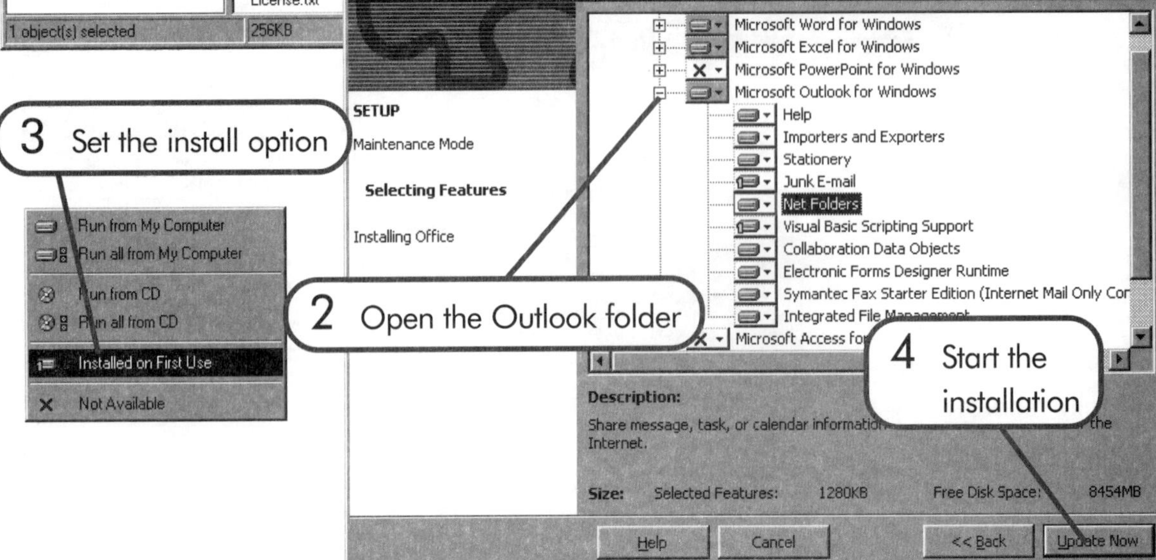

Basic steps

1 Click Next to get going.
2 Select the e-mail software to draw from.
3 Click Next.

- ❑ If the wizard needs to make any changes to your system, you will be asked to OK them.

Take note

If your PC had no e-mail software on it before installing Outlook, you will be asked for the details of your e-mail connection.

Startup Wizard

When Outlook starts for the first time, the Startup Wizard will run to help you configure Outlook 2000. It is brief and to the point, it's main purpose being to collect details of your e-mail connection, Address Book and other existing settings. Just tell the wizard which e-mail software to draw the information from, and set it off.

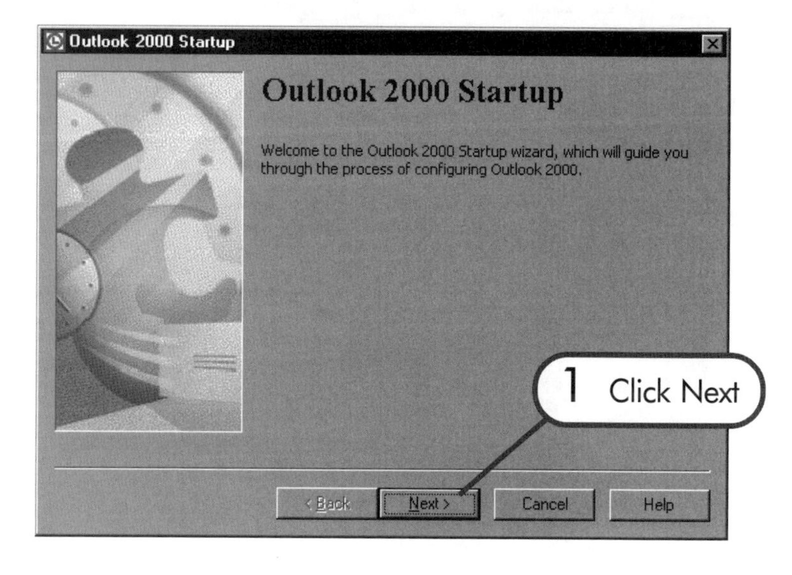

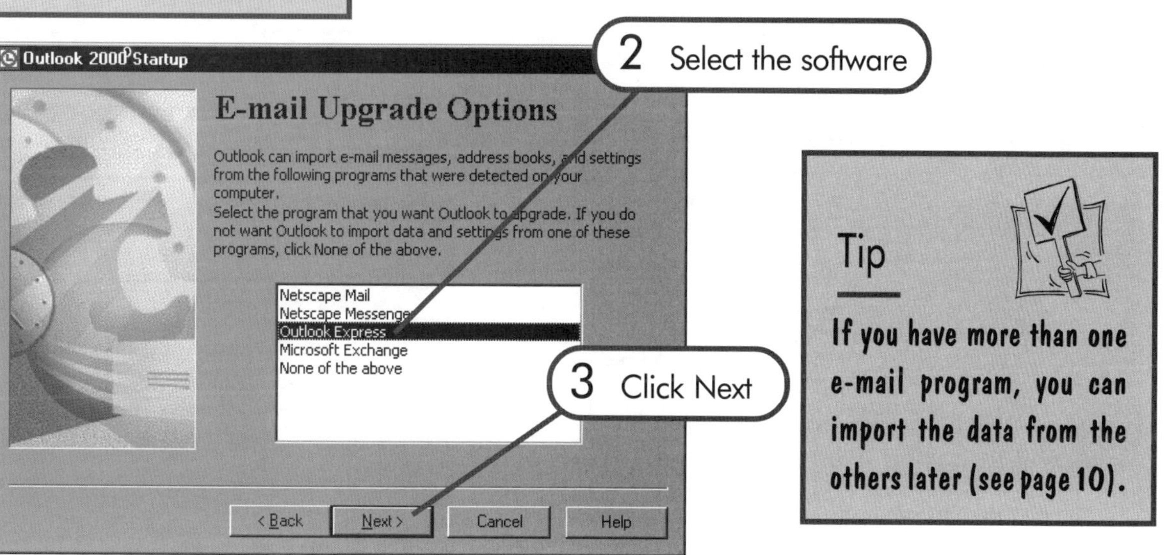

Tip

If you have more than one e-mail program, you can import the data from the others later (see page 10).

Importing data

Basic steps

The Startup Wizard will bring in the main data from your existing e-mail software, but you may well have other e-mail related data on your system. The Import and Export Wizard can pull in data from a variety of sources – and export it in different formats if needed.

1 Open the File menu and select Import and Export …

❑ Importing e-mail data

2 Select Import… and the type of data.

3 Select the application.

4 Set the options – these vary with the action.

5 At the Import Summary dialog box, click Save in Inbox and click OK.

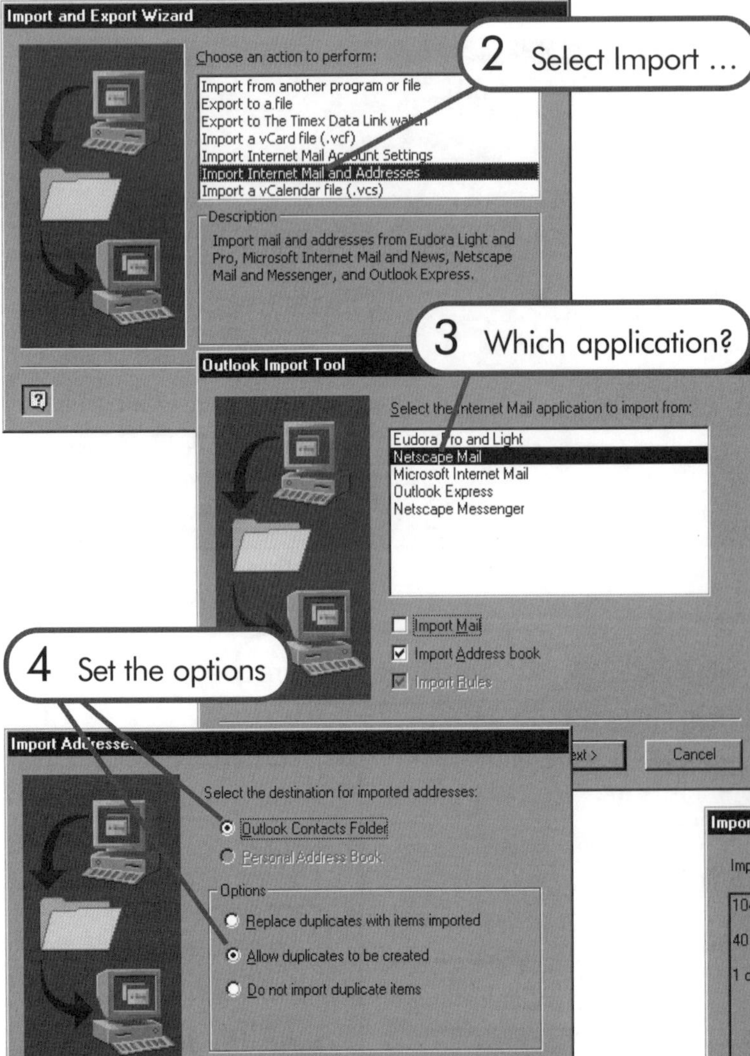

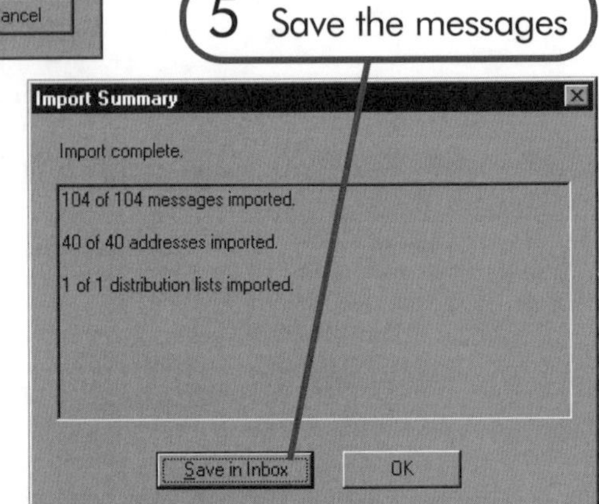

- ❑ Importing files

6 Select Import from another program or file.

7 Select the file type.

8 Browse for the file and decide how you want duplicates to be treated.

9 Select the folder to import into.

10 Check the details, and if you are sure you want to go ahead – imports cannot be undone – click Finish.

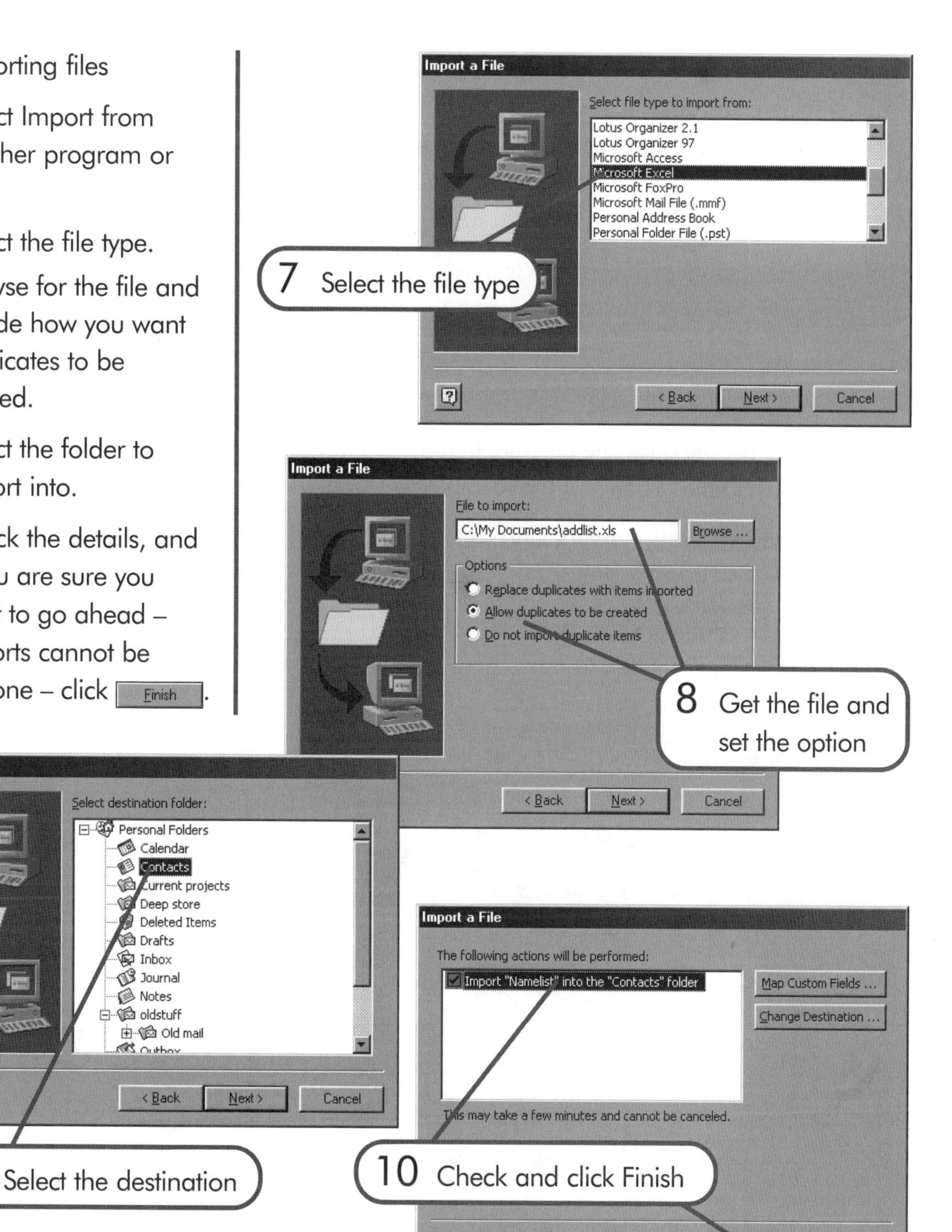

Common features

Though Outlook is powerful and packed with features, it is not difficult to use. One of the main reasons for this is that many of the same features and tools – perhaps with minor variations – are present in different modules. Master one module, and you are over half-way to mastering the rest.

There are three examples of common features on this page. You will meet many more as you work through the book.

- You can use the same Find (or Advanced Find) routines to find contacts, messages, appointments or notes.
- You can use the Back and Forward buttons, and the drop-down list to move between the modules as you work.
- You can start a new entry for any module from within any other.

Click New to start a new entry for the current module …

… or pick from the full set of New options in the drop-down list

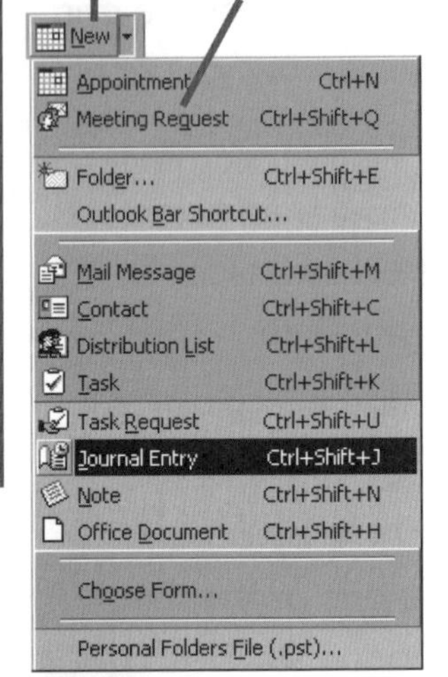

Back and Forward let you switch quickly between modules

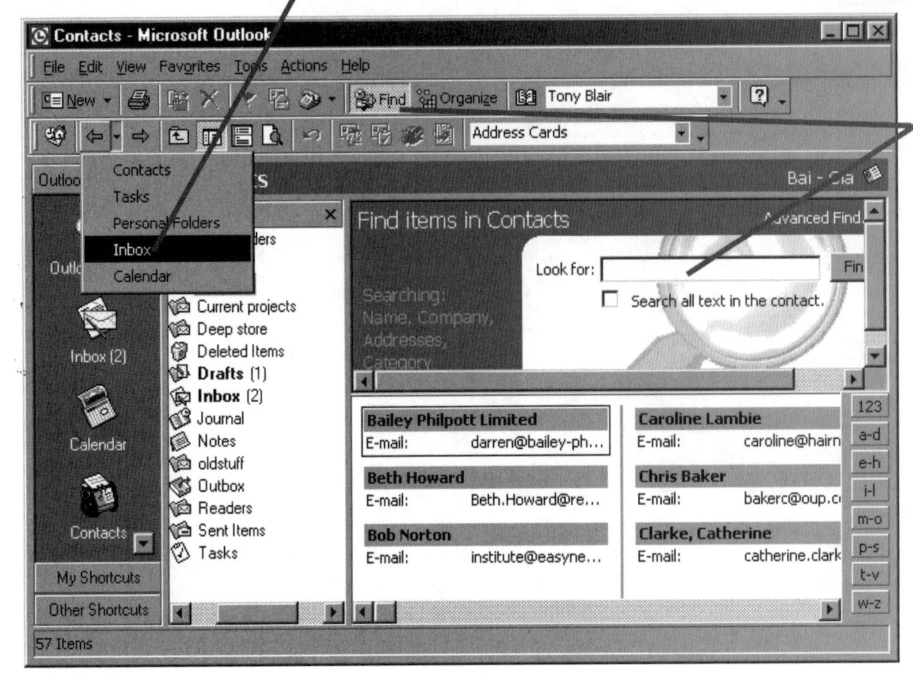

The Find routine looks and works the same in all modules

Common tools

Take note

These common tools are covered in Chapter 3, when we look at the first of the modules.

Some tools are present in all (or most) modules, and are always used in the same or very similar ways.

The tools in the **Standard** toolbar mainly apply to the currently selected item – e-mail message, individual contact, meeting or task details and the like.

The tools in the **Advanced** toolbar mainly apply to the layout of the screen and the details within it.

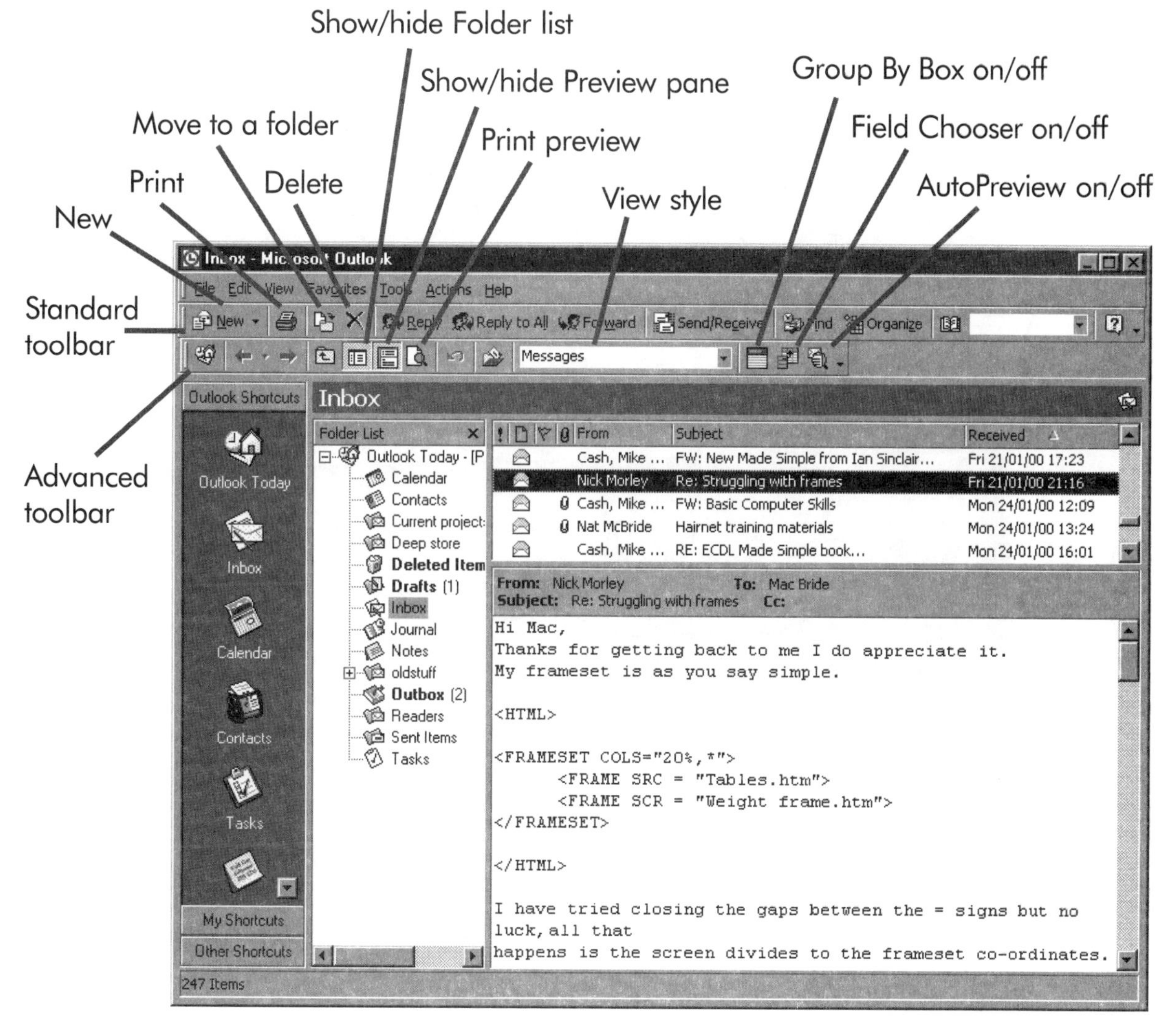

The Outlook Bar

Basic steps

The shortcuts in the Outlook Bar offer a one-click way to switch between modules – and beyond. There are ready-made shortcuts to *My Computer*, *My Documents* and *Favorites*, and you can add links to selected folders on your computer.

Outlook starts with three shortcut groups. You can move the shortcuts around between them, add new groups or remove any that you do not use. It's useful to know early on how to add and remove shortcuts.

- ❑ Adding a shortcut

1. Open the bar and right-click on its background – not on an existing shortcut.
2. Select Outlook Bar Shortcut…

To use a shortcut, click on it

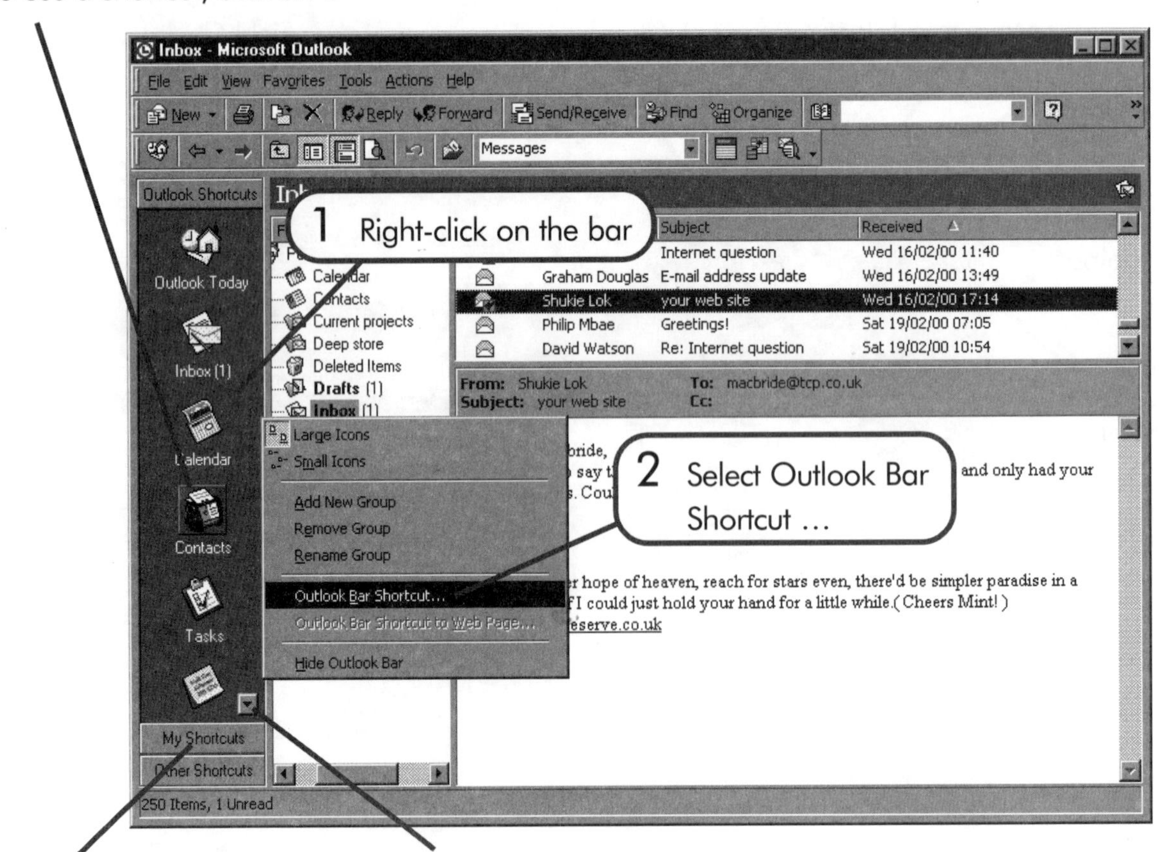

To open a different bar, click on its name

Click the arrows to reach the shortcuts that are out of sight

- To link to a module

3 Select it from the display or from the drop-down list.

Or

- To add a link to a folder

4 Select File System from the Look in: list, then browse through your system for the folder.

5 Click OK.

- Removing a shortcut

6 Right-click on it and select Remove from Outlook Bar from the pop-up menu.

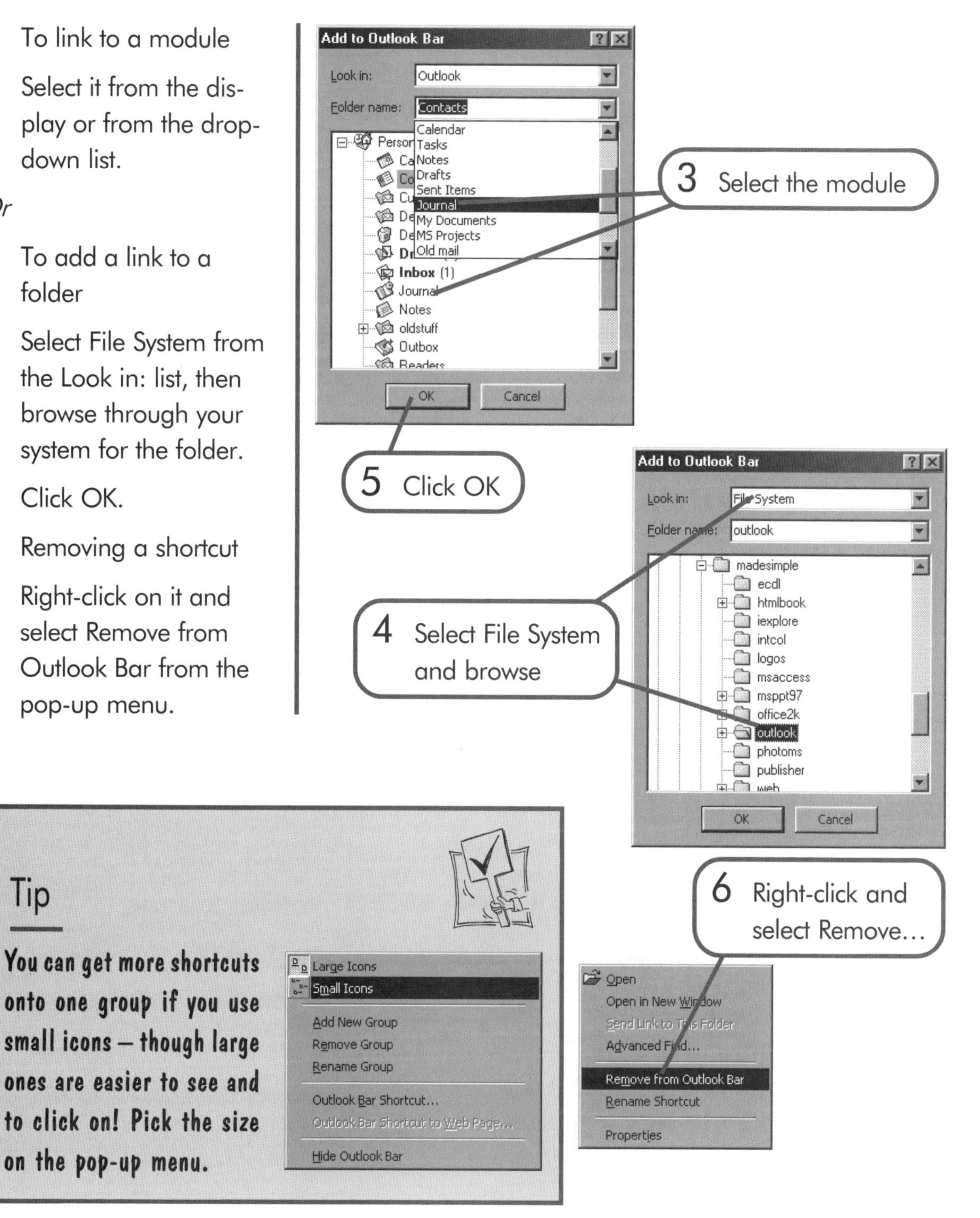

Tip

You can get more shortcuts onto one group if you use small icons – though large ones are easier to see and to click on! Pick the size on the pop-up menu.

Customising the Bar

Basic steps

1. Open the Outlook Bar and right-click on the background.
2. Select Add New Group.
3. The new group will appear at the bottom of the Bar with 'New Group' highlighted, ready for editing. Replace this with a suitable name.

Adding a new group

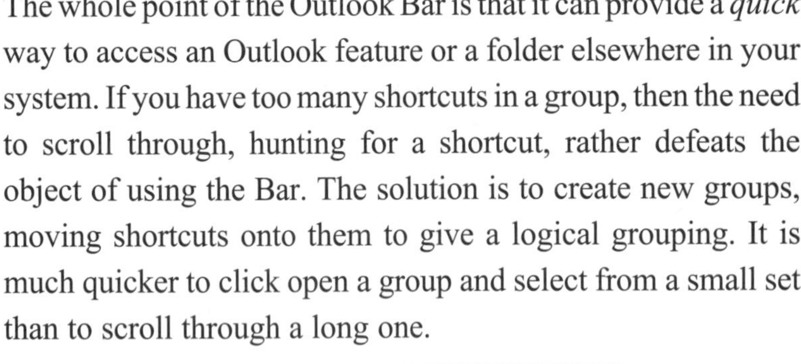

The whole point of the Outlook Bar is that it can provide a *quick* way to access an Outlook feature or a folder elsewhere in your system. If you have too many shortcuts in a group, then the need to scroll through, hunting for a shortcut, rather defeats the object of using the Bar. The solution is to create new groups, moving shortcuts onto them to give a logical grouping. It is much quicker to click open a group and select from a small set than to scroll through a long one.

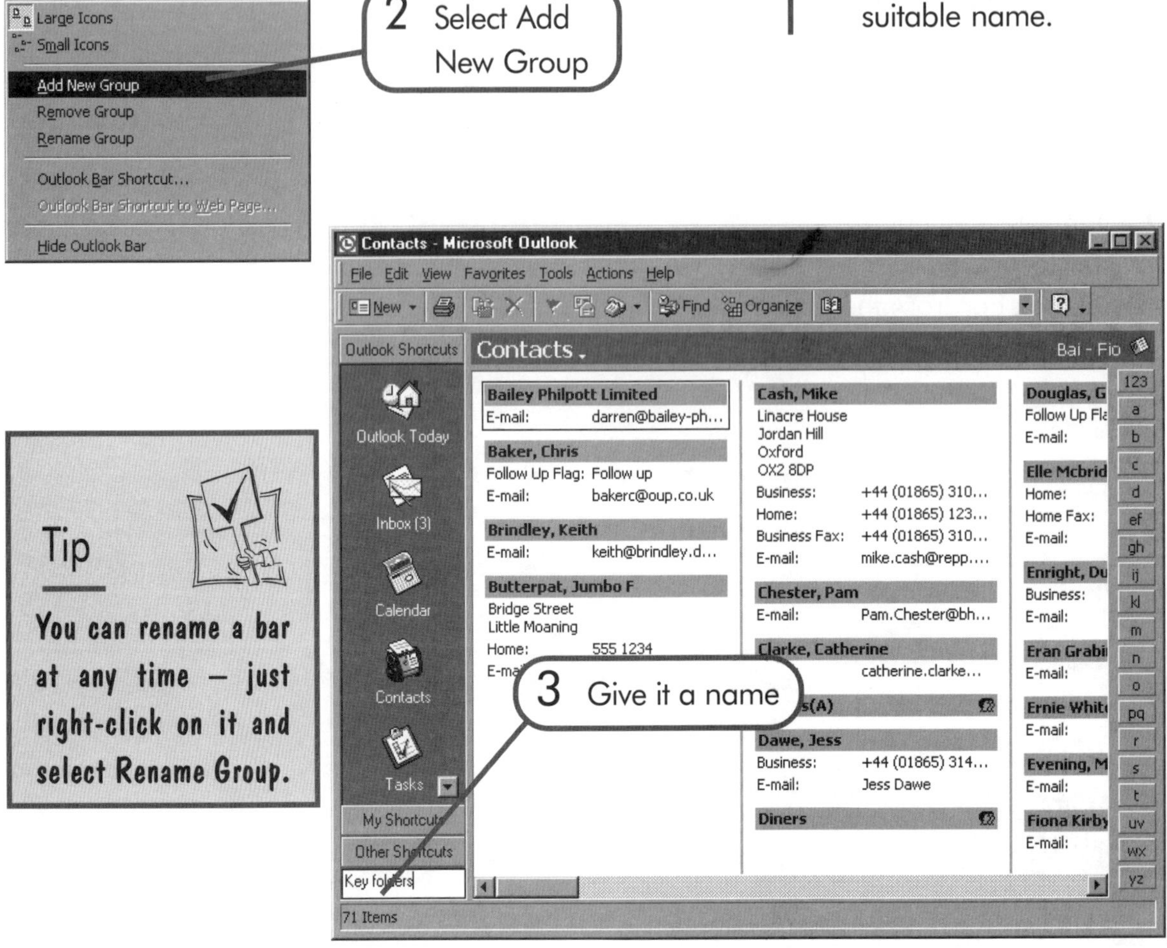

Tip

You can rename a bar at any time – just right-click on it and select Rename Group.

Basic steps

1. Click on the shortcut.
2. Drag it up or down the bar – a thin line will show you where it will go when released.
3. To move it onto a different group, point to the group's name and wait for it to open.
4. Release the mouse button when the shortcut is where you want it to go.

Moving shortcuts

Shortcuts can easily be moved, both within a group and from one group to another – simply drag them to where you want them.

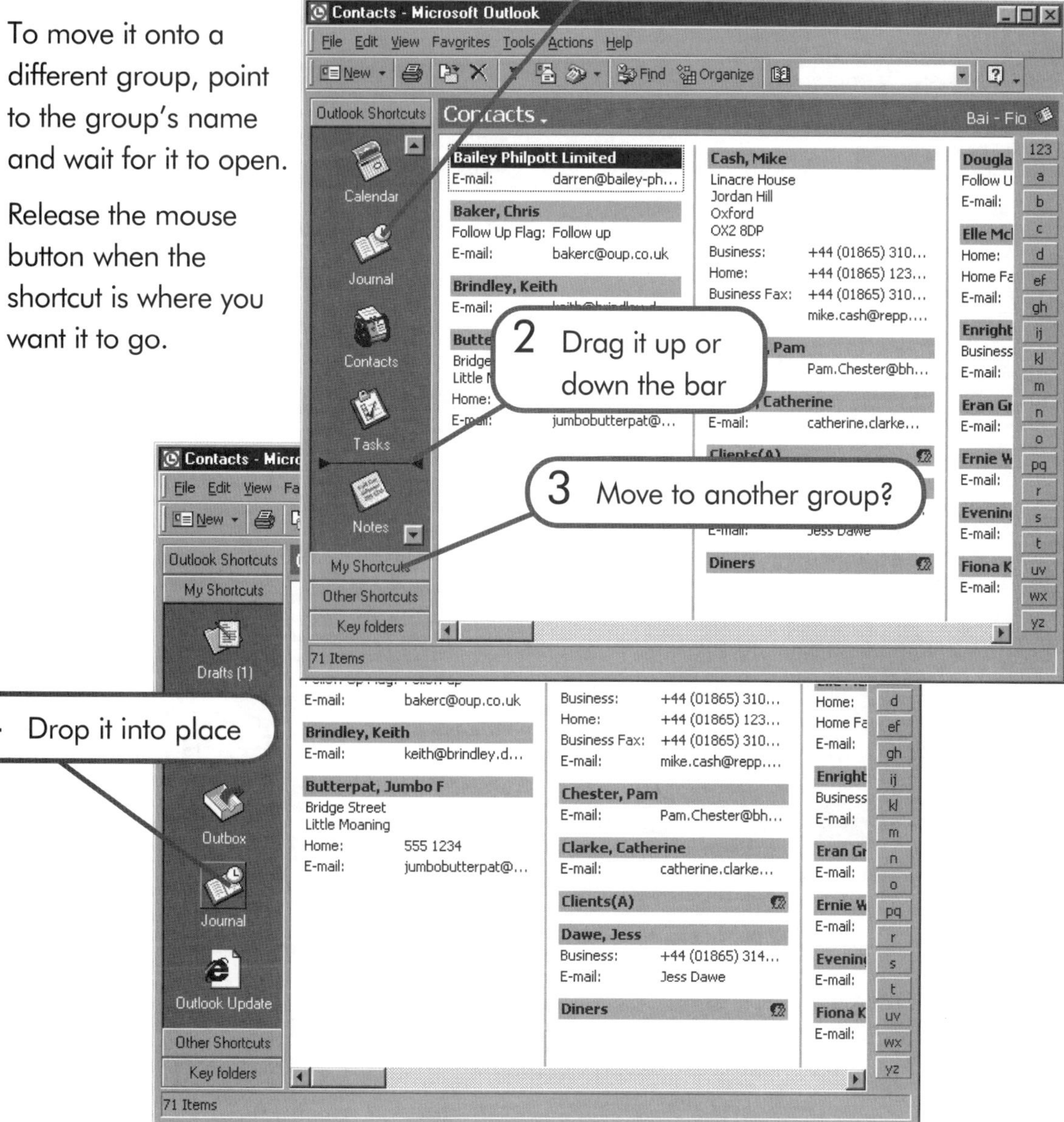

Outlook Today

Basic steps

This displays summaries of the things that need dealing with today and in the near future. You can choose what information to display, and how, through the simple Customise routine.

Outlook Today can be set as the start-up screen, to help you to get organised at the start of the day.

1. Click the Outlook Today icon in the Outlook Bar.
2. Click Customize Outlook Today...
3. Tick Startup if wanted.

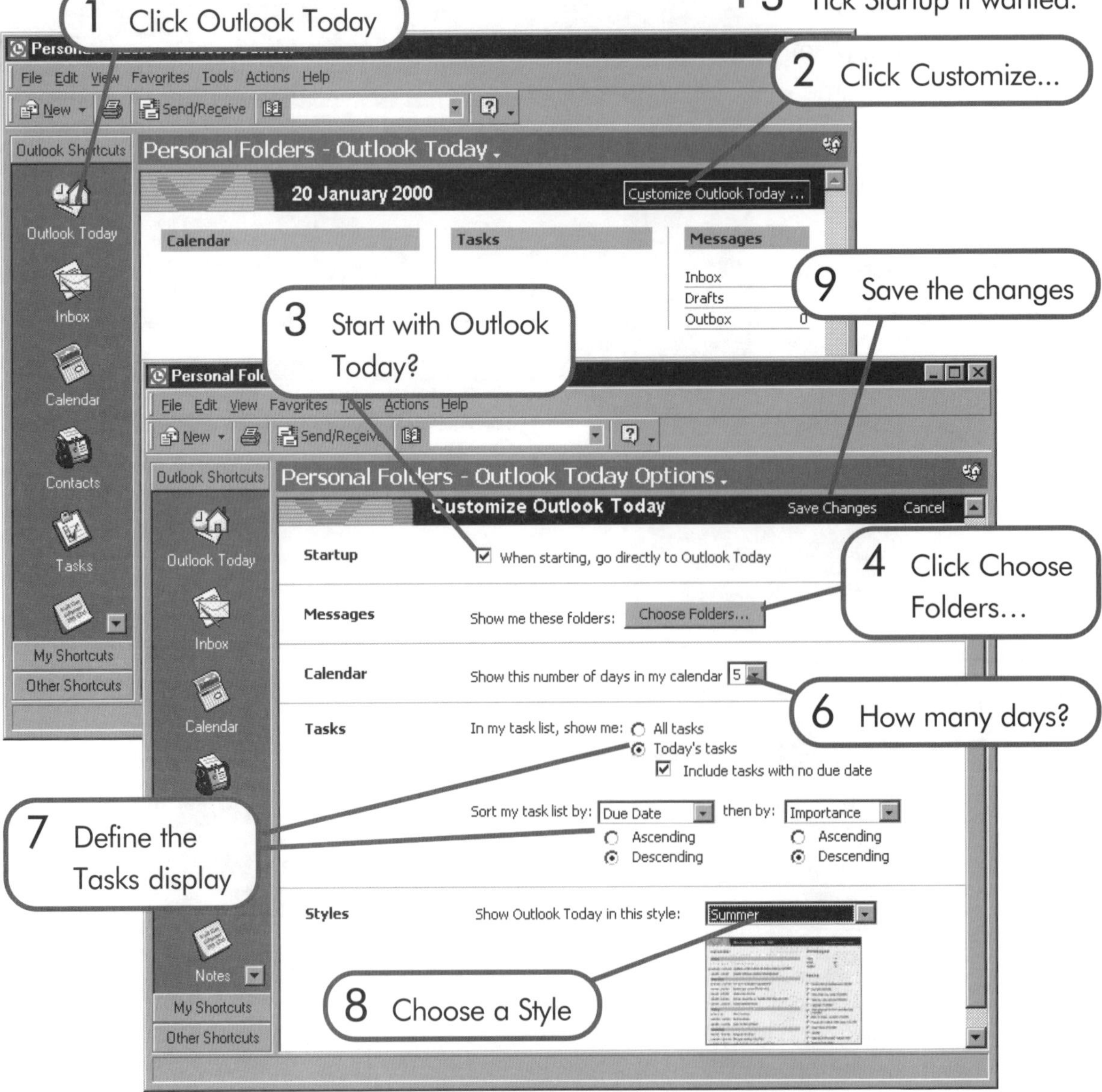

4 Click the Choose Folders… button.

5 Tick the folders you want to include then click OK.

6 For the Calendar, set the number of days to show.

7 Choose which Tasks to show, and how to arrange them.

8 Choose a Style.

9 Click Save Changes.

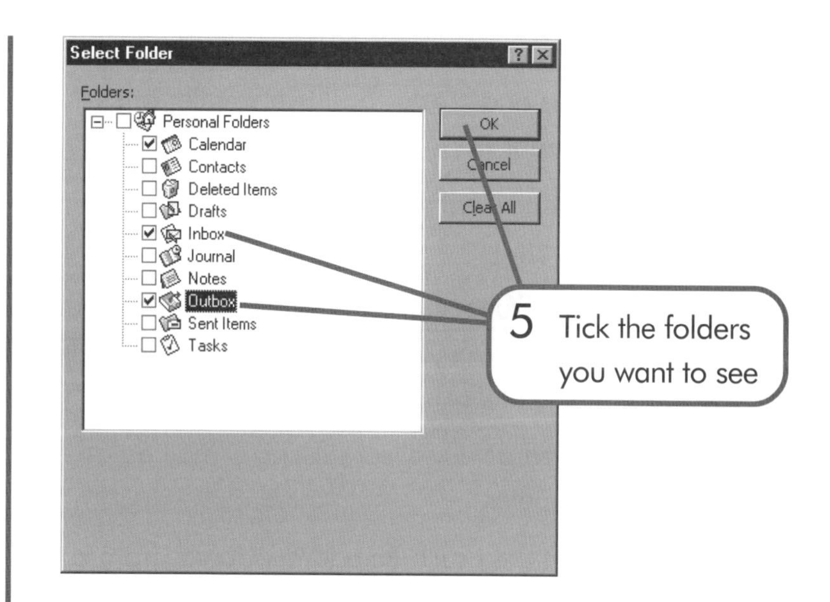

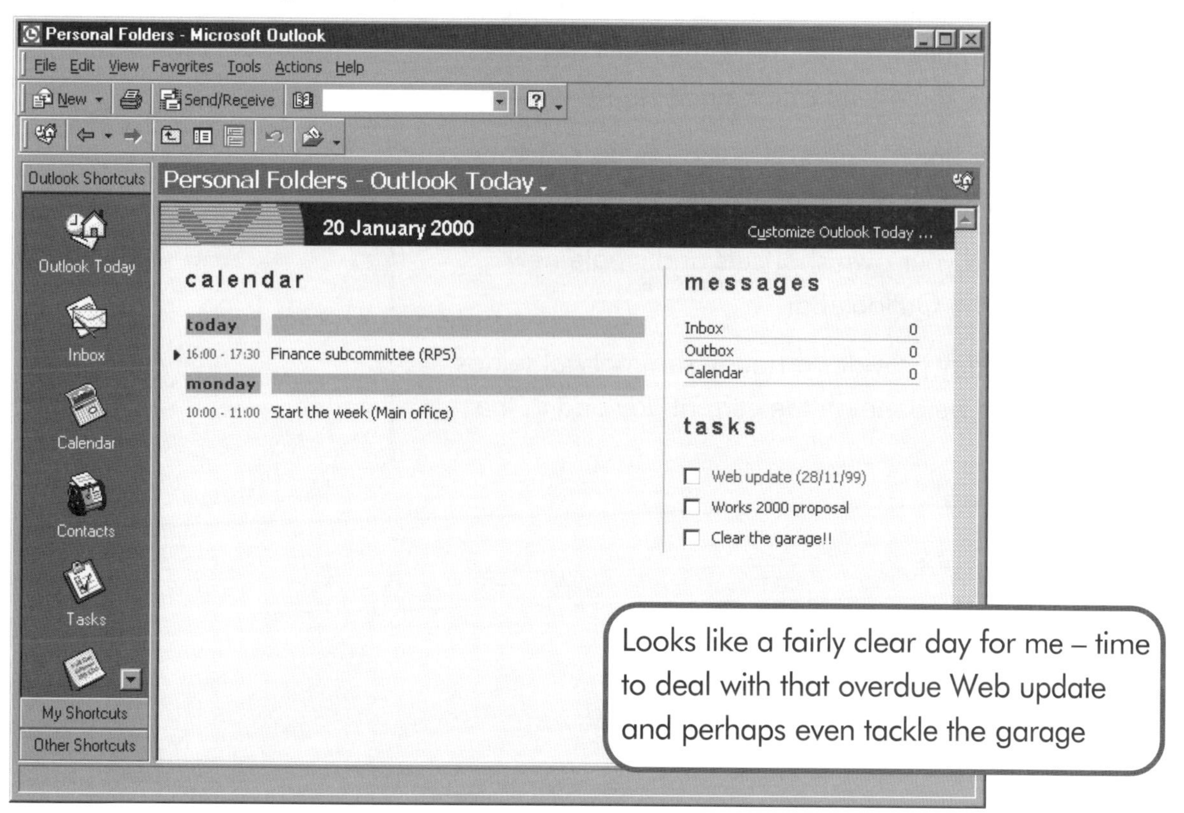

Summary

- ❑ Outlook consists of four major modules – Inbox, Calendar, Contacts and Tasks, and two smaller ones – Notes and Journal.
- ❑ You can start a new entry for any module from within any other.
- ❑ When installing Outlook, if you are not sure that you will need a feature, you can set it to be installed on first use, or run from the CD.
- ❑ The Startup Wizard will collect existing e-mail data from your computer.
- ❑ You can Import data such as address books, from a range of applications for use with Outlook.
- ❑ All of the modules have many features in common. You will normally find that the same routine is used wherever the same kind of job needs to be done.
- ❑ The Outlook Bar gives you a quick way to switch between modules and to open frequently-used folders.
- ❑ You can add your own shortcuts and create new groups on the Outlook Bar.
- ❑ Outlook Today provides a handy summary of things that need to be done on the current day and in the near future.

2 Help!

Office Assistant

Office Assistant is a friendly front-end to the Help system. It keeps an eye on what you are doing, so that, when you call on it for help, it will be ready with some likely topics. If it has guessed wrong – as it often does – you simply tell it what you need help with, and it will come up with the goods.

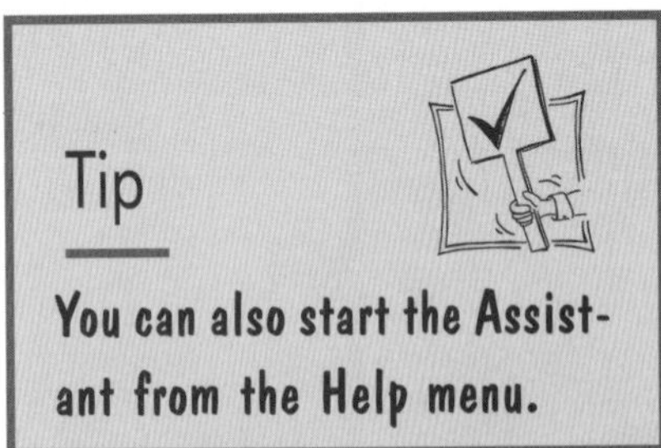

Tip

You can also start the Assistant from the Help menu.

Basic steps

1. If the Assistant is not visible, click the query icon to wake it up.
2. If a relevant topic is listed, click on it to display the page.

Otherwise

3. Type a word or phrase to describe the Help you want.
4. Click Search.

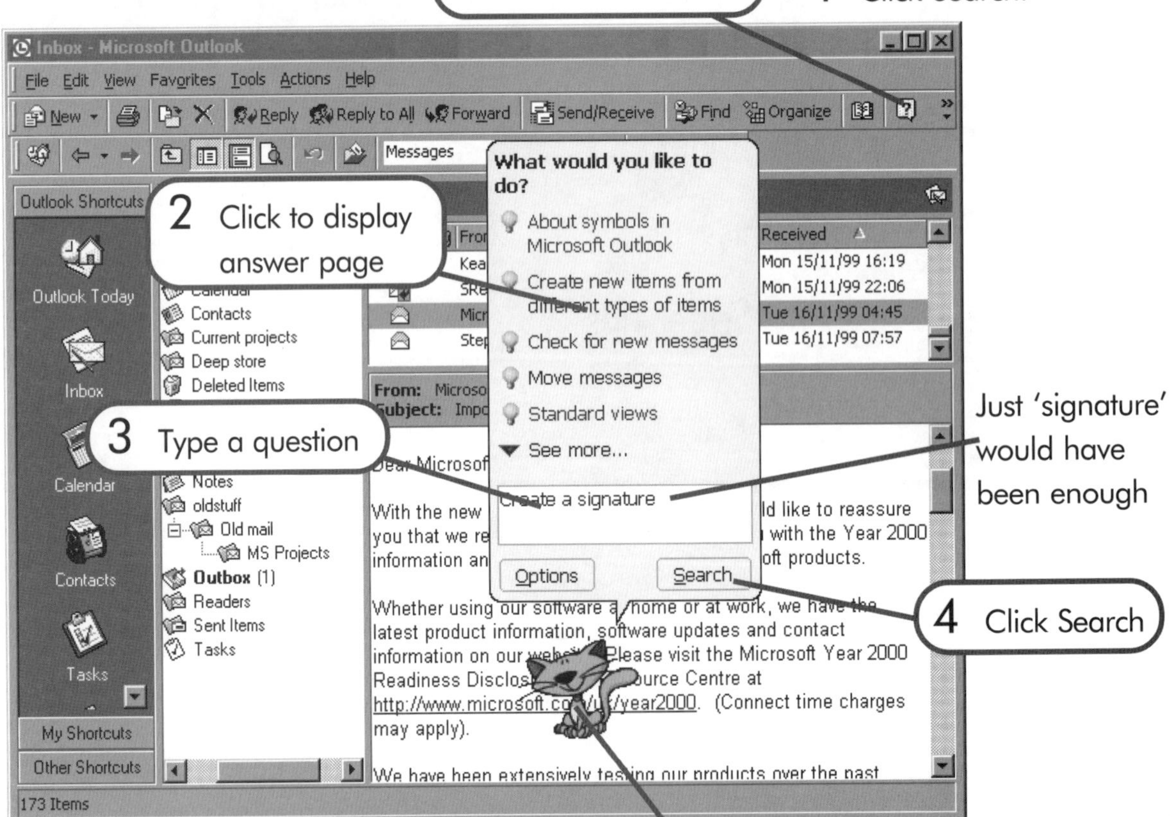

5 You will be offered a list of topics – click the one that is closest to your question.

6 If you are offered a set of links to pages, click on one to read it.

7 Read the page, following any underlined links if they look useful.

8 Click [print icon] for a printed copy of the Help page.

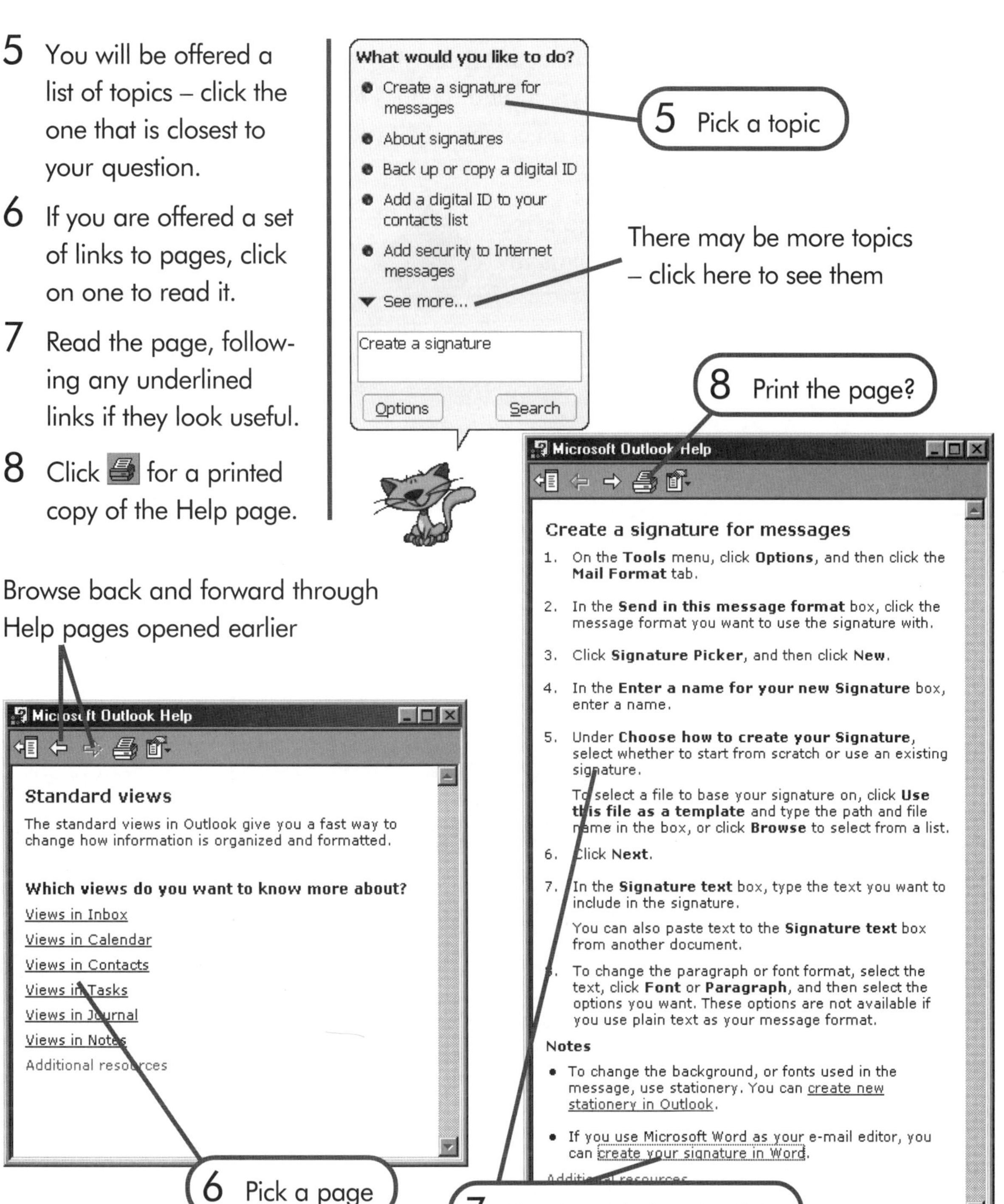

Customising Office Assistant

Basic steps

The Assistant has eight alternative ‘personalities’ for you to choose from, and – rather more usefully – a set of options to control how it works. And you can turn it off completely if you find it more irritating than entertaining!

The Logo is the least obtrusive

The Genius is one of the best animations

1. Click Options on the Assistant’s dialog box or its right-click menu.
2. Select an image on the Gallery panel.
3. Set the Options as required.
4. Click OK.

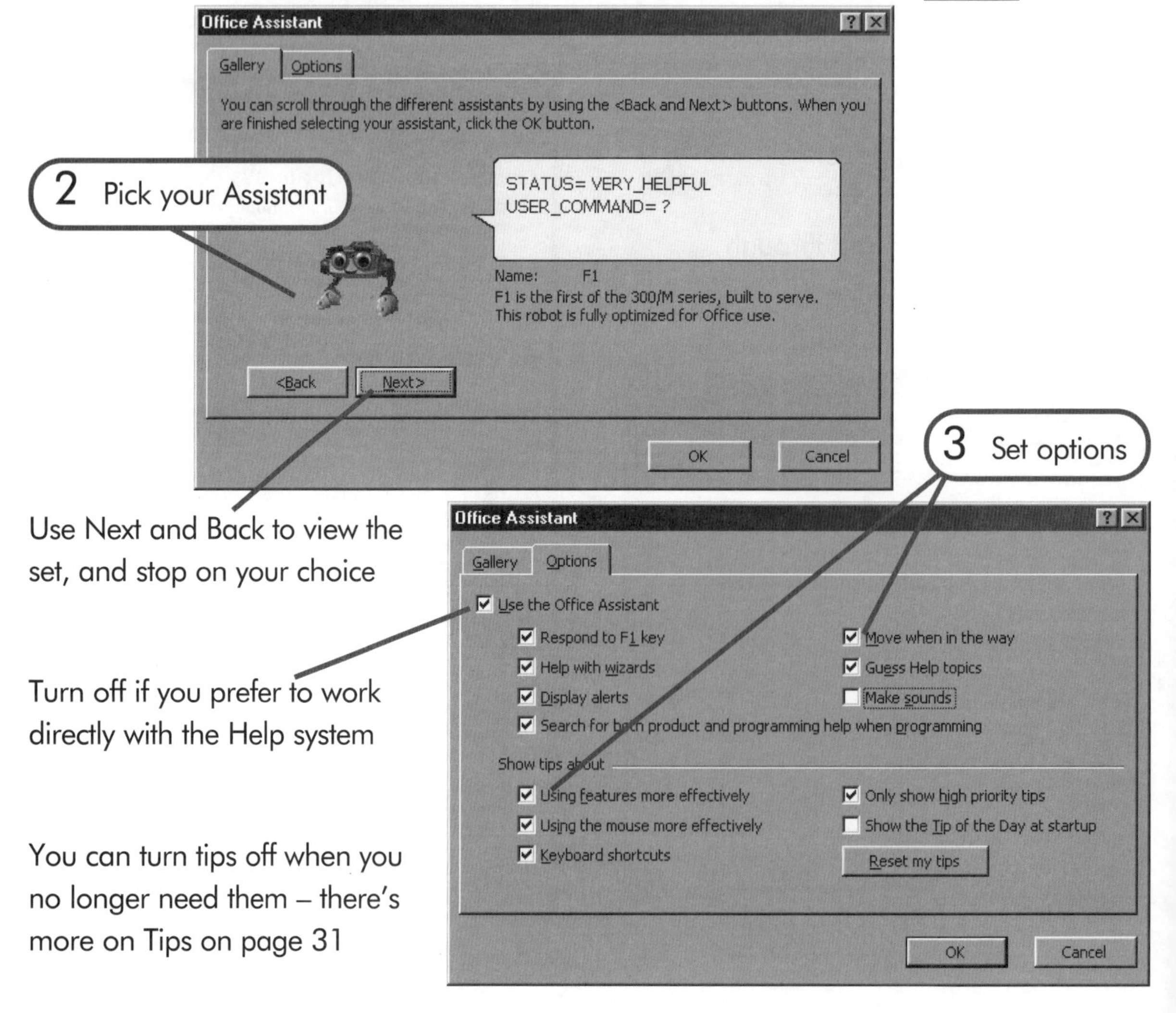

The Help menu

Basic steps

1 Open the Help menu.

2 If you want to use Detect and Repair click [»].

3 Select an option.

This is the route into the full Help system. The menu has seven options, of which five are immediately visible:

- **Microsoft Outlook Help** opens the Help system or displays the Office Assistant if used – the [?] button also opens this.
- **Show/Hide Office Assistant** toggles its display.
- **What's This?** provides quick explanations of the buttons and options on the main screen and on dialog boxes.
- **Office on the Web** links to pages at Microsoft's Web site. These are mainly for new Web users, but if you cannot find the answers you need in the built-in Help – and if you have an Internet connection – you might try here.
- **About Microsoft Outlook** displays copyright and other details – there's also a link to Technical Support.

If you click [»], another option appears.

- **Detect and Repair** check the application and restores any lost or corrupted program files – you will need your Office CD if you want to use this.

Take note

Pressing [F1] starts up the Office Assistant.

Pressing [Shift] and [F1] activates What's This?

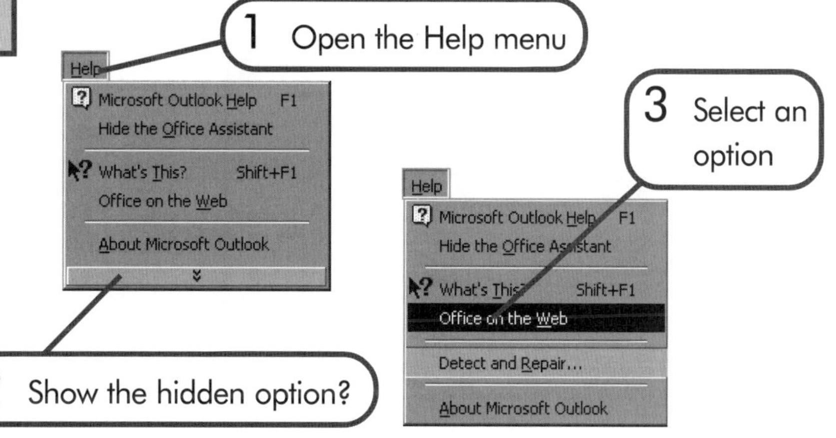

The Help system

If you use the Office Assistant to access the Help system, all you normally see is a page of Help, but there is more to it than this. Click the Show button, on the left of the toolbar, and a new panel opens. Its tabs gives you three ways to find Help.

Contents tab

This approach treats the Help pages as a book. Scan through the headings to find a section that seems to cover what you want, and open that to see the page titles. (Some sections have sub-sections, making it a 2 or 3-stage process to get to page titles.)

Some Help topics are stand-alone pages; some have a top page with a set of links to pages on different aspects of the topic.

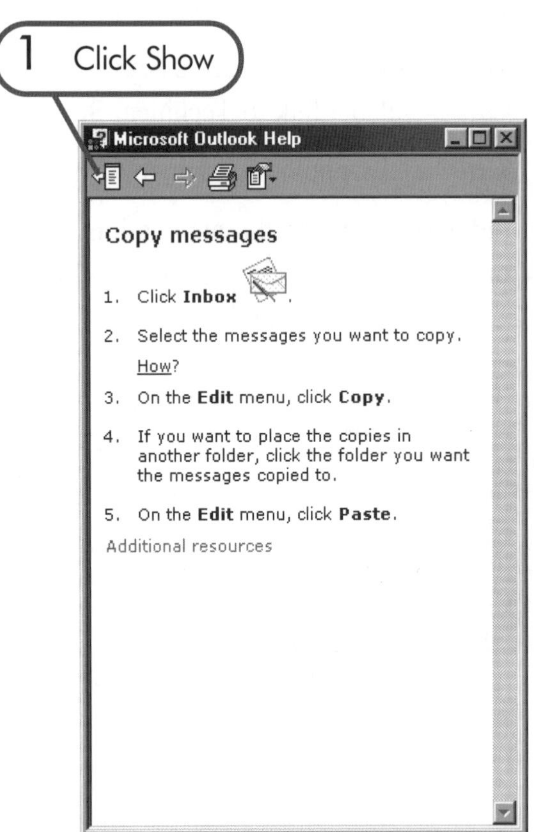

Basic steps

1. Click the Show button.
2. Click the Contents tab if this panel is not at the front already.
3. Click ⊞ to open a book – or ⊟ to close one.
4. Click or the page title to see a page.
5. Click on underlined text to go to the linked page – following up links as necessary.
6. Use the and buttons to move between visited pages.
7. When you have found the Help you want, click on the application window to hide Help or click to close Help.

Take note

If you turn the Office Assistant off, the tabs panel is displayed automatically.

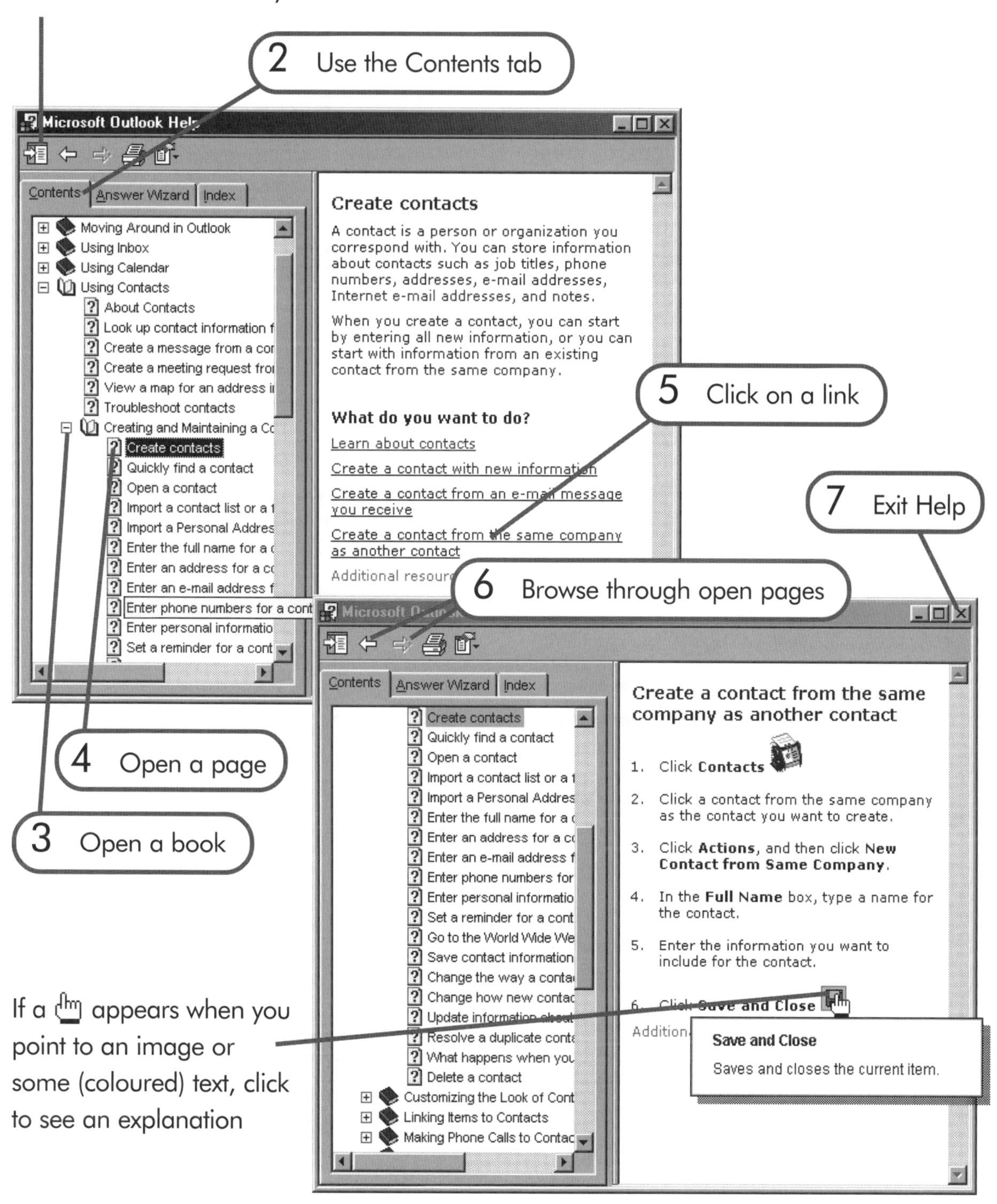
Click to hide the tabs if you want them out of the way
2 Use the Contents tab
Microsoft Outlook Help
Contents
Answer Wizard
Index
Moving Around in Outlook
Using Inbox
Using Calendar
Using Contacts
About Contacts
Troubleshoot contacts
Create contacts
Quickly find a contact
Open a contact
Create contacts
A contact is a person or organization you correspond with. You can store information about contacts such as job titles, phone numbers, addresses, e-mail addresses, Internet e-mail addresses, and notes.
When you create a contact, you can start by entering all new information, or you can start with information from an existing contact from the same company.
What do you want to do?
Learn about contacts
5 Click on a link
7 Exit Help
6 Browse through open pages
4 Open a page
3 Open a book
Create a contact from the same company as another contact
1. Click Contacts
2. Click a contact from the same company as the contact you want to create.
3. Click Actions, and then click New Contact from Same Company.
4. In the Full Name box, type a name for the contact.
5. Enter the information you want to include for the contact.
Save and Close
Saves and closes the current item.
Delete a contact
Linking Items to Contacts
If a appears when you point to an image or some (coloured) text, click to see an explanation

Answer Wizard

This is almost identical to asking a question through the Office Assistant. The main difference is that all the possible topics are displayed in the panel.

You can type in complete questions, or simply the most significant words. In the example below 'table columns change' produces exactly the same set of topics as 'How do I change columns in a table?'

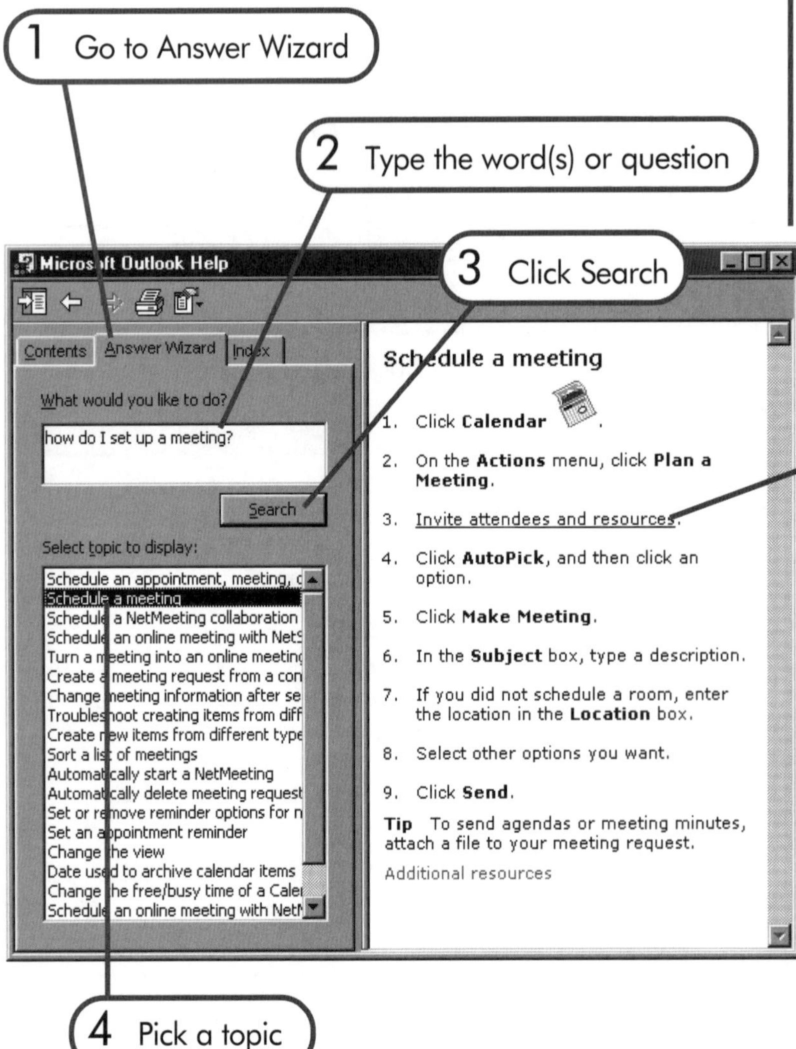

Basic steps

1. Switch to the Answer Wizard tab.
2. Type a word or phrase to describe the Help you want.
3. Click Search.
4. You will be offered a list of topics – click the one that is closest to your question.
5. If you are offered a set of links to pages, click on one to read it.

Take note

If there is only a single relevant topic page, the Help system will take you directly to it after Step 4.

Basic steps

Using the Index

1 Click the Index tab.

2 Start to type a word in the keyword box, then select it from the list.

3 Click Search.

4 Enter a second word and search again.

5 Select a topic.

The Answer Wizard will locate the main Help pages on any topic, but if you want to dig deeper, try the Index. Searching for a word here will track down every page on which it occurs – and the Help system is very thoroughly indexed! The best way to use it is to give two or more words, to focus onto the most relevant pages.

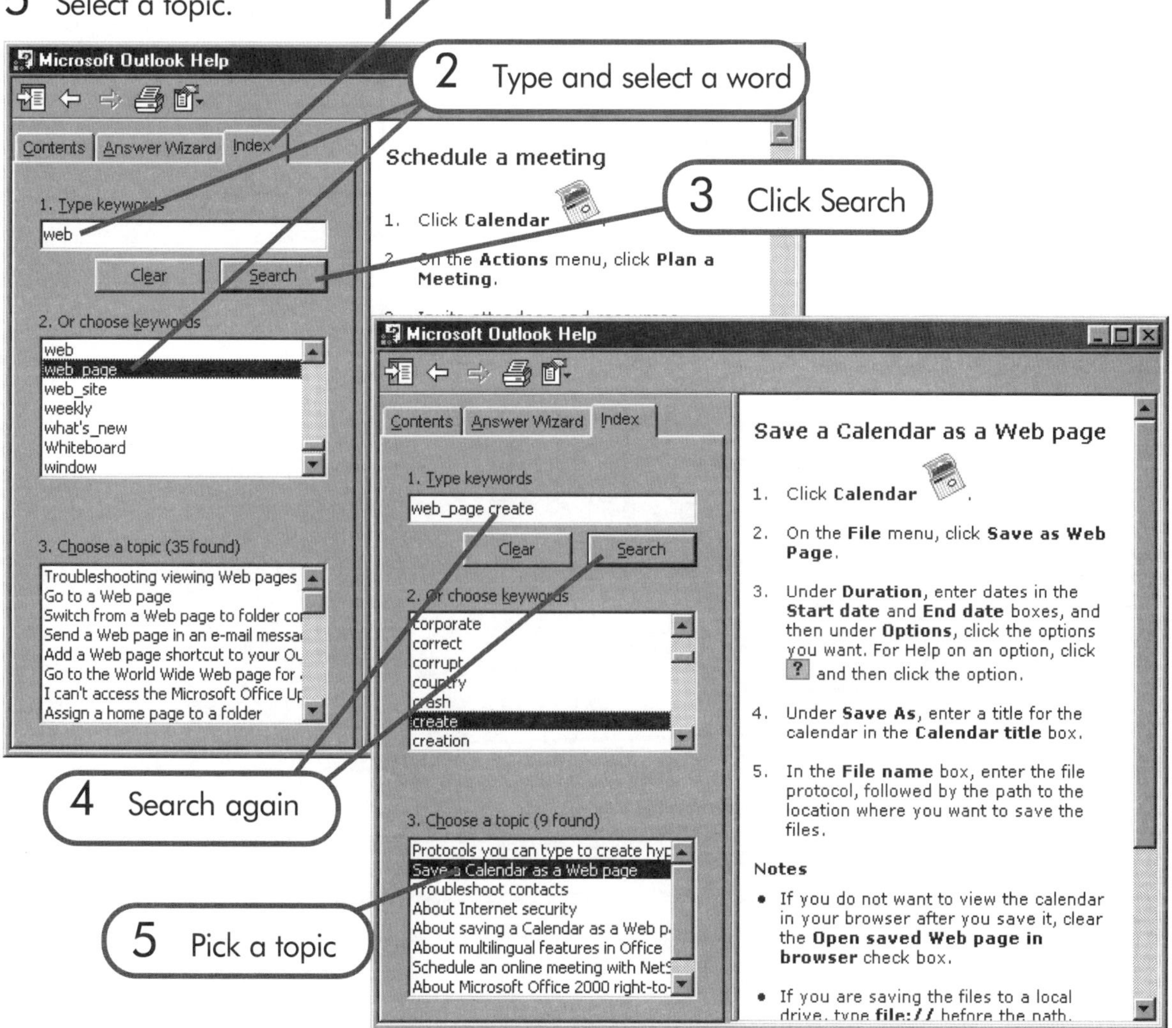

What's This?

Basic steps

Office's icons, menus and dialog boxes are designed to be intuitive – which is great, as long as you know how to intuit! However, when you first start to use these applications, you may need a little prompting. *What's This?* will tell you about the buttons and menu items in the main application window.

Once you open a dialog box or menu, you can no longer get to the What's This? command, but the Help is still at hand. Most dialog boxes have a query icon ? at the top right, which does the same job, and – no matter what you are doing – pressing **[Shift]** and **[F1]** will usually start the What's This? Help.

- ❑ In the main window
1. Open the Help menu and select What's This?
- ❑ On a dialog box
2. Click ? or ?.
- ❑ On a menu (or anywhere)
3. Hold down [Shift] and press [F1].
4. Click the ? cursor on the item that you want to know about.
5. After you have read the Help box, click anywhere to close it.

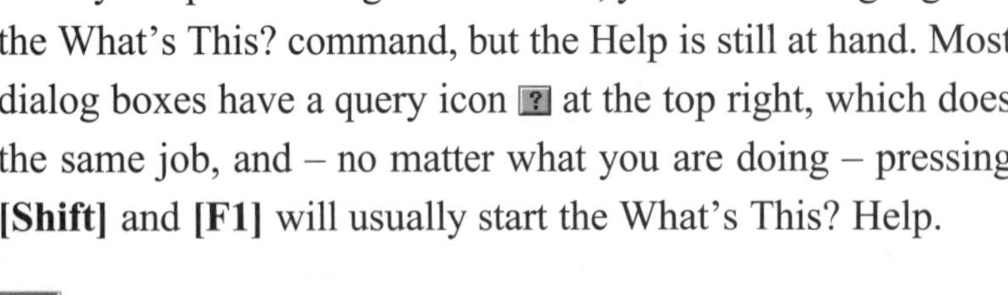

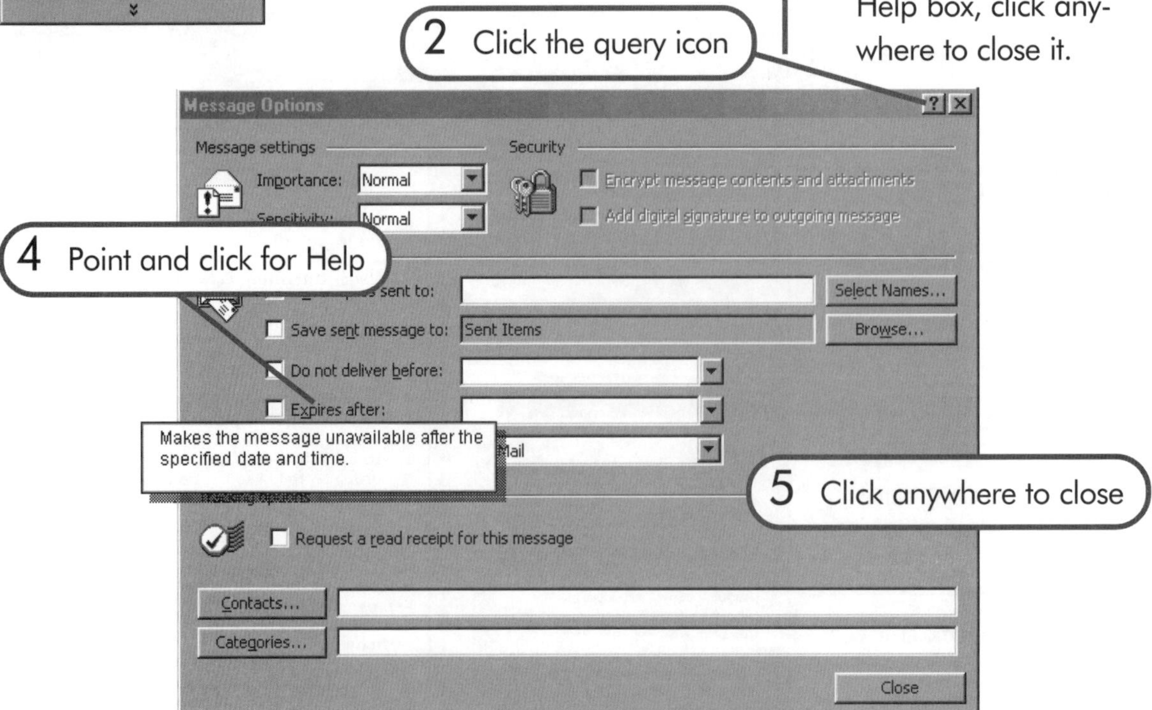

Basic steps

Tips and ScreenTips

- ❑ When the light is on

1. Click on the Office Assistant or the light icon to get the tip.
2. Select the new – or an earlier – tip.
3. If the tips don't help, ask a question and search as normal.

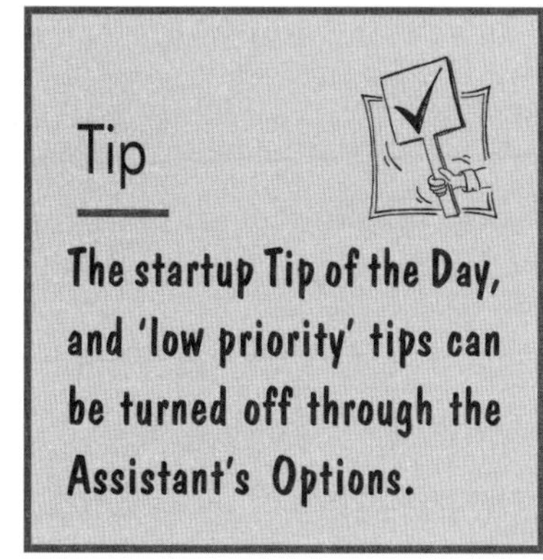

The startup Tip of the Day, and 'low priority' tips can be turned off through the Assistant's Options.

If ever you see 💡 on Office Assistant, it has a tip related to your last action or to the last error report. The tips that crop up during a session are stored in the bubble, and can be read at any time.

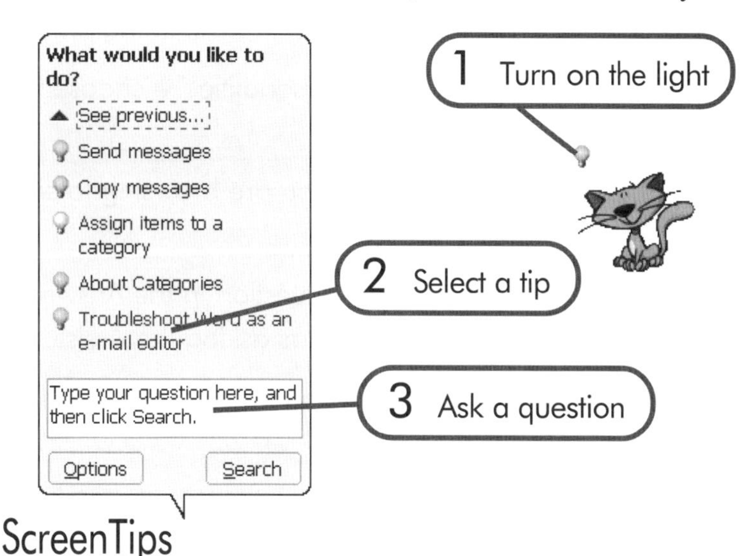

ScreenTips

These are little prompts that appear when you pause the mouse over a tool button, to tell you its name and its shortcut keys. The tips can be turned on or off through the **Options** tab of the **Toolbars – Customize** dialog box.

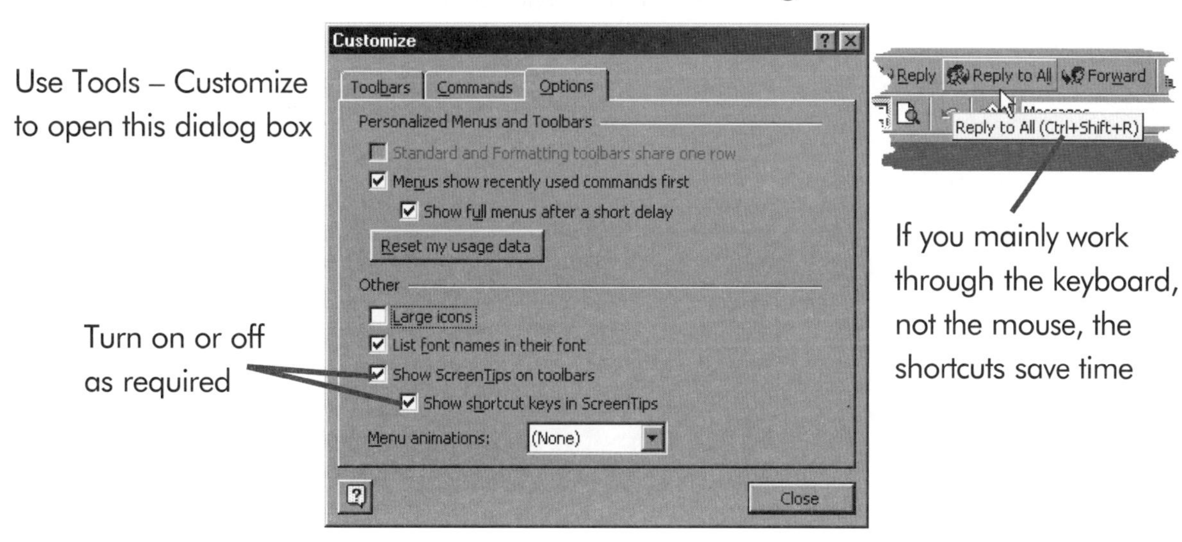

Use Tools – Customize to open this dialog box

Turn on or off as required

If you mainly work through the keyboard, not the mouse, the shortcuts save time

Summary

- ❑ Help is always available.
- ❑ Office Assistant is a friendly front-end to the Help system. It will offer appropriate Help when needed, and can handle questions written in simple English.
- ❑ Office Assistant has several 'personalities' – choose the one that suits you.
- ❑ Use the Contents panel when you are browsing to see what topics are covered.
- ❑ You can get Help by asking a question in the Answer Wizard tab – it works the same as asking the Assistant.
- ❑ Use the Index to go directly to the Help on a specified operation or object.
- ❑ For help in a dialog box or panel, use What's This? or click the query icon and point to the item.
- ❑ If you hold the cursor over an icon, a brief prompt will pop up to tell you what it does.
- ❑ The Tip of the Day at start up can be switched off if no longer wanted. Tips are stored and can be reviewed at any time.

3 Contacts

Viewing Contacts

Basic steps

When Outlook is installed (page 8) it will normally collect existing e-mail addresses from your system, so you should find some entries in Contacts when you first open it. This is good, as it means you can explore Contacts – and see what information it can handle – before you start to add the details of new entries.

Contacts has seven alternative displays, which can be selected from the Current view list:

- **Address cards** (the default) display the key information for each person – name, address, e-mail address and phone numbers.
- **Detailed address cards** show all the information on the General tab of the Contacts cards (see page 37).
- **Phone list** shows names, phone numbers and a few other key details in a simple table layout.
- **By Category**, **By Company**, **By Location** and **By Follow-up flag** all use the same table layout, but group entries by the information in the selected field.*Category* (see page 38) and *Company* are probably the two most useful for organising your list. *Follow-up flags* can be set for any item, so that you can easily pick up those entries that need more work, and can be marked as completed or cleared once the work is done.

In the table views, the order of the columns can be adjusted by dragging the column headers.

1 Click Contacts in the Outlook Bar.

❑ Changing views

2 Click the arrow to drop down the Current view list.

3 Select a new view.

❑ Moving columns

4 Click and hold on the header of the column you want to move.

5 Drag it across to its new position – pulling off screen if necessary.

❑ Sorting into order

6 Click once on a header to sort by that column in ascending order – or click again for descending order.

Take note

You will need to edit your existing entries to take advantage of what Outlook has to offer. Double-click on an entry to open it for editing, then add details as for a new entry – see page 37.

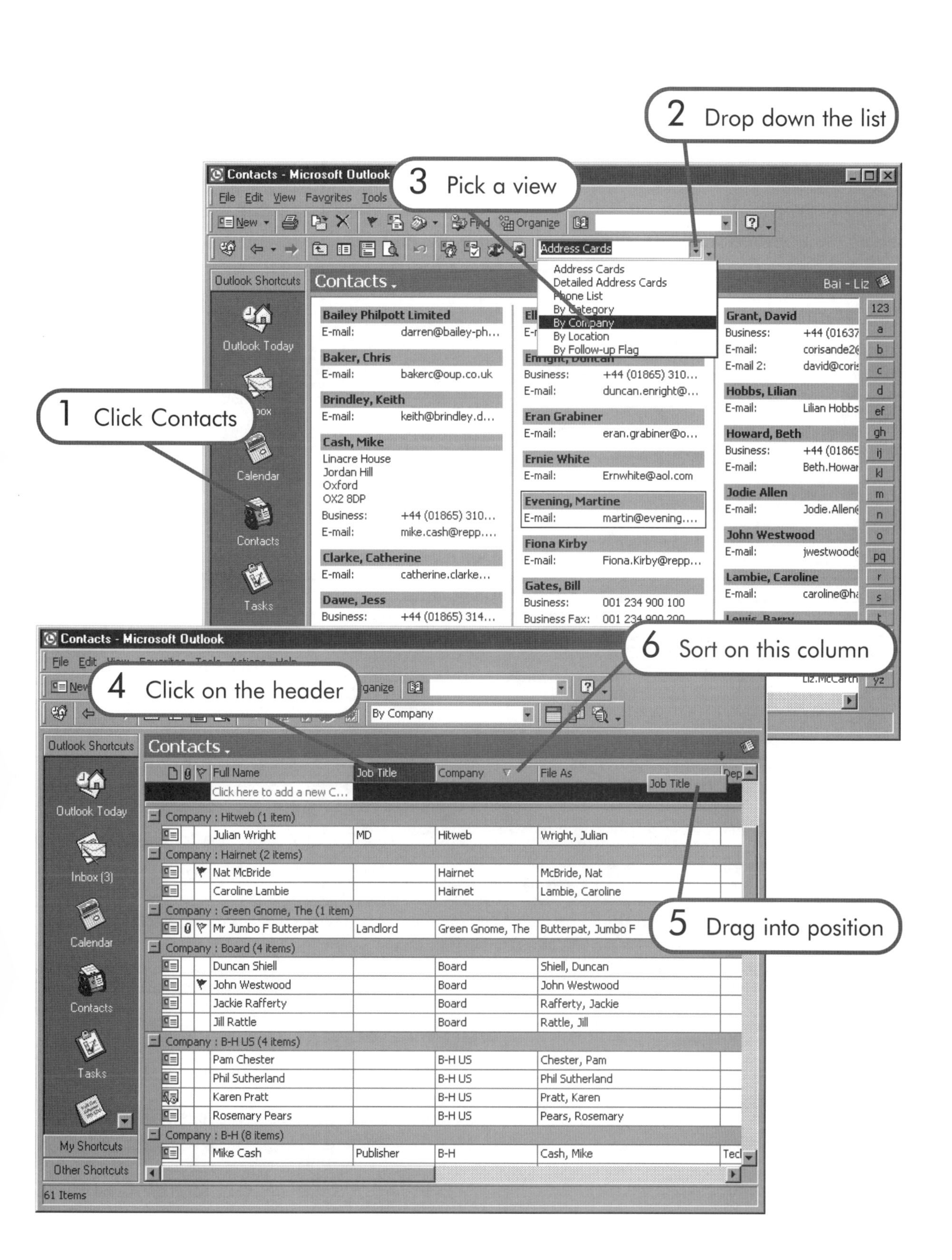
1 Click Contacts
2 Drop down the list
3 Pick a view
4 Click on the header
5 Drag into position
6 Sort on this column

Entering Contacts

This is probably the most straightforward part of Outlook to set up. Mind you, it will take a while if you give all the details that it can hold – home and business address, phone and fax, birthdays, spouse, assistant, dog's name…

The information is entered into a card with five tabs. Only the first two are relevant at this point.

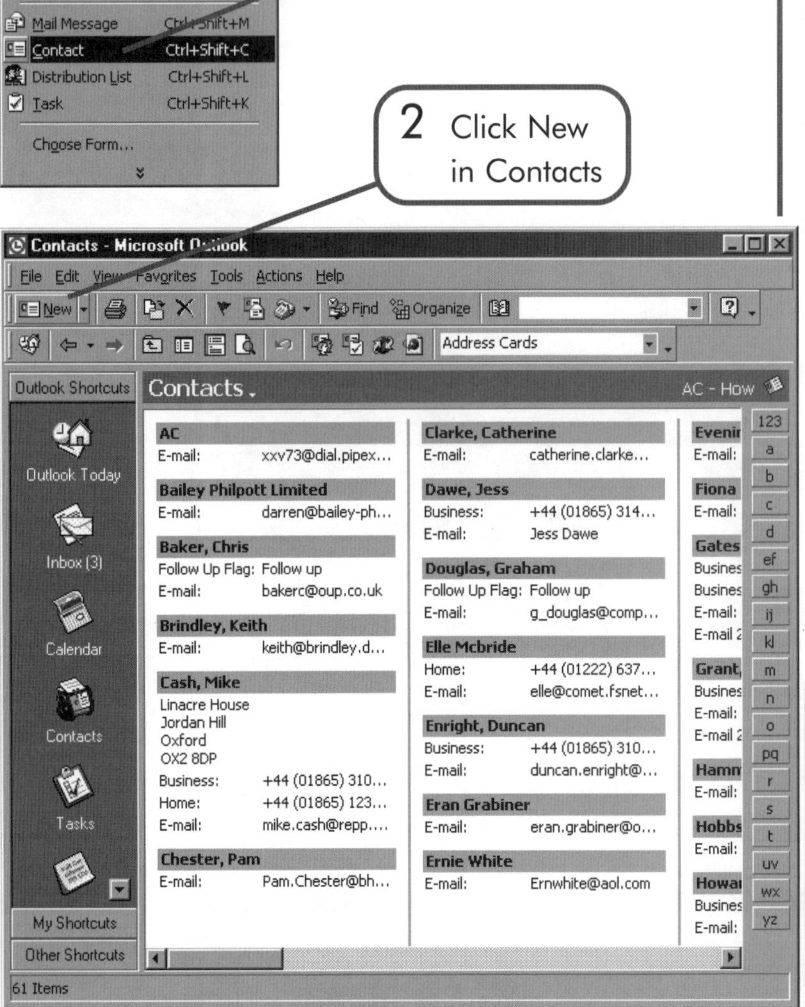

Basic steps

1. In any module, open the New drop-down list and select Contact.

or

2. Open Contacts and click New.
3. Type in the name

or

4. Click Full Name... enter the name there.
5. Enter other information as required.
6. Select a File As line – this sets its normal place in the list. The options are made up from the Full Name and Company details
7. Switch to Details to add more if wanted.
8. Click Save and Close.

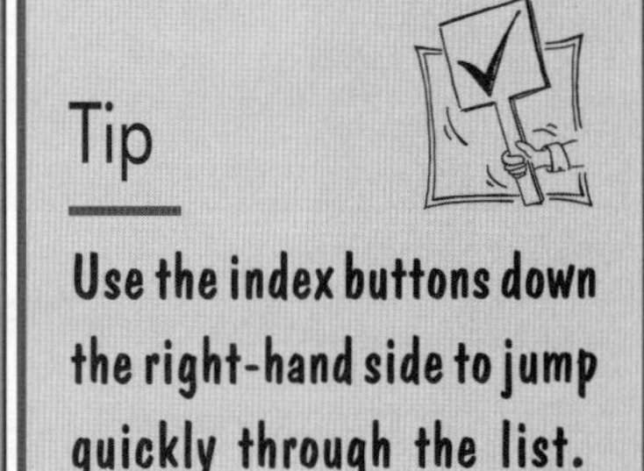

Tip

Use the index buttons down the right-hand side to jump quickly through the list.

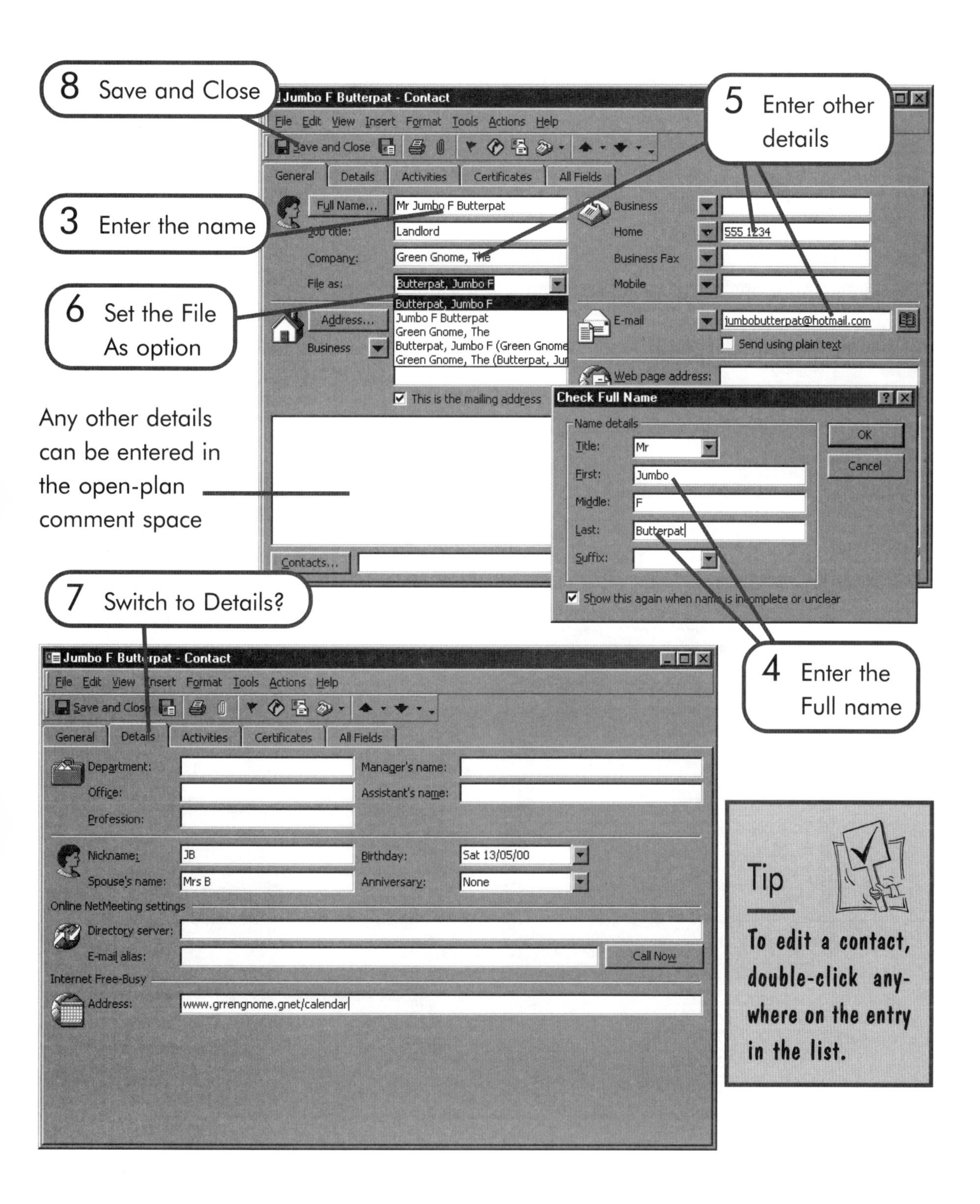

Tip

To edit a contact, double-click anywhere on the entry in the list.

Using Categories

Basic steps

Categories are not exclusive to Contacts. You will find them in the other modules, where they are used in exactly the same way. Categories help you to keep organised. In Contacts, they will allow you to group people together according to a common feature, or the way that you relate to them.

Outlook has about a dozen pre-defined categories, but you can easily create your own if there are no suitable ones already.

1 On the General tab of a person's Contact card, click Categories... .

2 Tick those categories that apply.

❑ Adding categories

3 Type in a name and click Add to List .

❑ Deleting categories

4 Open the Categories panel and click Master Category List... .

5 At the Master List, select a category and click Delete .

or

6 Click Reset to remove all your added categories.

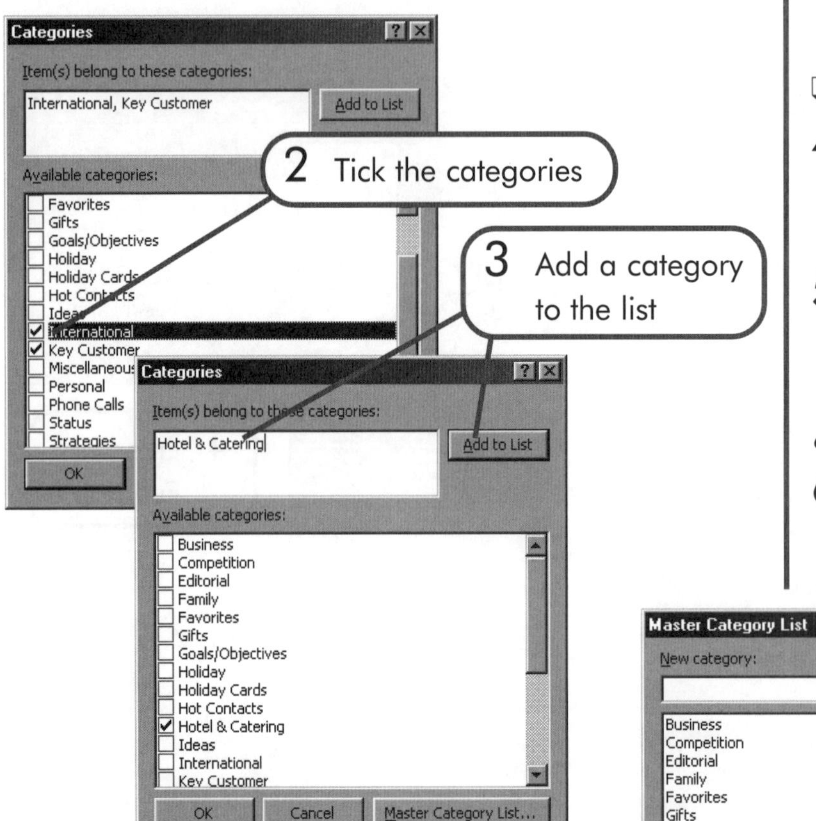

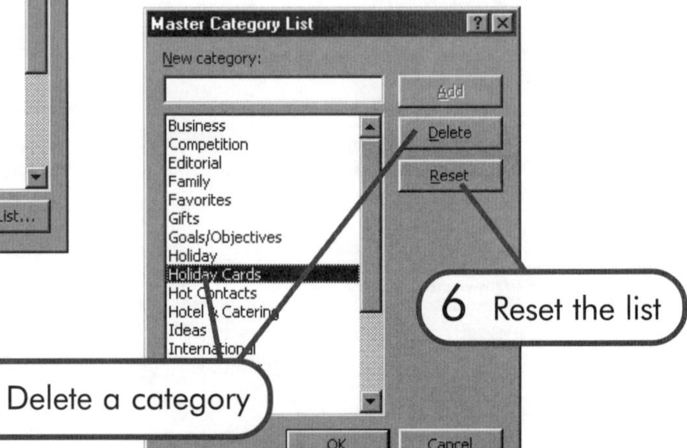

Basic steps

1 Select the person.

2 Open the Action menu and choose an option.

or

3 Click a toolbar button.

❑ What happens next varies with the action.

Getting in touch

The main point of Contacts is to make it easier to keep in contact with others, so what tools have we got for this?

The options are listed on the **Actions** menu, with the more commonly-used ones duplicated in toolbar buttons. You can send an e-mail or a letter, make a phone call, set up a meeting (in the real world or through NetMeeting), assign a task, make a journal entry – and more.

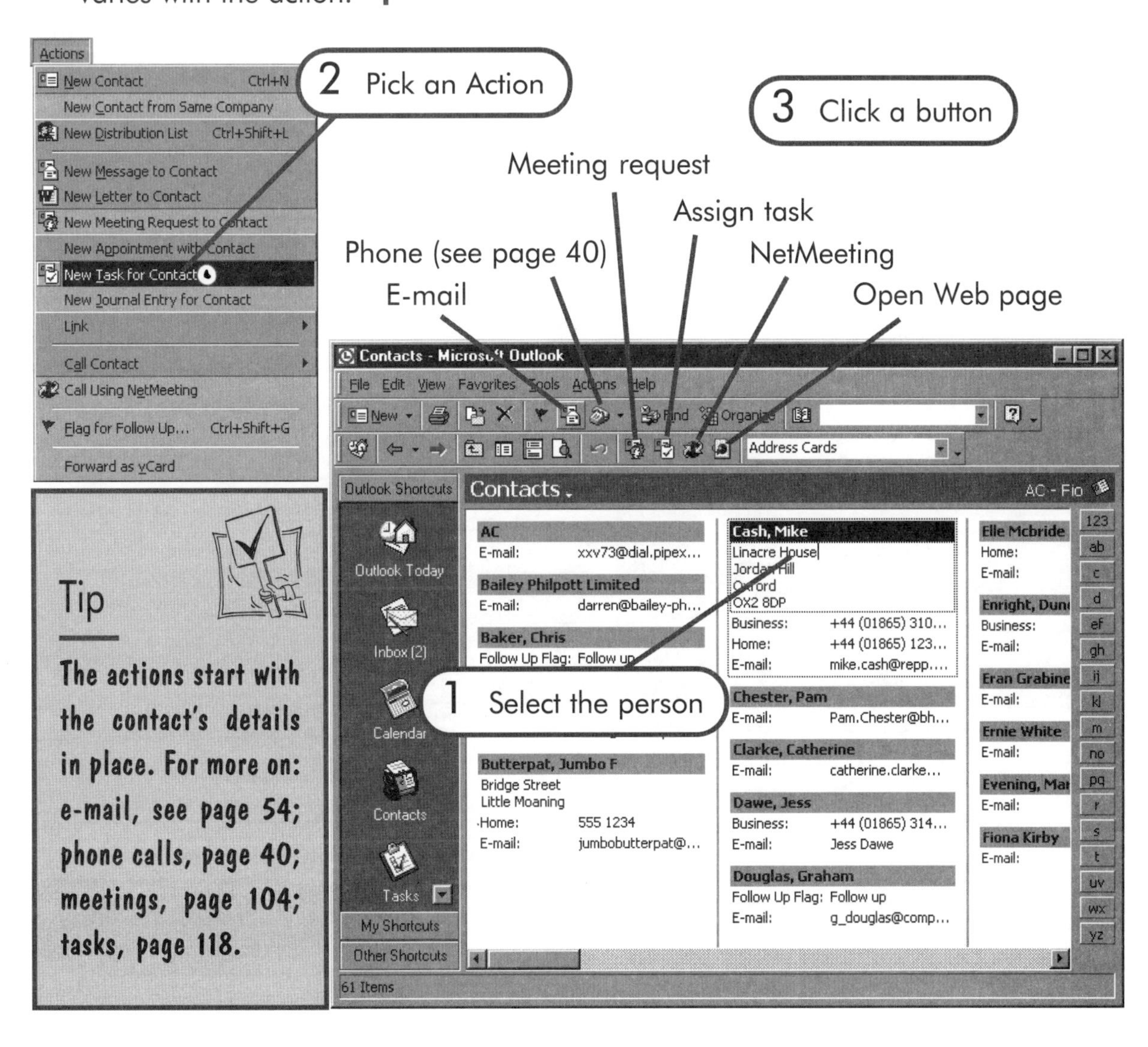

Tip

The actions start with the contact's details in place. For more on: e-mail, see page 54; phone calls, page 40; meetings, page 104; tasks, page 118.

Phone dialling

If your phone is connected through the PC's modem, you can get Outlook to dial for you. You can also get it to create a journal entry for the call. We'll come back to these later – at this point just note how calls can be logged.

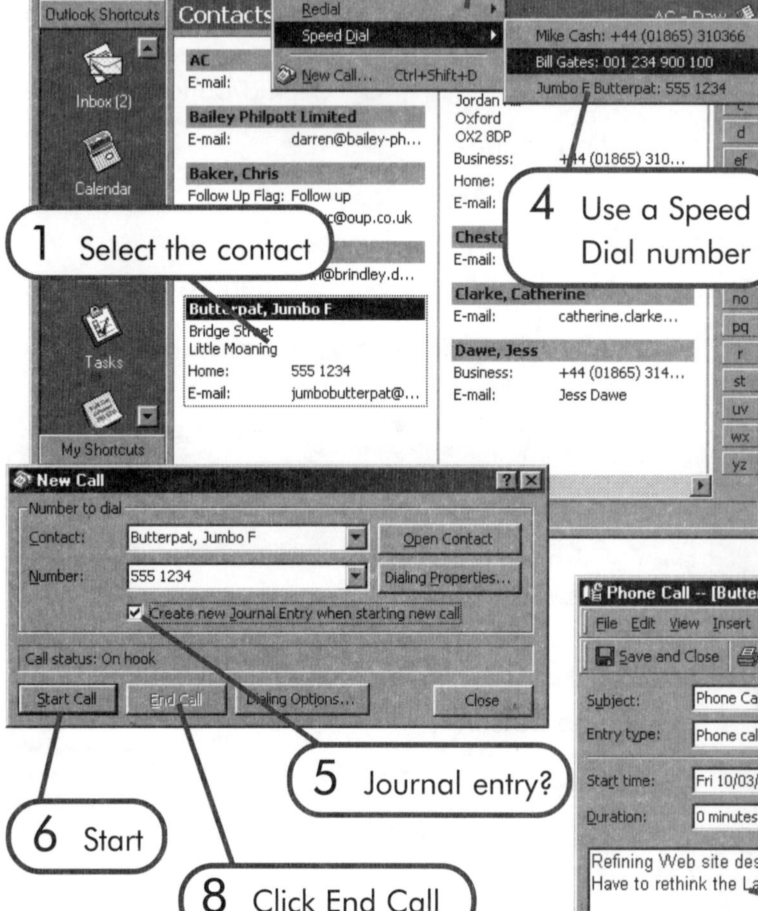

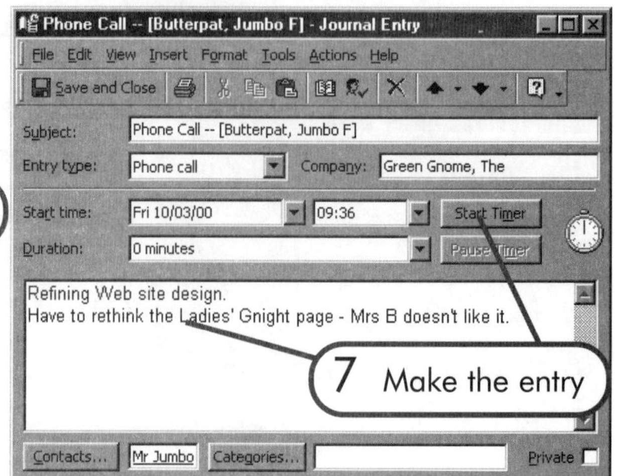

Basic steps

1 Select the person.

2 Click [Dial button].

or

3 Redial a number from the Dial menu or its Redial sub-menu.

or

4 Click the number in the Dial – Speed Dial list.

5 Tick Create new Journal Entry... if wanted.

6 Click Start Call and lift the phone.

7 If making a Journal Entry, add any notes and click Start Timer.

8 When you have finished, click End Call.

Basic steps

1 Open the Actions menu, point to Call Contact then select New Call …

2 At the New Call dialog box, click Dialing Options… .

3 Enter the first part of the Name and press [Tab]. The rest of the name and its phone number should be filled in for you.

4 Click Add .

5 Repeat 3 and 4 as needed then click OK .

Speed dial

If contacts are on your Speed Dial list, it's even easier to place a call to them. To add contacts to the list, you have to track it down to where it is hiding, just off the New Call dialog box. Its Dialing Options button takes you to the dialog box where contacts can be added to your Speed Dial list.

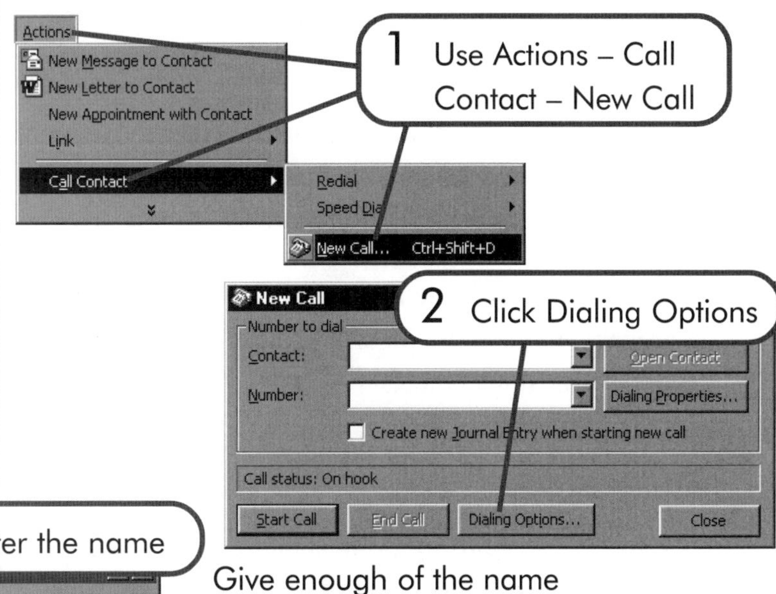

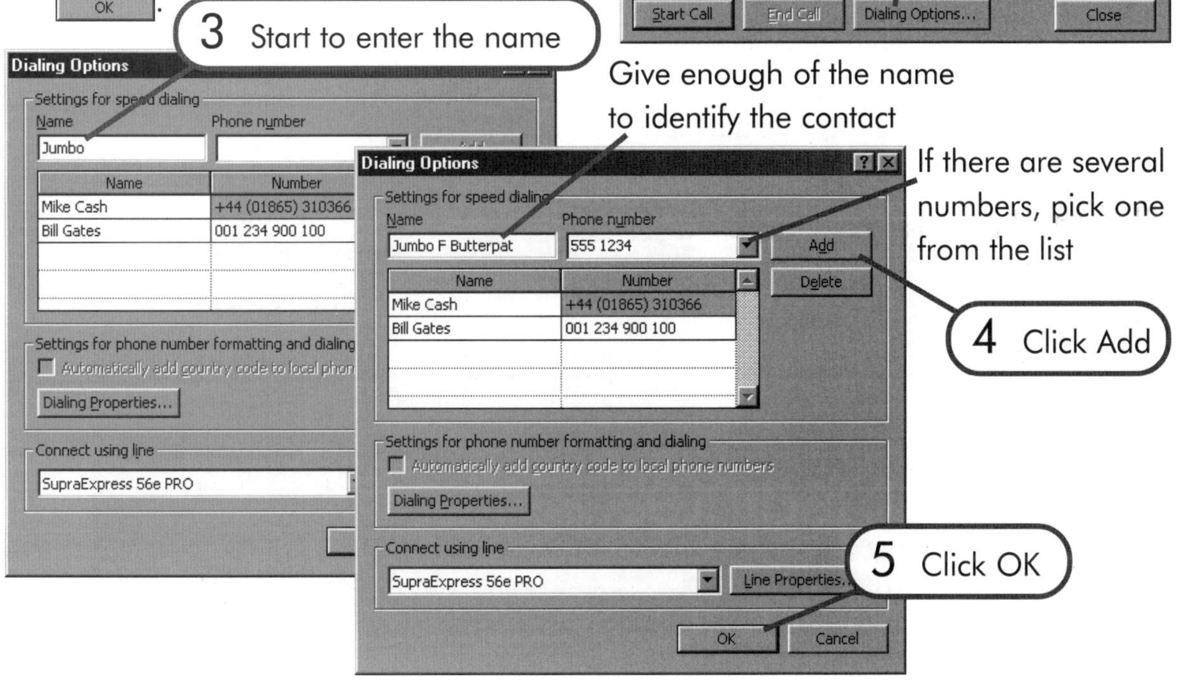

Custom Views

Basic steps

We saw on page 34 that Contacts can be viewed in seven different ways, but there's more… Each view can be customized to your own particular needs and tastes.

There are six aspects which may be customised. Not all of these apply to all views, and two are of very little value in any Contacts display – we'll leave those until we look at Inbox.

- **Fields** specifies which columns of information are shown.
- **Group By** (list views only) brings together those items with the same data in a given field or fields.
- **Sort** lists items in order of the data in one or more fields.
- **Filter** shows only those items that meet set criteria. This is probably more useful for sifting through your messages than for selecting contacts.
- **Other Settings** define the fonts used and the layout of lists or cards.
- **Automatic Formatting** defines the fonts to be used for those items that meet certain criteria. This variation on the Filter is also more useful in the Inbox than in Contacts.

1. Open the View menu, point to Current View then select Customize Current View …
2. At the View Summary panel click the button for the aspect that you want to define.
3. Complete the dialog box as required and move onto the next aspect.
4. When you are happy with all your changes, click [OK].

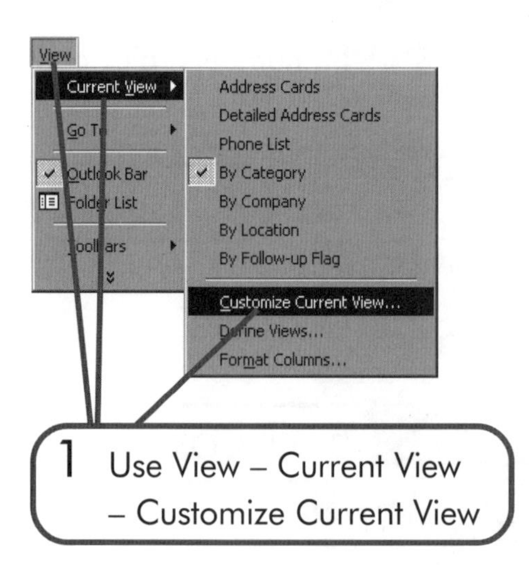

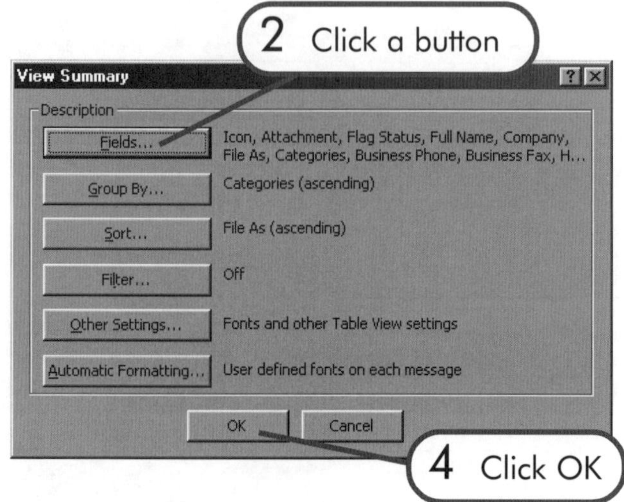

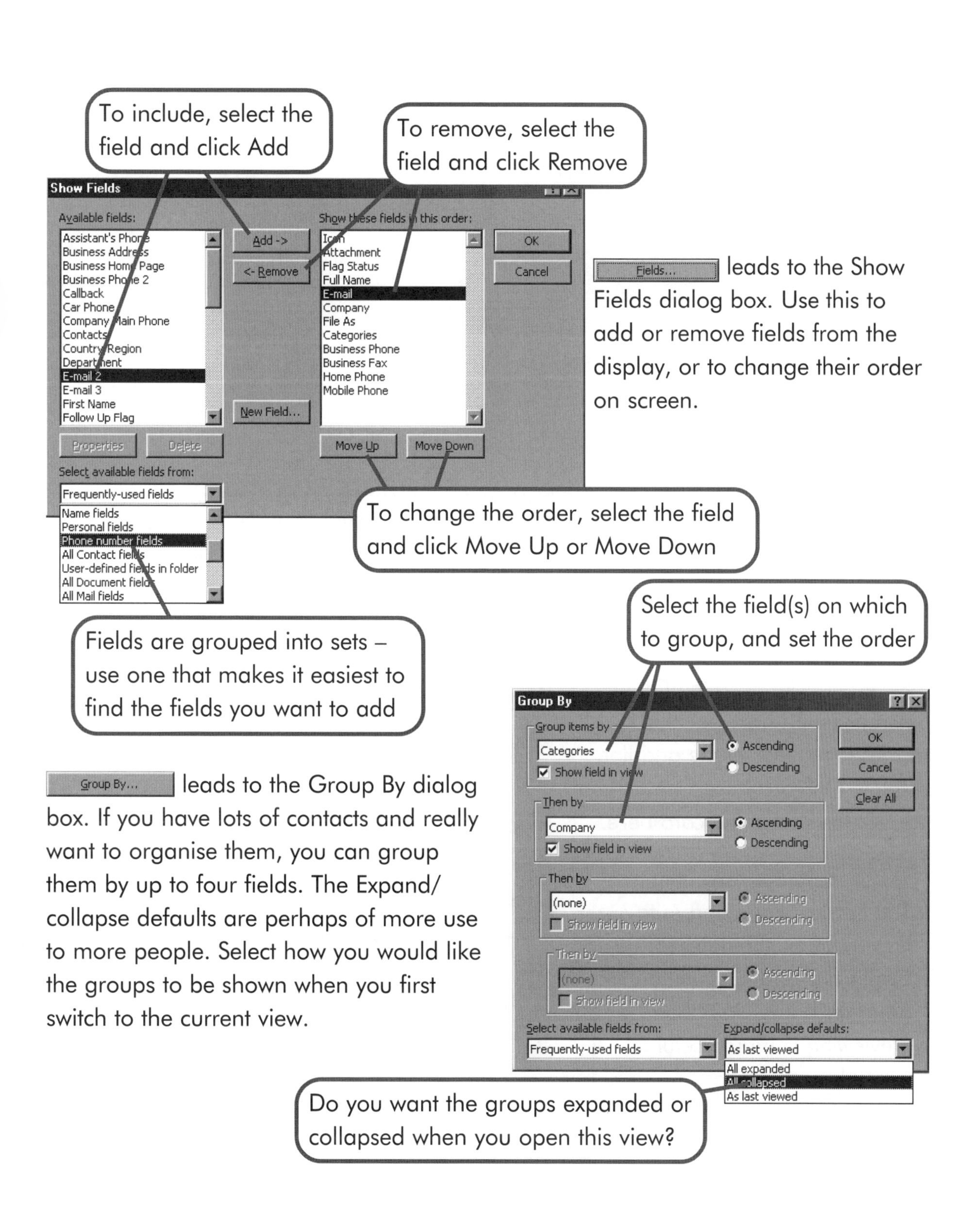

Fields... leads to the Show Fields dialog box. Use this to add or remove fields from the display, or to change their order on screen.

Group By... leads to the Group By dialog box. If you have lots of contacts and really want to organise them, you can group them by up to four fields. The Expand/collapse defaults are perhaps of more use to more people. Select how you would like the groups to be shown when you first switch to the current view.

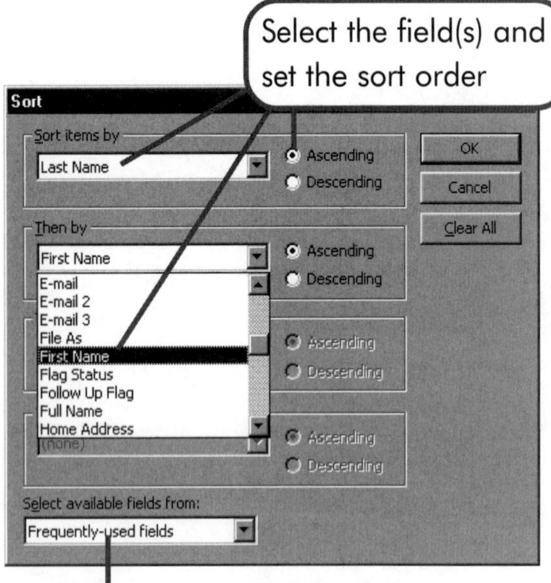

Tip

The settings only apply to the current view. Each view must be defined separately.

Sort... leads to the Sort dialog box. Contacts are normally sorted by their File As values. You can sort on any field – and sort within that on up to three more – ascending or descending.

Other Settings... leads to the Other Settings dialog box. Use this to format fonts and set the grid line display. On card-based views, you can set the size of the card here.

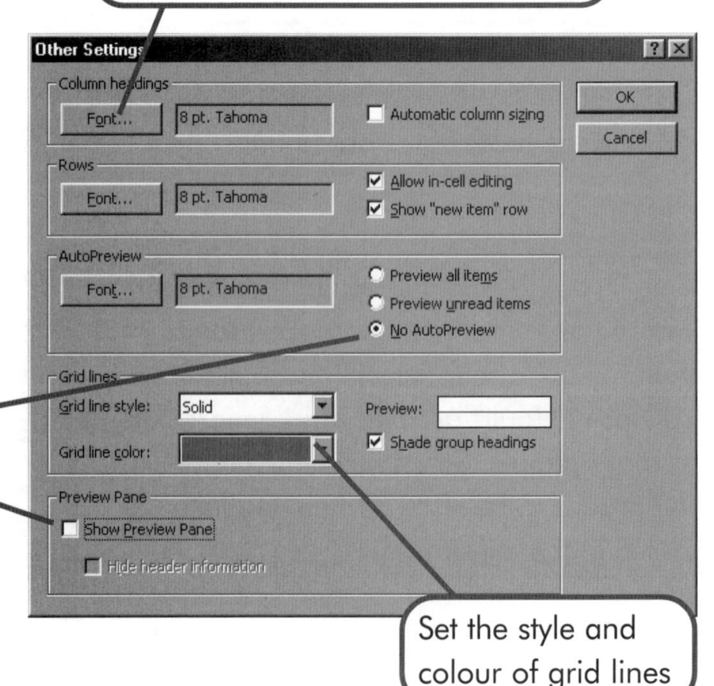

The Preview Pane and Auto-Preview show the notes in Contacts – and you wouldn't normally bother with them. Previewing is more useful with Inbox messages.

Basic steps

Defining Views

1 Open the View menu, point to Current View then select Define Views … .

❑ Modifying a view

2 Select the view and click [Modify…].

❑ Creating a new view

3 Click [New…].

4 Give the view a name.

5 Select the type of view.

6 Set where it can be used.

7 Click [OK].

The Customize Current View routine is a neat way to tweak the existing display, but there is another approach you can take if you want to give the views a more drastic overhaul. At the **Define Views** dialog box you can select any view for modification, or set up an entirely new view. In both cases, once you have got past the initial steps, the process is the same as for customising the current view.

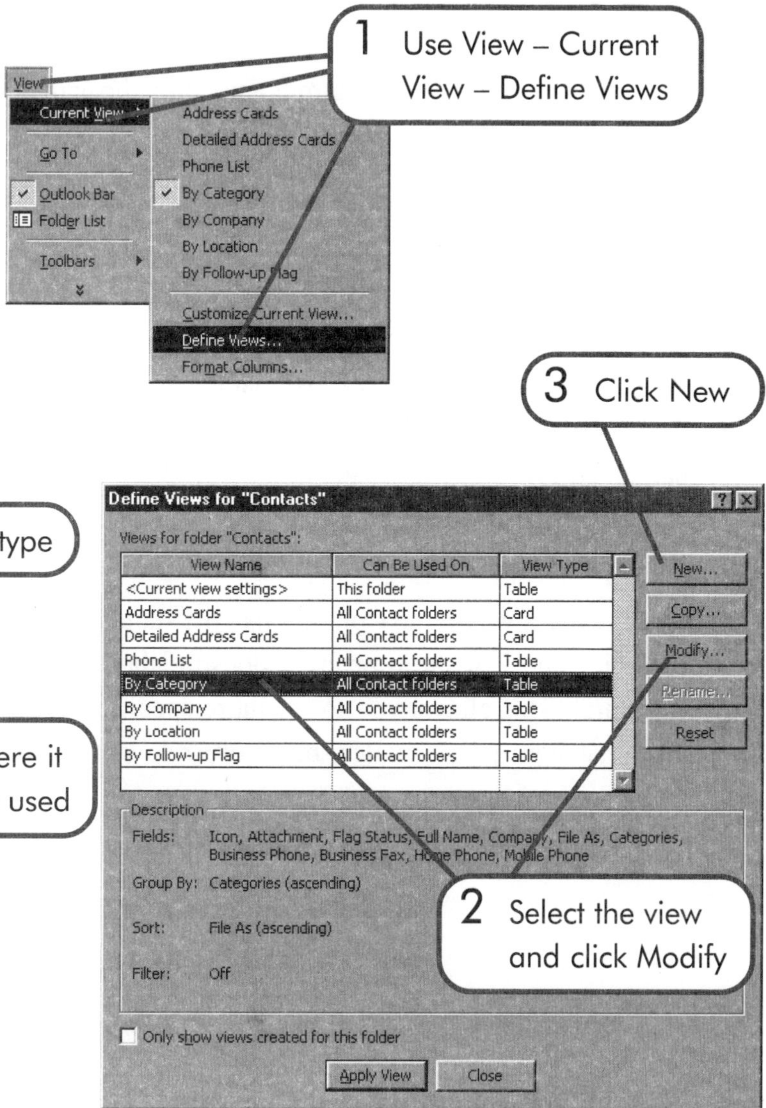

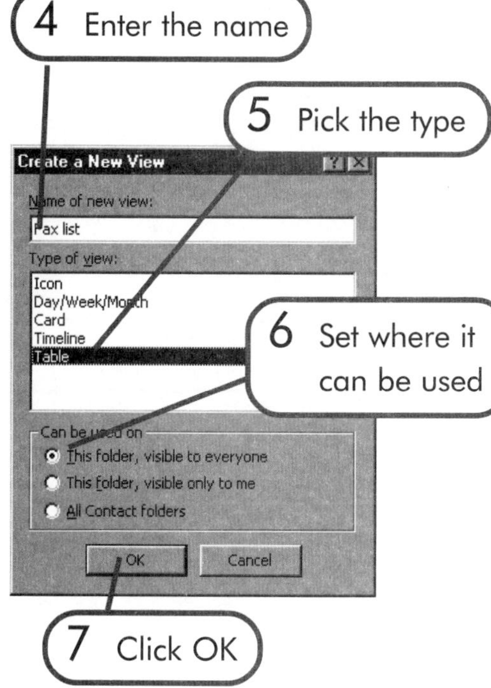

The Find routine

Basic steps

If you are methodical in organising your Contacts list, you should have little use for this routine – but most of us will find it quite handy for tracking down lost contacts.

Even if you are methodical, you may need this to locate those contacts that were added either through Inbox's Add Contact routine or its automatic adding facility – how these are filed will depend upon how the contacts set up their address details on their own e-mail systems.

- The Find routine will search through not only the names, but also all the other text fields, so can be used to track down people on the basis of their company, e-mail address, real address or category.
- If required, the search can be extended to cover the free text in the comment space.
- You can give all or part of the text that you expect to find – though with partial searches you can get more than you bargained for. 'hot', for instance, will find all your *hot* contacts, anyone with a *hot*mail address, and contacts in *hot*els or p*hot*ography.

Unless you have a a very large Contacts list, the standard Find will do the job most of the time. If it doesn't, then try the Advanced Find. This allows you to set more specific search criteria so that you get a smaller, but more relevant set of results.

1. Click [Find] or open the Tools menu and select Find.
2. Enter all or part of the name or other text into the Look for slot.
3. Tick Search all text... if you want to include the comment space.
4. Click [Find Now].
5. If you want to do another search, click Clear Search to re-store the full Contact list display.
6. If you get nothing, or too many results, click Go to Advanced Find... (see page 48).

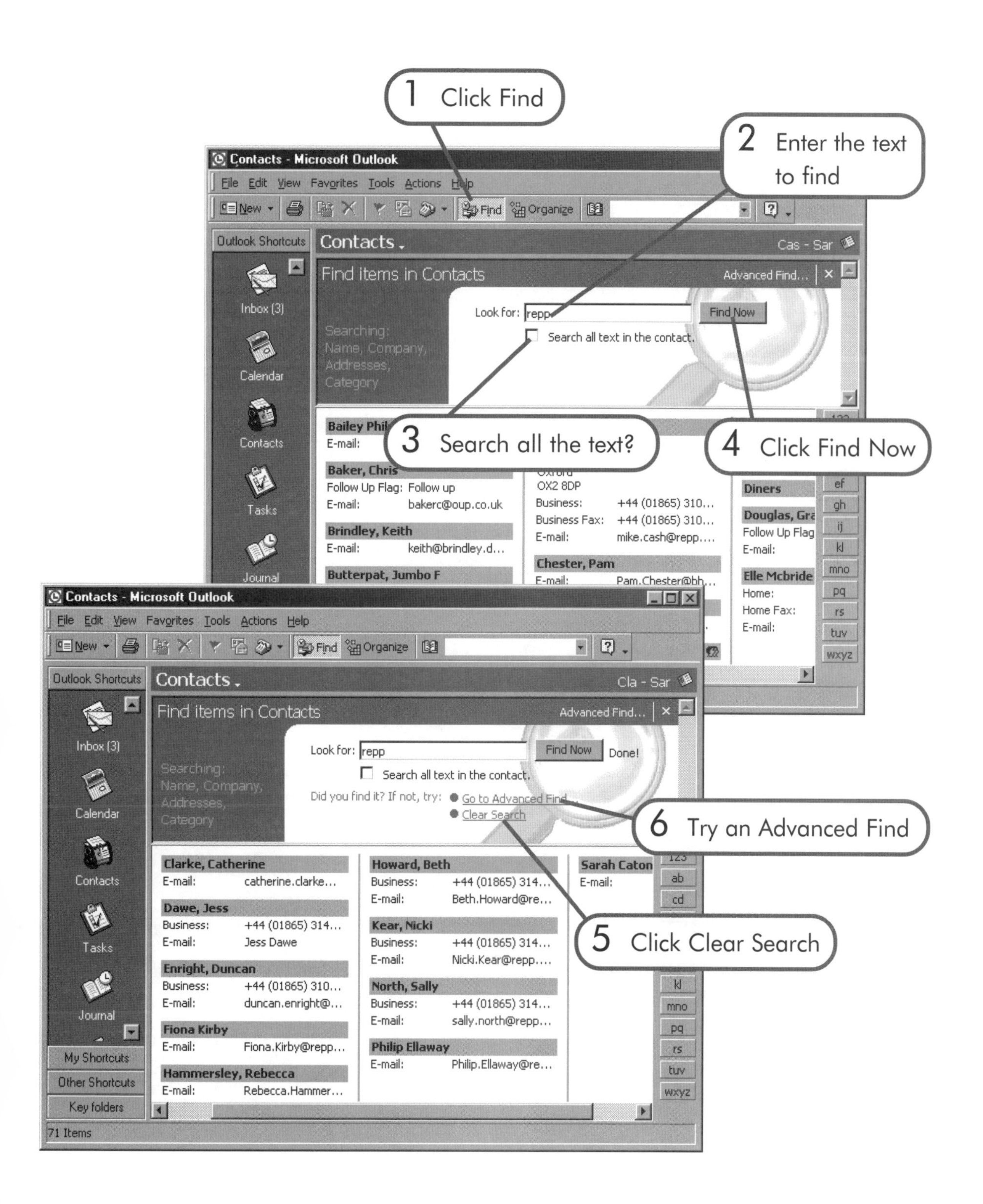
1 Click Find
2 Enter the text to find
3 Search all the text?
4 Click Find Now
5 Click Clear Search
6 Try an Advanced Find

Advanced Find

On the Contacts tab you can specify what to look for and where to look, and set a time frame.

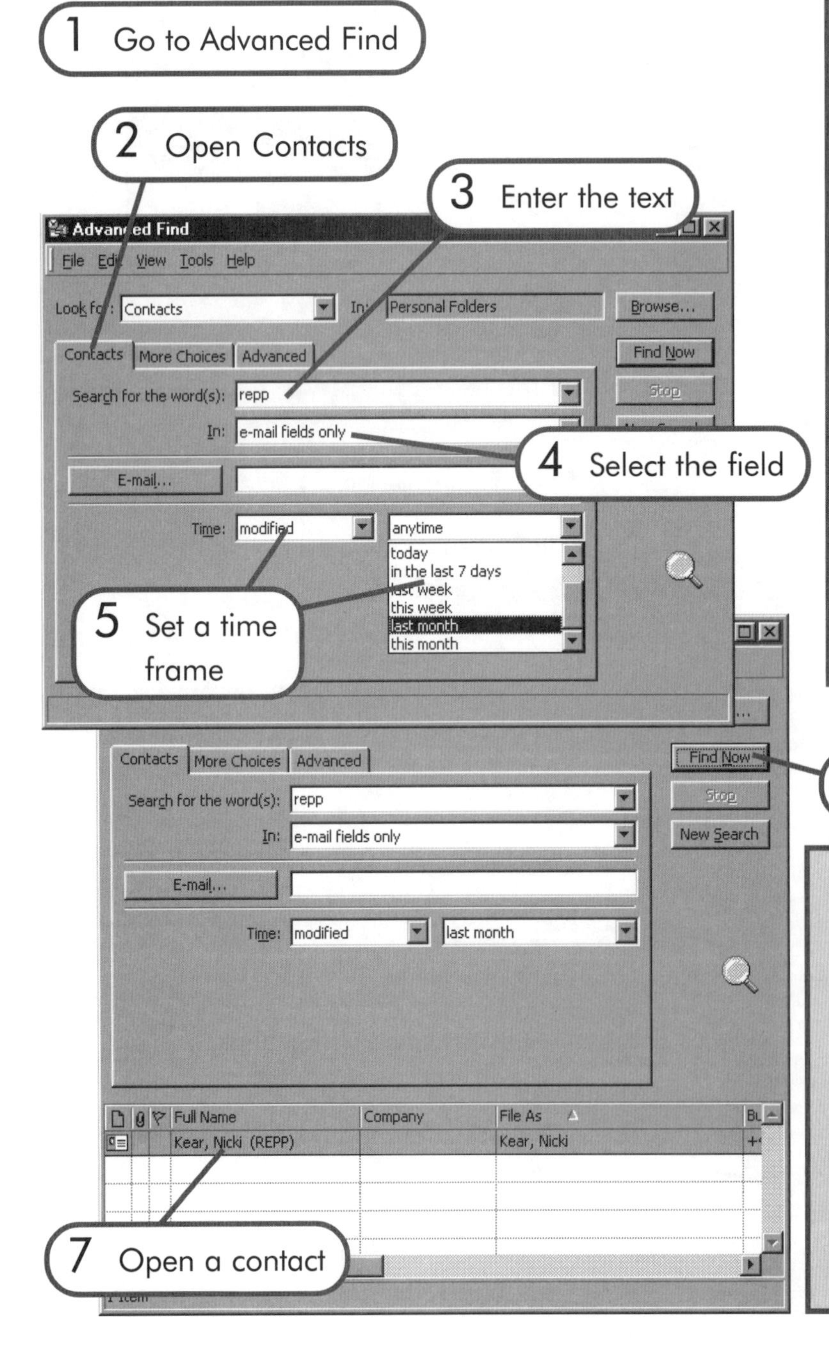

Basic steps

1. On the Find panel click Go to Advanced Find…
2. Switch to the Contacts tab if it is not on top.
3. Enter the text in the Search for slot.
4. Drop down the In list and select the field or fields to search.
5. To set a time frame, select *created* or *modified* in the Time slot, then set the limit.
6. Click Find Now.
7. Double-click to open a contact in the list.

Take note

The Advanced and More Choices and tabs are of little use with Contacts, but are far more useful for finding e-mail messages, so we'll deal with them in Chapter 4.

Basic steps

1. Click [Organize].
2. Switch to the Using Categories tab if it is not already selected.
3. Select the contact(s).
4. Select a category from the drop-down list.
5. Click [Add].

or

6. Type a new category name and click [Create].

Getting organised

There are three ways to organise Contacts:

- **Using Folders** serves no visible function.
- **Using Views** is the same as selecting an option from the **View – Current View** menu.
- **Using Categories** gives you a quick way to add people to categories. Here's how.

Use the normal Windows techniques if you want to select several people at once:

Hold down **[Ctrl]** while you click to select a scattered set.

Click on the first, hold down **[Shift]** and click on the last to select a continuous set.

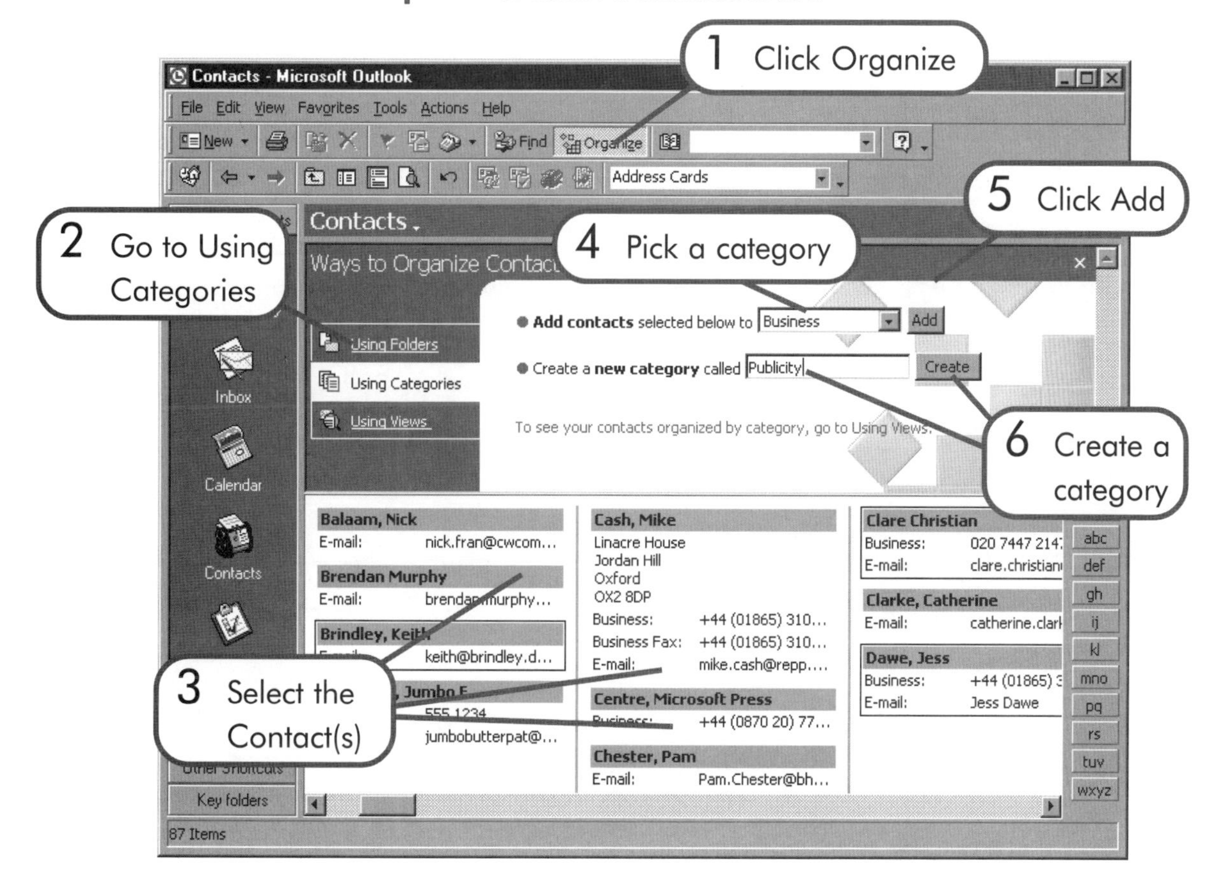

Summary

- ❑ The Contacts list can be used to record very complete details of your contacts.
- ❑ The list can be viewed in different ways to help you locate people more easily.
- ❑ New Contacts can be entered at any point, including as much detail as you like.
- ❑ Categories provide a way of grouping contacts for easier handling.
- ❑ You can get in touch with someone by e-mail, phone or NetMeeting from within Contacts.
- ❑ You can dial phone numbers in your Contacts list by clicking the dialler button.
- ❑ Views can be customised to display the information you want, and new views can be defined if required.
- ❑ The Find routine can help you track down Contacts.
- ❑ The Organize panel is useful for adding people to categories.

4 Using Inbox

The screen display

Basic steps

The screen layout can be adjusted in many ways, but one based on the default display – the one shown below – is probably the best for most purposes.

You need the **Folder List** for filing old mail or switching between mail folders; the **Outlook Bar** is handy for moving around within Outlook; the **Preview Pane** is a convenient way to read all but the largest messages; and the **Advanced Toolbar** contains some useful tools.

With this layout, you can reach a message in a few clicks.

1. Switch to Inbox in the Outlook Bar.
2. Select a folder from the Folder List.
3. Click on a message header in the Header Pane.
4. Read it in the Preview Pane.

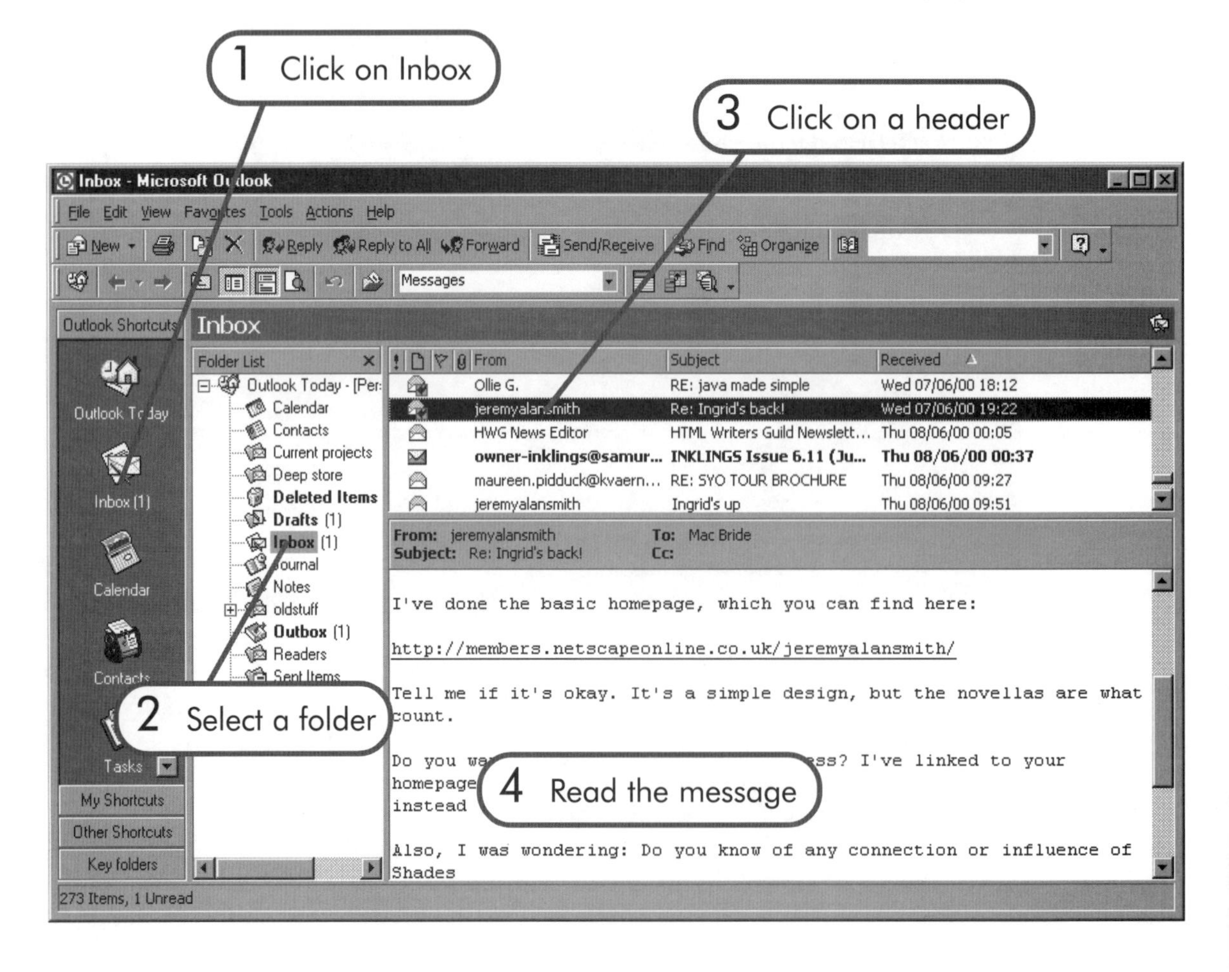

Basic steps

1. Open the View menu.
2. Wait a moment for the menu to open fully.
3. Point to Toolbars if you want to control their display.
4. Click on an element to turn it on or off.

Adjusting the display

The major elements can all be turned on and off by simple switches on the **View** menu.

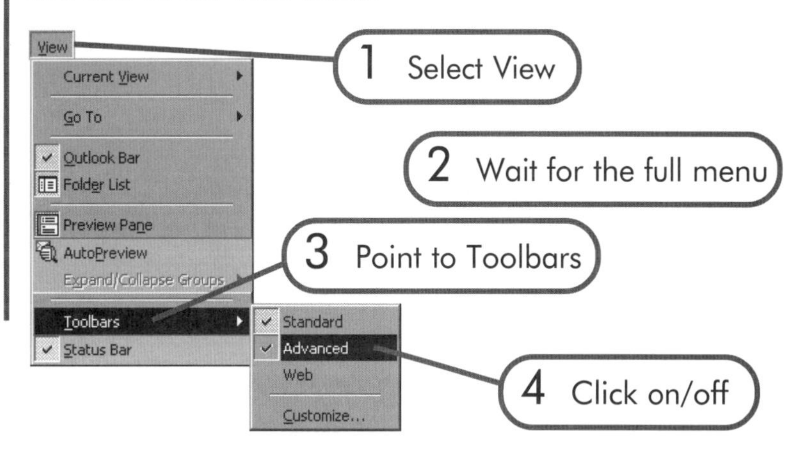

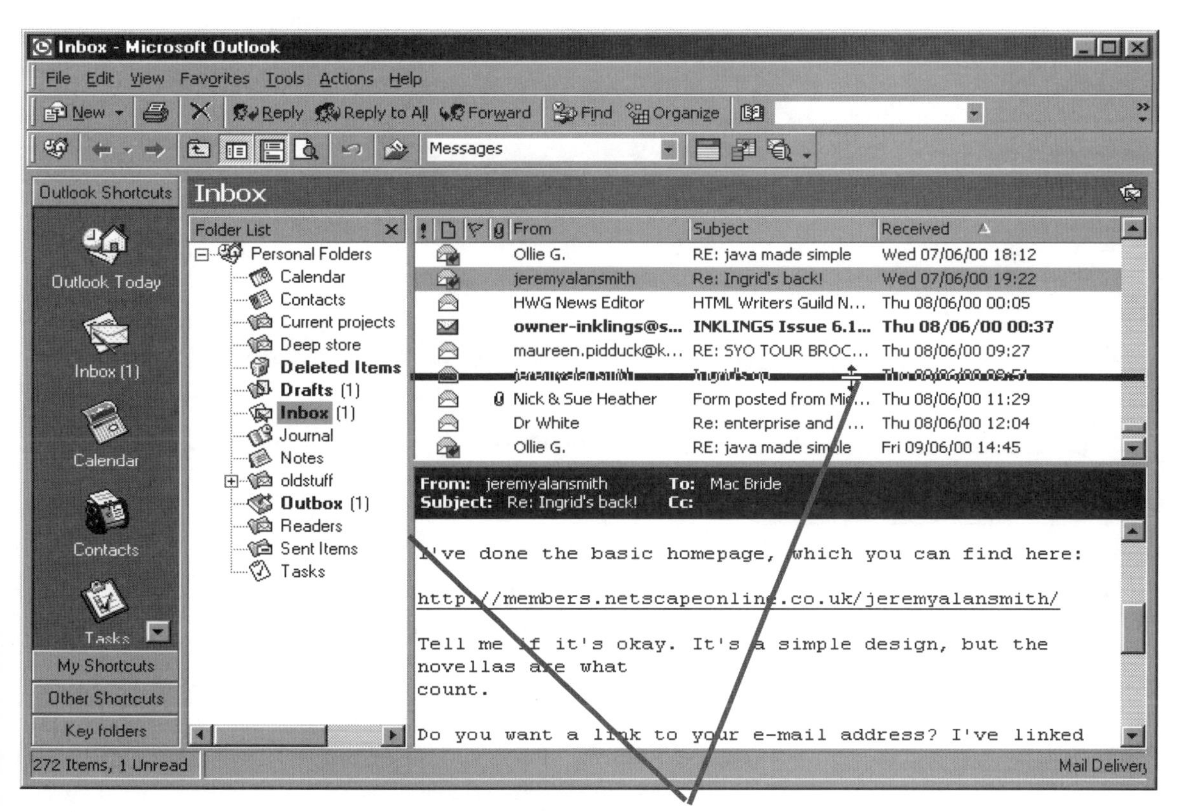

To adjust the relative size of two panes, drag on their dividing line

Sending messages

Basic steps

To send e-mail, all you need is the address – and something to say! Messages can be composed and sent immediately if you are on-line, or composed off-line and sent later. If you are writing to someone who also uses Outlook or other modern e-mail software, you can add impact with HTML formatting.

1 Click New, or select Mail Message from the drop-down list.

2 Type the To: address.

or

3 Click the To... button to open the Select Names dialog box.

4 Select the names and click To-> or Cc-> to copy them to the Recipients lists.

5 Click OK.

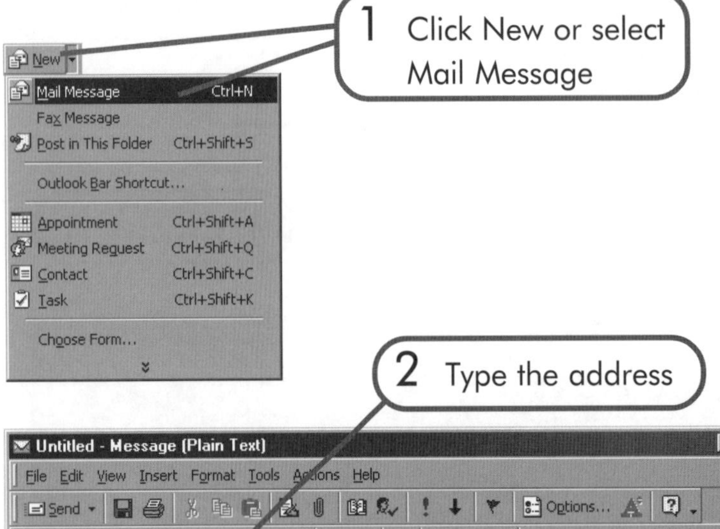

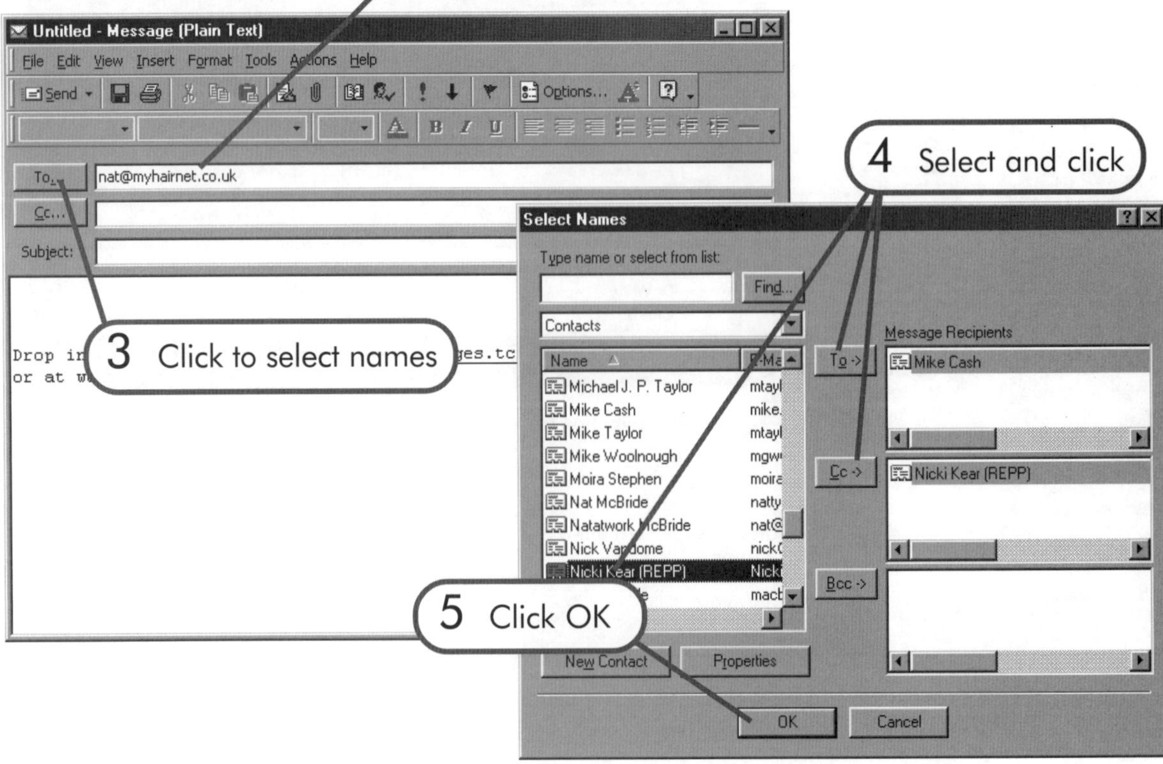

6 Type a Subject.

7 Type your message.

8 If you are using HTML, format the text as required.

9 Click Send to send the message.

- The message will be sent immediately, or stored in the Outbox until you go on-line.

Take note

Subjects help your recipients to organise their messages. Make them brief, but clear.

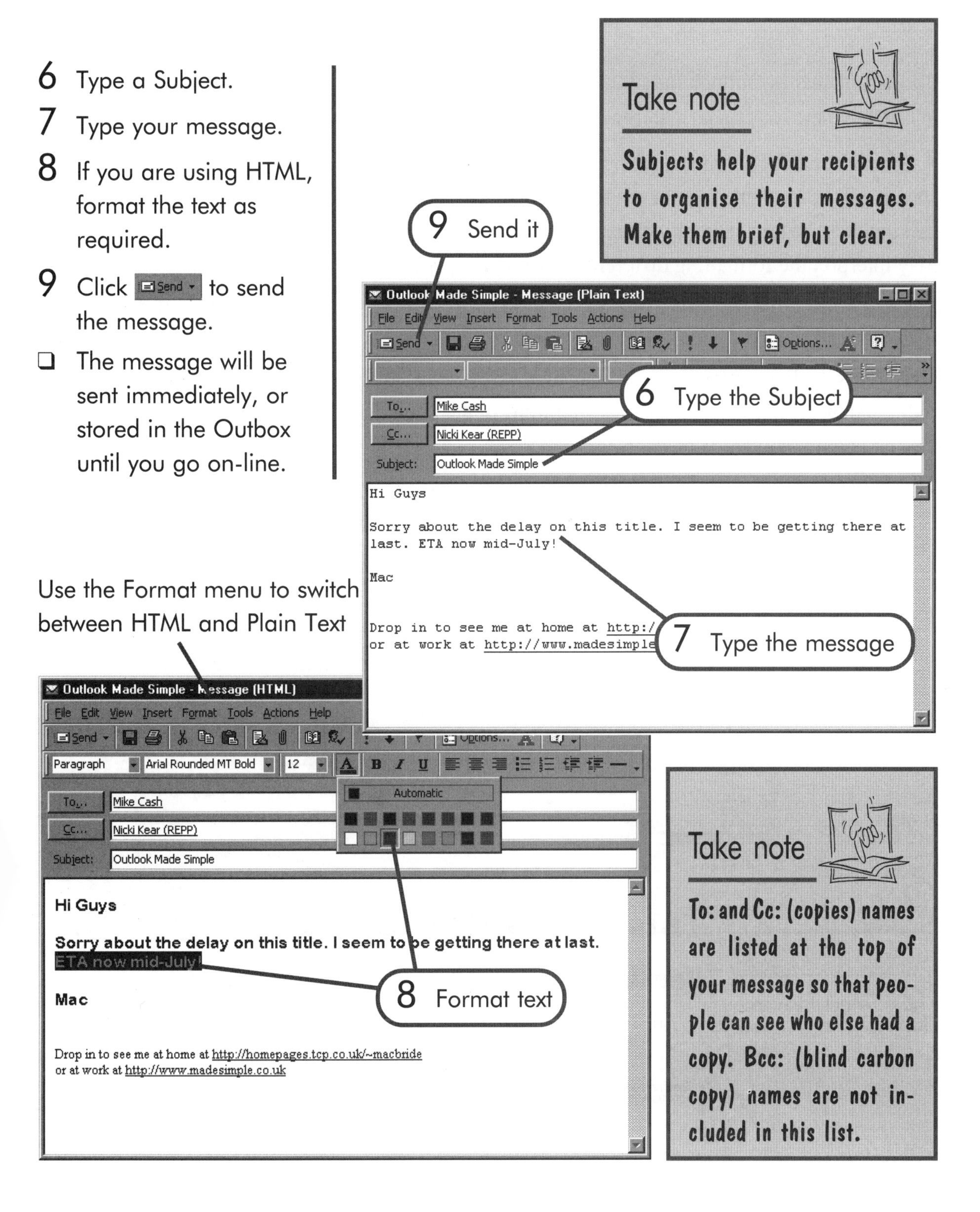

Take note

To: and Cc: (copies) names are listed at the top of your message so that people can see who else had a copy. Bcc: (blind carbon copy) names are not included in this list.

Formatted messages

Formatting text in Outlook may look similar to formatting it in Word, but there is a crucial difference – this is based on HTML.

A Word document is (normally) printed, and what you see on screen will be the same as your reader sees on paper. An e-mail message will be read in your recipient's e-mail software, which may interpret the formatting differently, or not display it at all.

It is better to use styles, rather than fonts. Fonts are very likely to vary – you cannot guarantee that your recipients will have the same fonts on their systems. Styles may also vary – they can be redefined by the user – but at least the hierarchy of headings and the list layouts will stay constant.

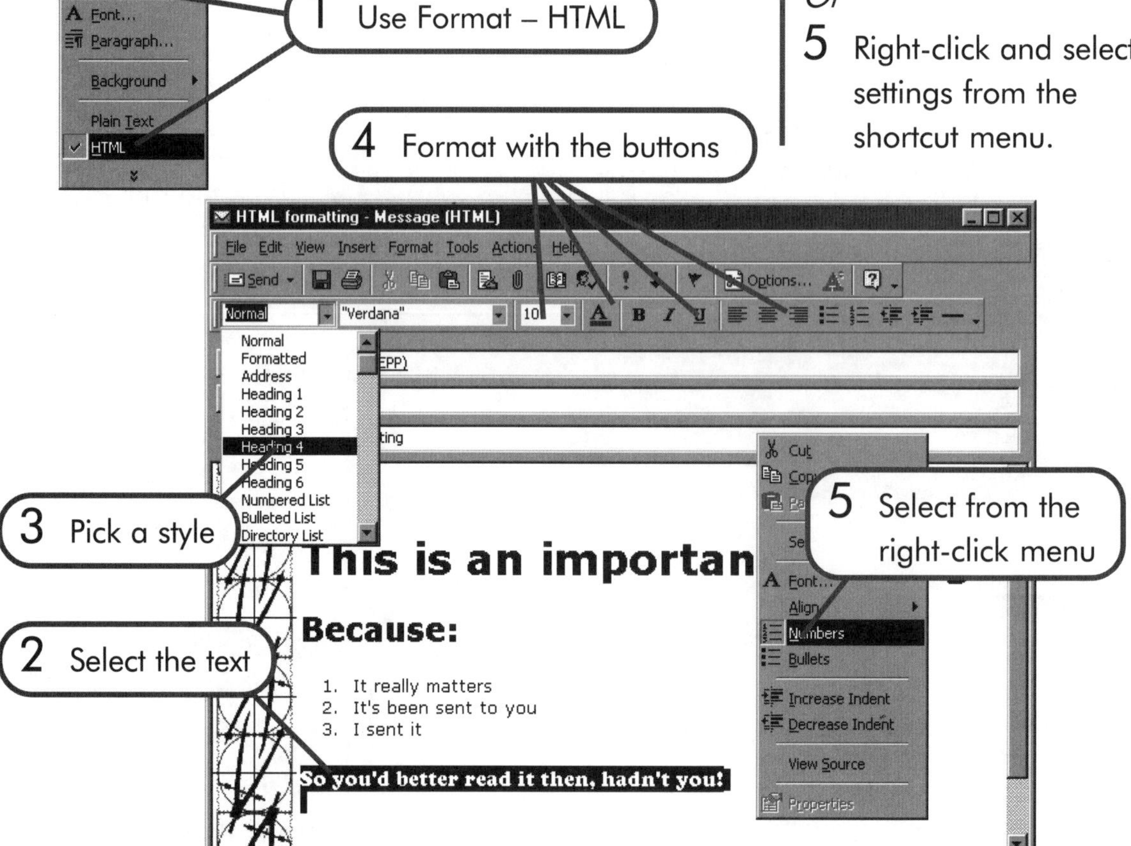

Basic steps

1 If the message is set for Plain Text, open the Format menu and select HTML.

2 Select the text to be styled.

3 Drop-down the style list and pick a style.

4 Set the colour, size or alignment by clicking the toolbar buttons.

Or

5 Right-click and select settings from the shortcut menu.

Basic steps

1 Open the Format menu, point to Background then...

2 Point to Color and select from the palette.

Or

3 Click on Picture...

4 At the Background Picture dialog box, click Browse...

5 Pick a picture and click Select.

6 Click OK.

Backgrounds

You can restrict your formatting to just picking out important bits in bold or a different colour, or you can go for a full-scale technicolour production – in which case, you'll need a fancy background.

You can set the colour, or add a picture, or both. There is a small selection of pictures available, or you can create your own. They must be in GIF or JPG format and should be small, and designed to be repeated down the page – most background pictures are a variety of stripe.

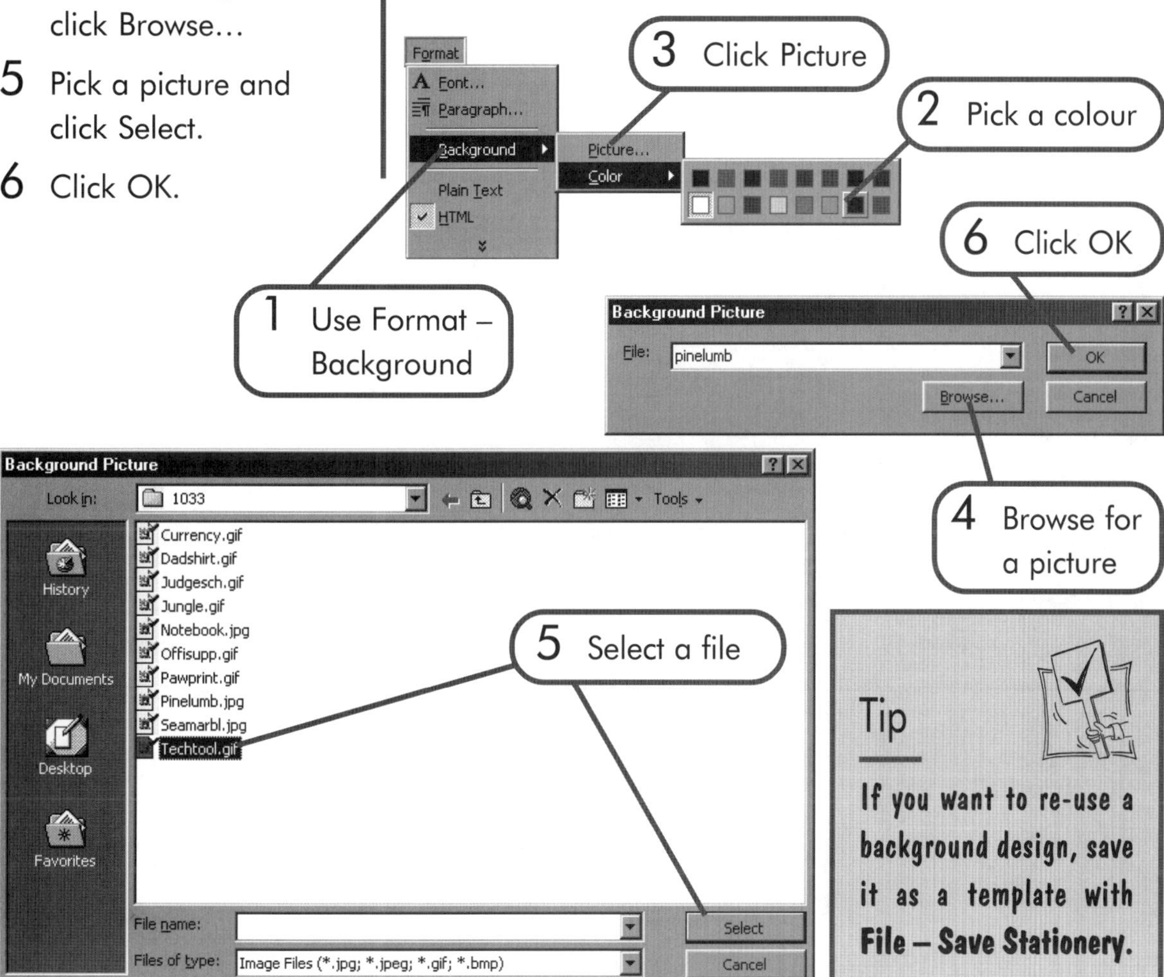

Tip

If you want to re-use a background design, save it as a template with File – Save Stationery.

Incoming mail

Basic steps

If you work in an office with a permanently open connection to the Internet, you can set Outlook to pick up incoming e-mail for you automatically (on the *Mail Delivery* tab of the **Options** dialog box, see page 86). If you get on-line through a dial-in connection, or want to check for new mail at an unscheduled time, use the Send/Receive routine to pick up your mail.

The Sender and Subject information in headers should tell you who messages are from and what they are about. Use the headers to decide which to read first – and to identify junk mail. Just click [X] to delete the current message.

1. Open the Tools menu, point to Send/Receive then select the account or click [Send/Receive] to check all your mail and fax accounts.
2. Click on a header to open its message in the Preview pane.

Or

3. Double-click to open a message in a new window.

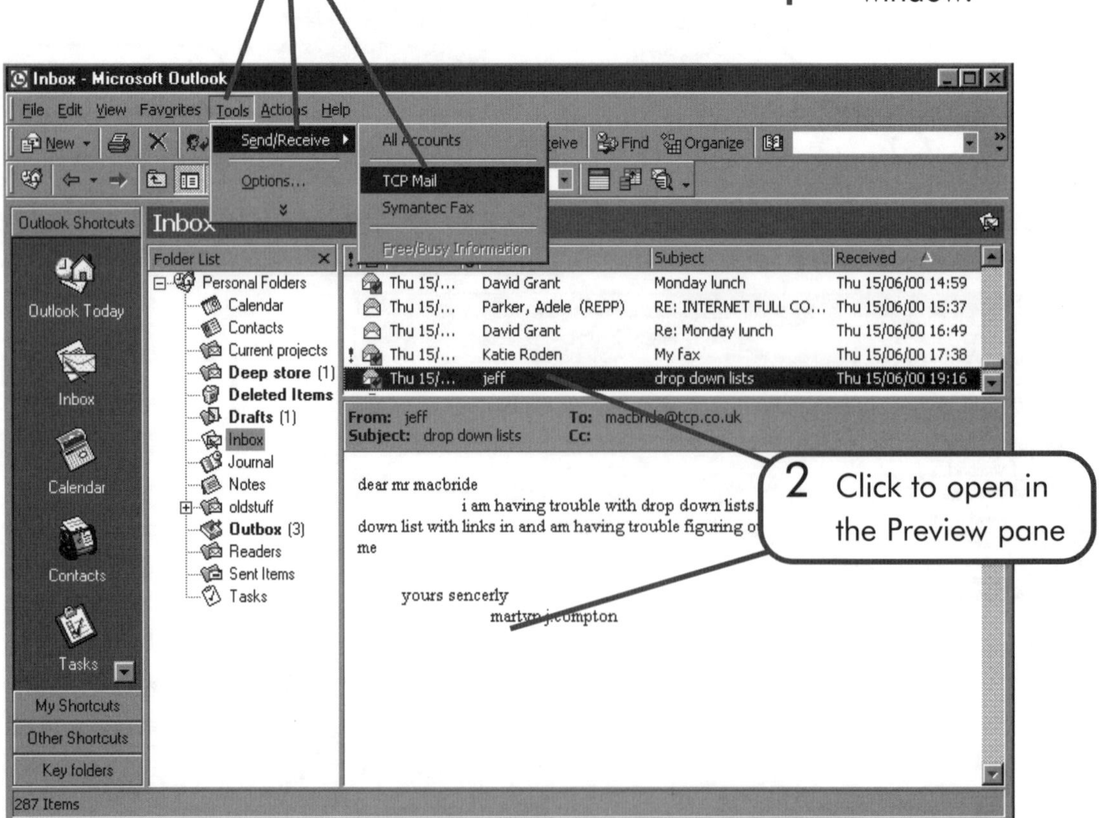

Basic steps

1. Select the message and click a reply or forward button.
2. When *replying*, the address will be copied in for you – when *forwarding* you must enter the address.
3. Delete unwanted text.
4. Add your own text.
5. Send the message as normal.

Reply and forward

The toolbar buttons offer a simple way to reply to or to forward on an incoming messages.

Reply	Reply to the sender
Reply to All	Reply to the sender and all who received a copy
Forward	Forward the message to another person

When forwarding, the original text is copied into the new message. This can also happen when replying – see page 84.

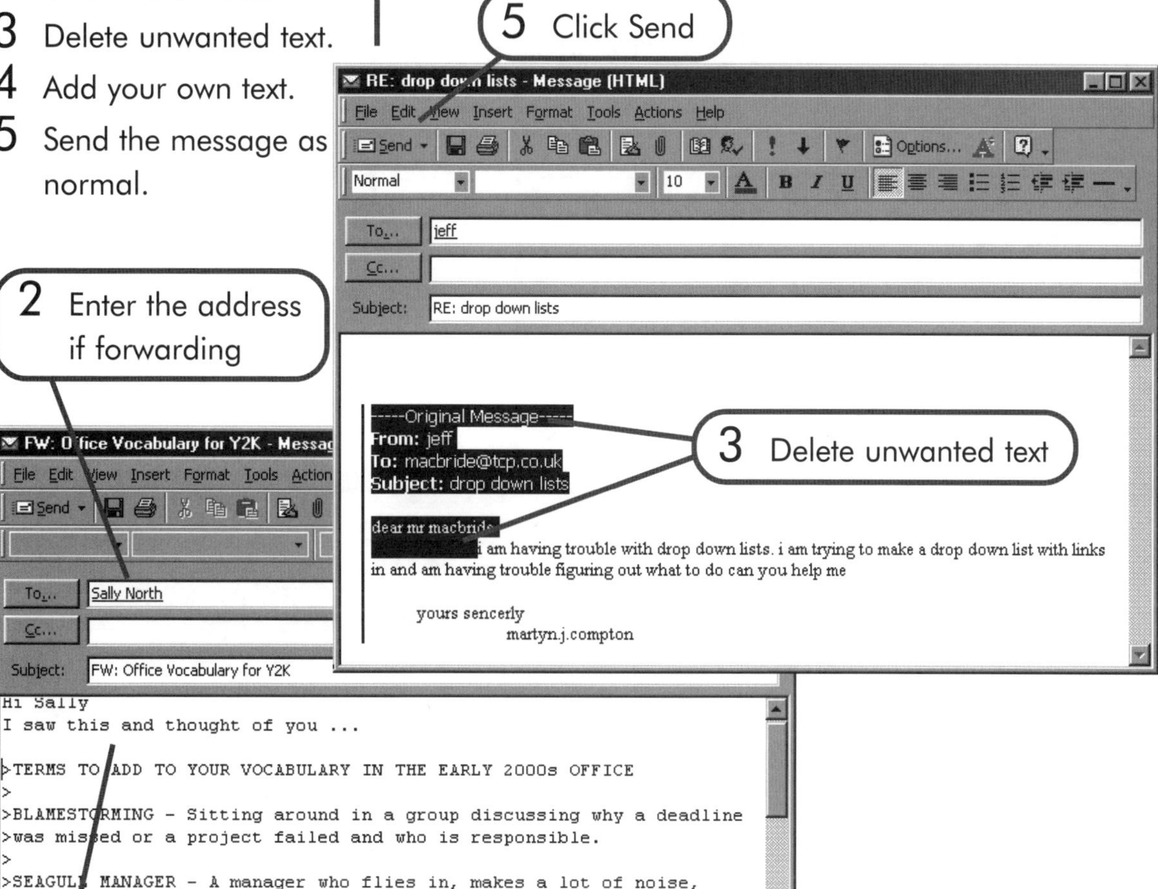

Names and nicknames

Basic steps

You have seen how to get an address into the To: slot by typing or by picking it from the Select Names box. There are also two other ways.

You can give a contact a nickname then type that in place of the address – Outlook will substitute it for you.

1. Click [Address Book icon] in the New Message window to open the Address Book.
2. Select the person and click [Properties].
3. Enter the Nickname, then click [OK].
4. When you want to send a message, type the nickname in place of the address.

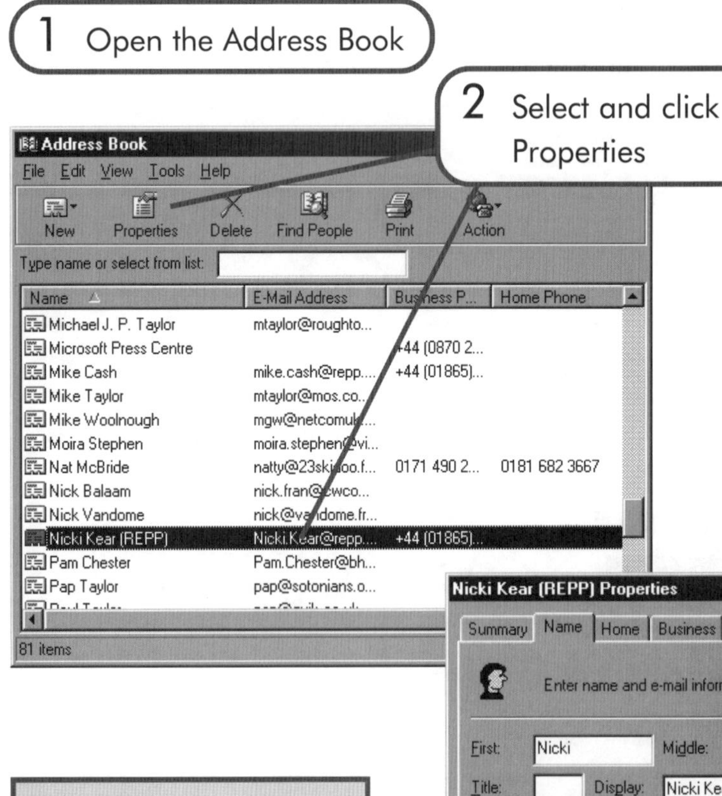

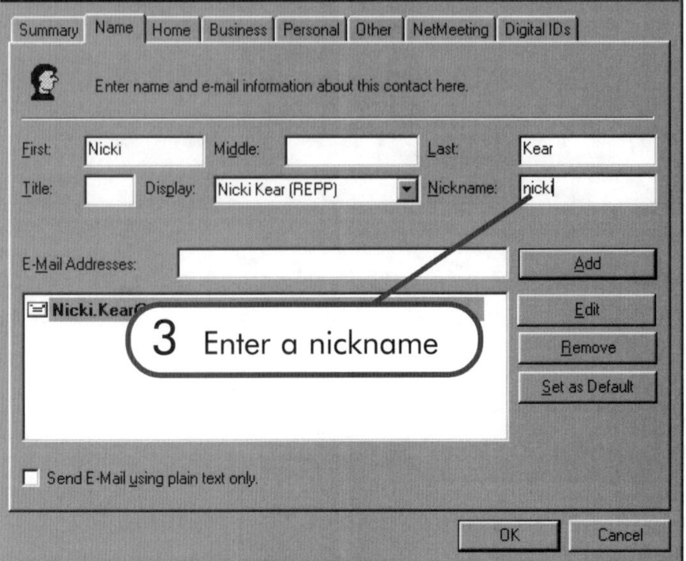

Take note

You can also set a nickname on the Details tab of a Properties dialog box in Contacts.

Basic steps

1 Type all or part of the name as the address.
2 Compose your message as normal and click [Send].
3 The Check Names dialog box will open if there are several matches. Pick the one you want.
4 Click [OK].

The Name Check

This is even easier! If you simply type part or all of a person's normal name, Outlook will search Contacts for any matches. If it only finds one, the contact's address will be copied in. If it finds several possible matches, it will then ask you which one you mean.

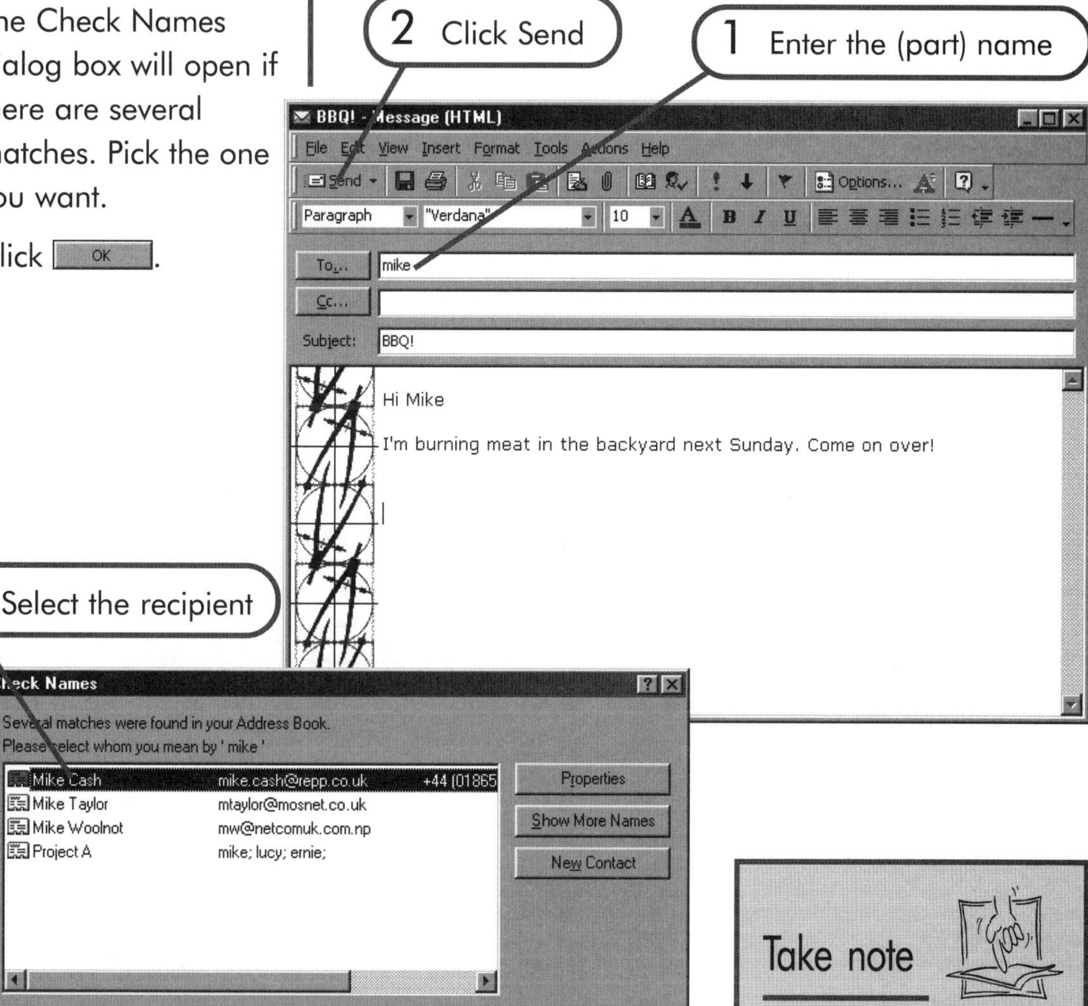

Take note

The Address Book is just a different way of looking at your Contacts.

Mail folders

Basic steps

There are initially four mail folders:

Inbox where new mail arrives;
Outbox for messages awaiting delivery;
Sent for copies of outgoing mail;
Deleted where messages are stored after deletion.

Messages in Deleted are removed at the end of the session if you have set the **Empty messages from 'Deleted Items'...** option (page 67).

It is useful to set up one or more new folders for long-term storage. You might have one for each project, topic or set of contacts – at the very least, you should have an *Old Mail* folder so that your Inbox doesn't get too cluttered.

- Creating a new folder

1 In the Mail window, open the File menu, point to Folder and select New Folder...

2 Select the folder in which to create it – select *Personal Folders* for a top-level folder.

3 Give it a name.

4 Click OK.

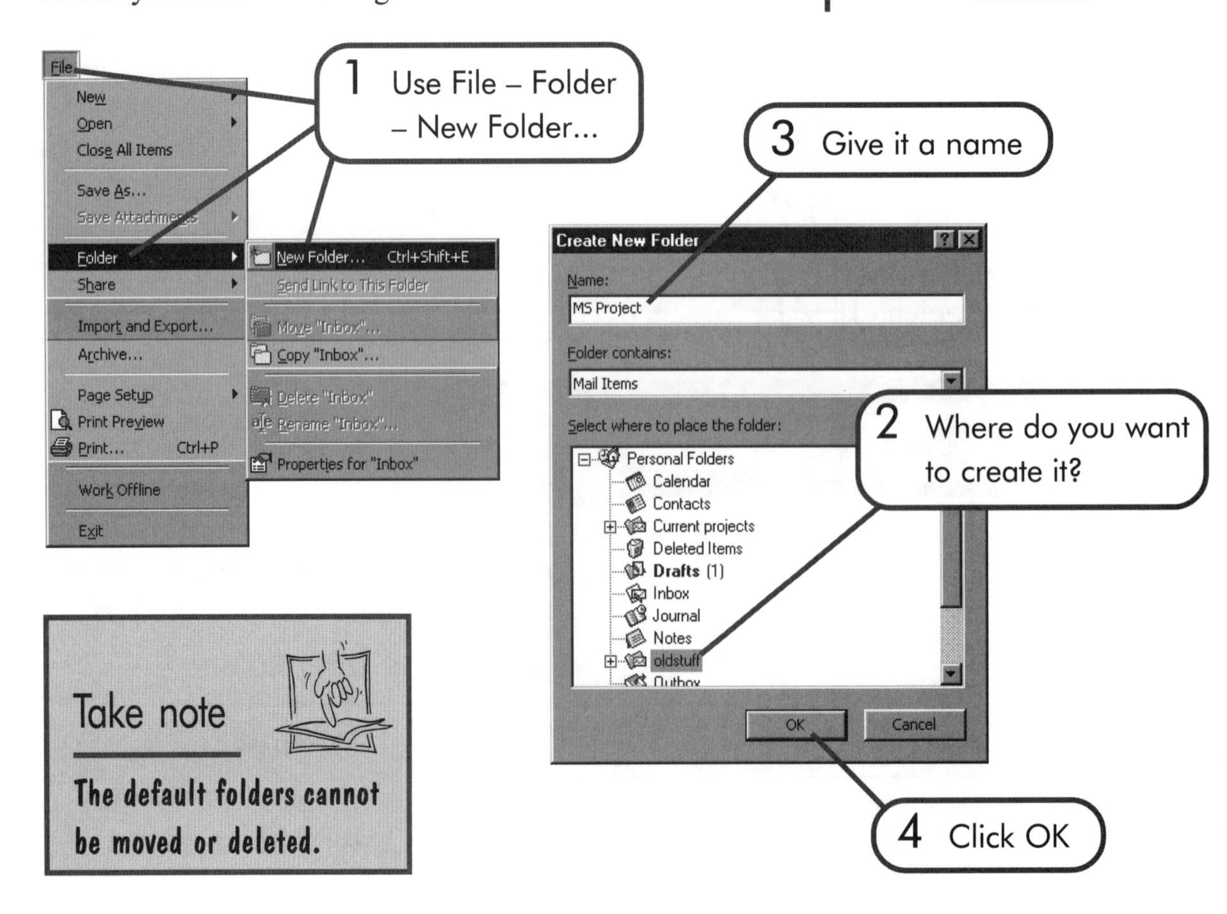

Take note

The default folders cannot be moved or deleted.

- Moving messages

5 Drag the message to the target folder.

Or

6 Right-click on the message and select Move to Folder from the shortcut menu.

7 Select the folder and click OK.

- Copying messages

8 Hold down the right button as you drag.

9 When you drop the message into its new folder a menu will open – select Copy.

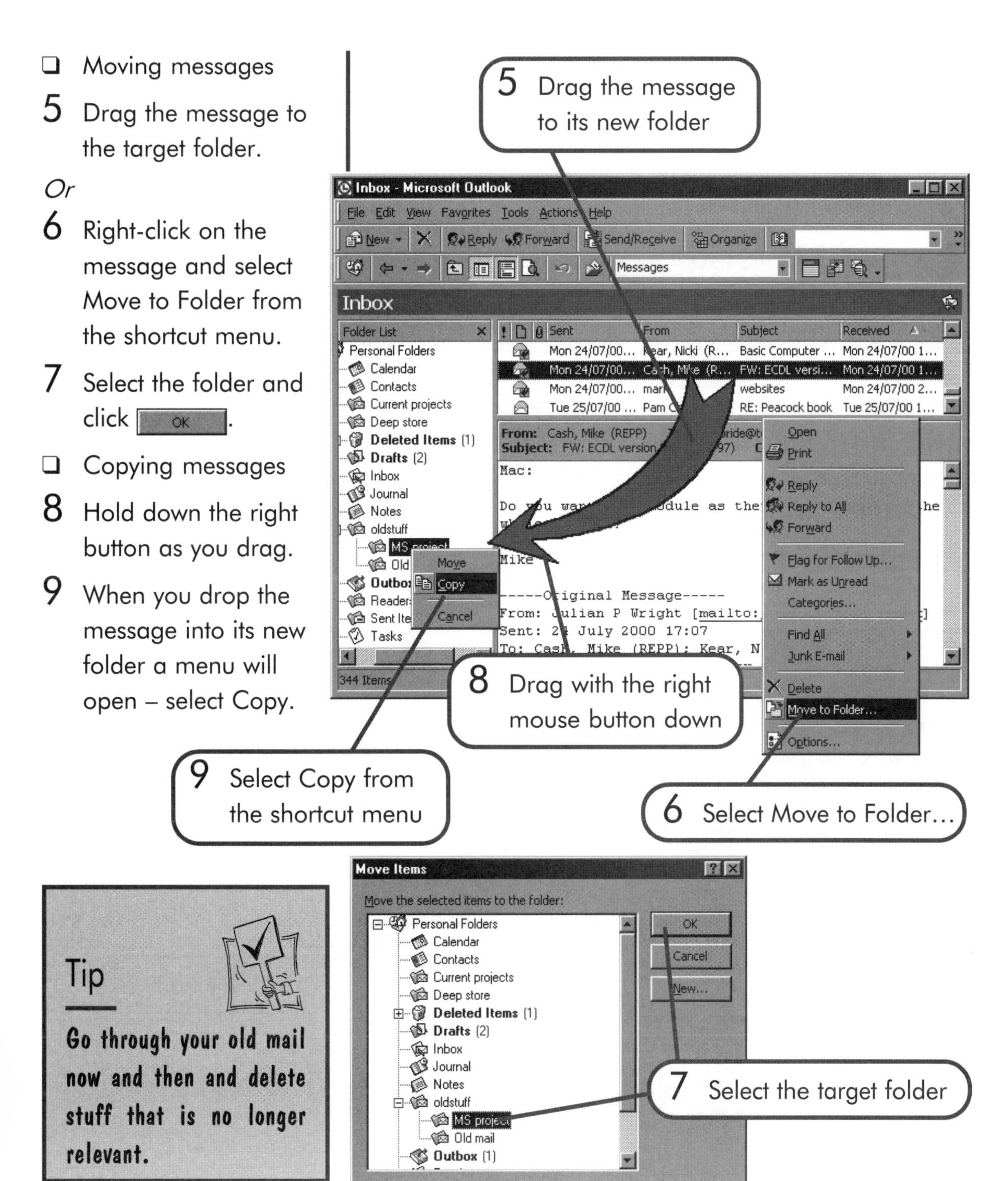

Tip

Go through your old mail now and then and delete stuff that is no longer relevant.

Lost in the mail?

Basic steps

The Find routine is almost identical to that in Contacts, but it is far more useful here – it is just so much easier to lose messages! (This is particularly true if, like me, you tend to leave messages in your Inbox for ages before you get round to deleting them or moving them into long-term storage.)

The standard Find will look for a word either in the **From** and **Subject** fields only, or in the message and all of the text fields. It will search only in the current mail folder.

The Advanced Find allows you to define the message more closely, including – very usefully – two ways to specify the time when a message was received, sent or otherwise processed. The search will normally be through all your personal folders, but can be restricted to a selected one if required.

1 Go to Inbox, or whichever mail folder you want to search.

2 Click Find or open the Tools menu and select Find.

3 Enter all or part of the name or other text into the Look for slot.

4 Tick Search all text... if you want to include the message body.

5 Click Find Now.

6 If you get nothing, or too many results, click Advanced Find...

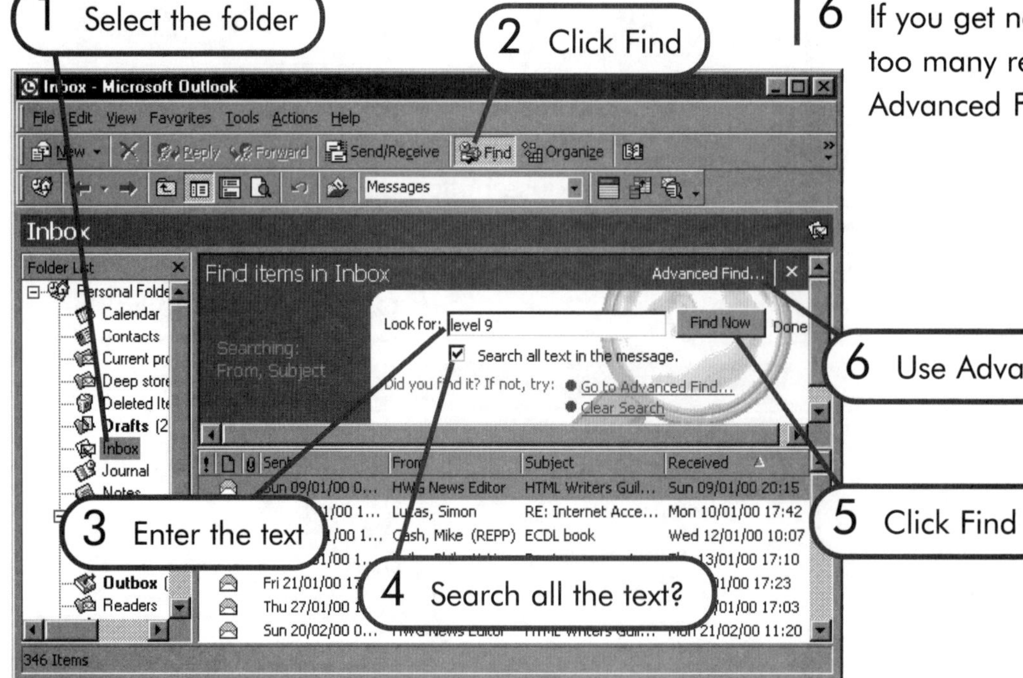

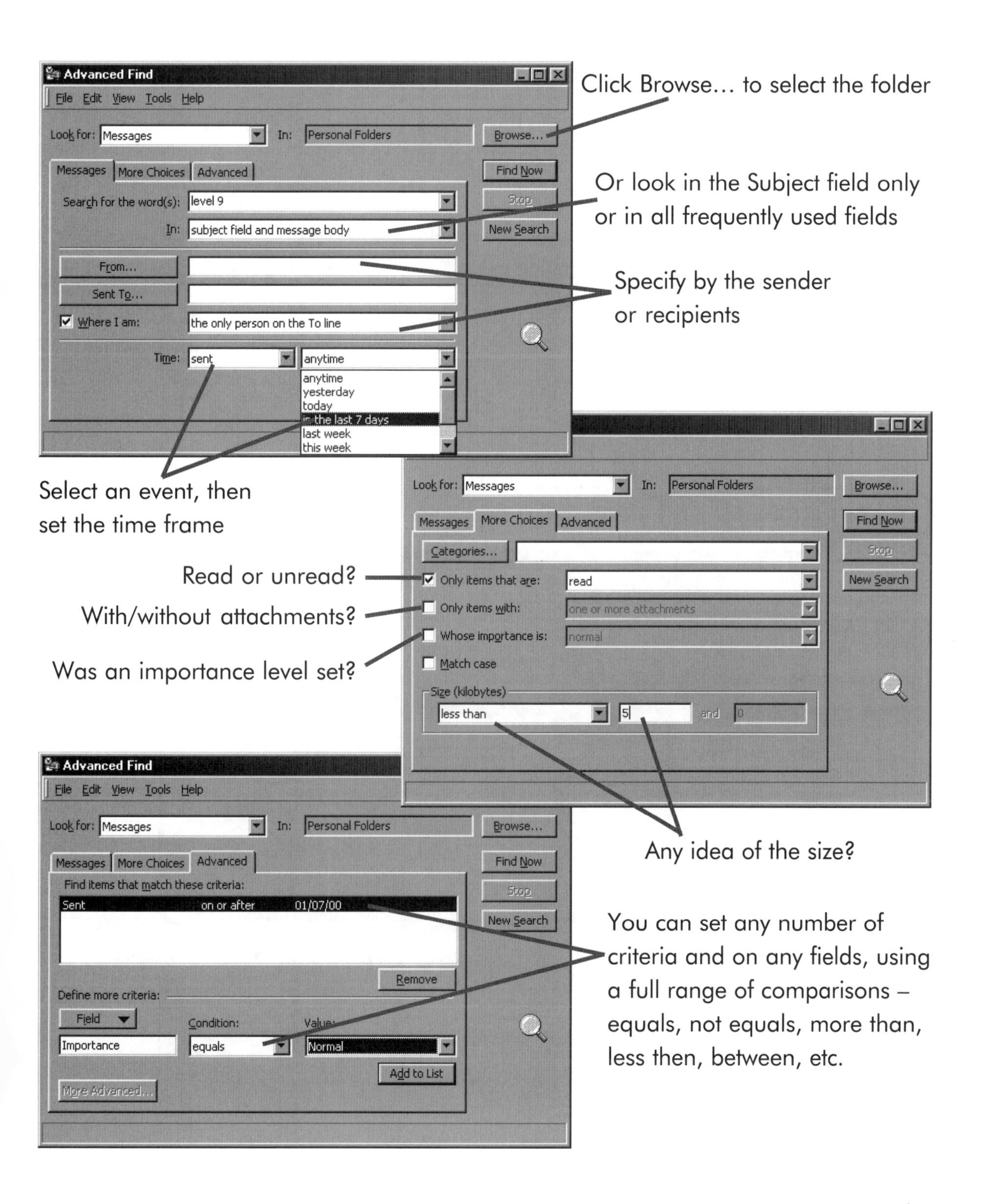
Advanced Find
File Edit View Tools Help
Look for: Messages
In: Personal Folders
Browse...
Messages
More Choices
Advanced
Find Now
Search for the word(s): level 9
Stop
In: subject field and message body
New Search
From...
Sent To...
Where I am: the only person on the To line
Time: sent
anytime
anytime
yesterday
today
in the last 7 days
last week
this week
Click Browse... to select the folder
Or look in the Subject field only or in all frequently used fields
Specify by the sender or recipients
Select an event, then set the time frame
Categories...
Only items that are: read
Only items with: one or more attachments
Whose importance is: normal
Match case
Size (kilobytes)
less than
5
and
0
Read or unread?
With/without attachments?
Was an importance level set?
Any idea of the size?
Find items that match these criteria:
Sent on or after 01/07/00
Remove
Define more criteria:
Field
Condition:
Value:
Importance
equals
Normal
Add to List
More Advanced...
You can set any number of criteria and on any fields, using a full range of comparisons – equals, not equals, more than, less then, between, etc.

Organising your mail

Basic steps

There are four aspects to the Organize routine in the Inbox:

- **Using Folders** offers a handy way to move messages to another folder, and a quick way to create rules (and we'll come back to this on page 82).
- **Using Colors** allows you to choose the colour that a person's messages are to be displayed in.
- **Using Views** offers a simplified selection of the options on the View menu.
- **Junk E-Mail** helps to reduce the flow of junk messages.

1 Click Organize.

❑ Using Folders

2 Select the messages you want to move.

3 Switch to the Using Folders tab.

4 Select the folder from the drop-down list.

5 Click Move.

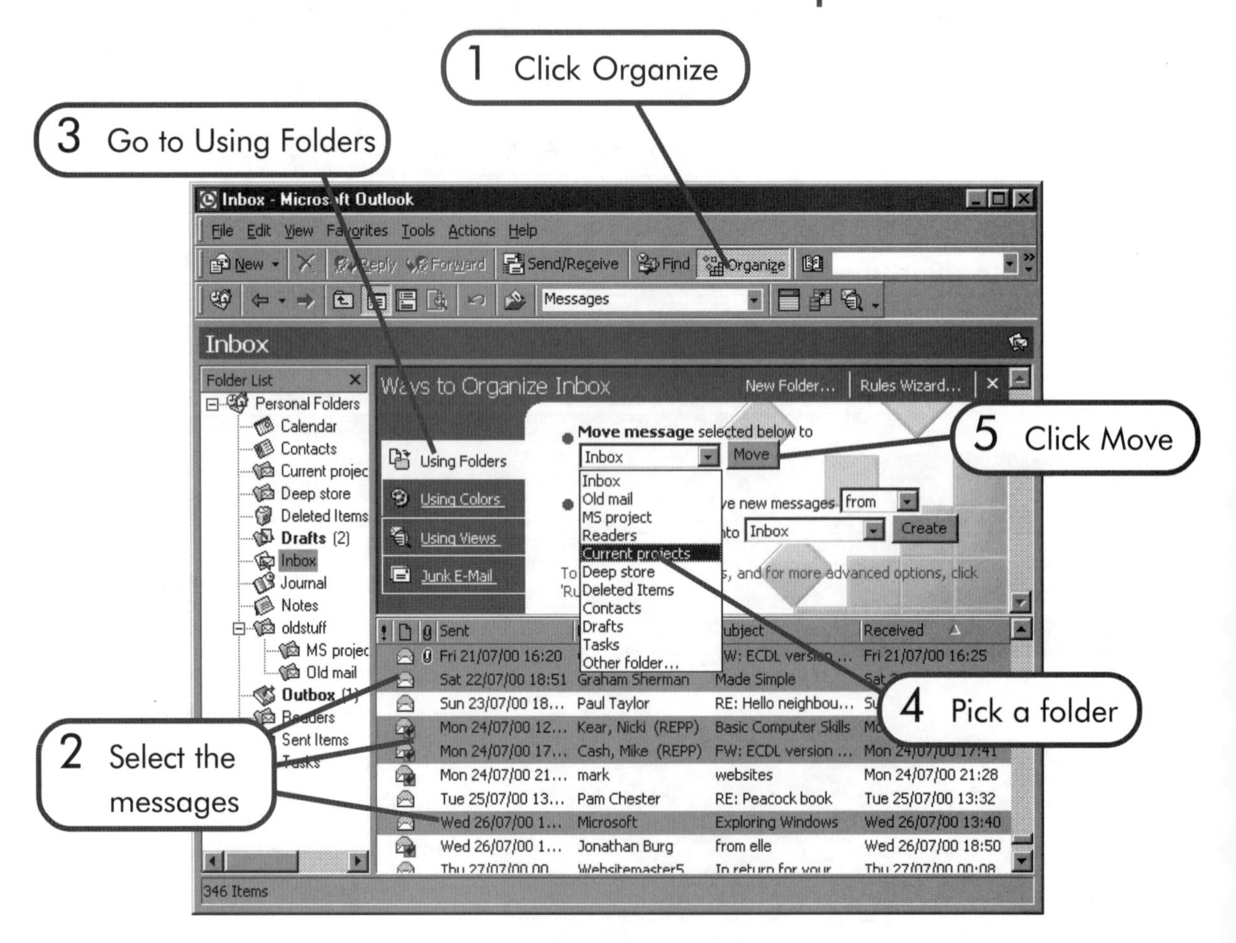

Basic steps

- ❑ Using Colors

1. Select a message from the person you want to highlight.
2. Switch to the Using Colors tab.
3. Select a colour from the drop-down list.
4. Click Apply Color.

- ❑ Using Views

5. Switch to the Using Views tab.
6. Select a style from the drop-down list.

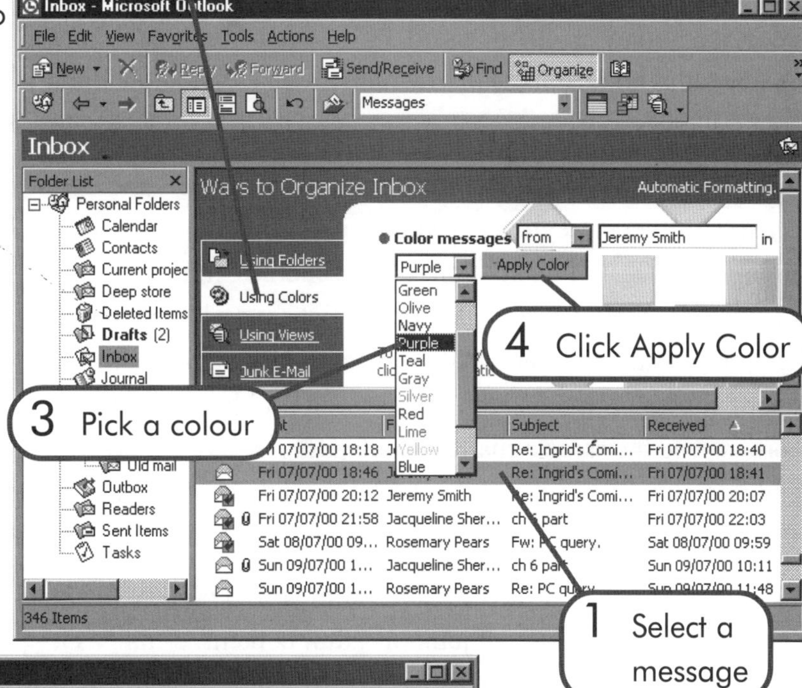

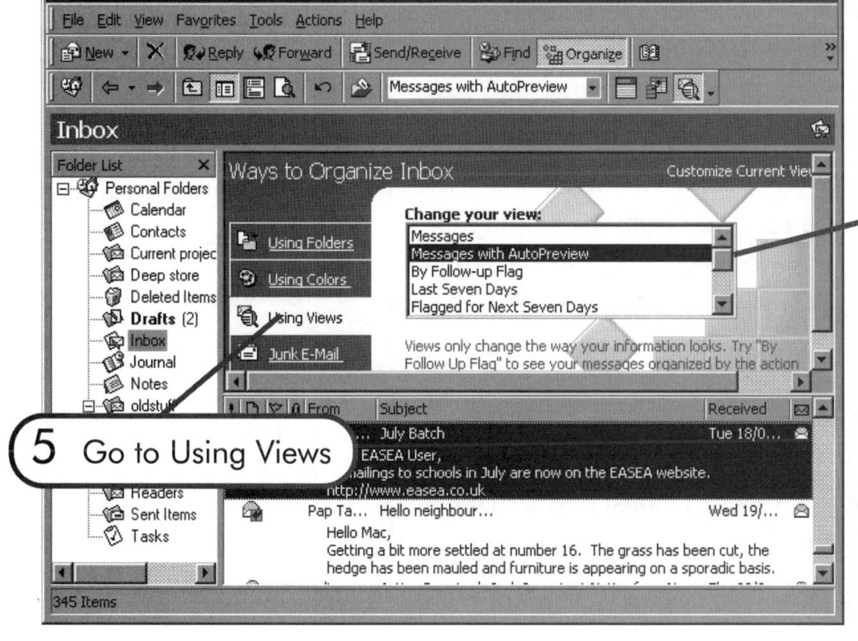

Junk E-Mail

Junk e-mail can be a major headache. It seems to be worse for people with some ISPs (Internet Service Providers) than it is with others, and it is worse for people who use the Internet actively, signing up for newsletters, update offers, Web site memberships and the like, all of which involve giving out their e-mail addresses.

Enterprising individuals compile lists of addresses and sell them on to other entrepreneurs who then send out details of their unmissable offers of make-money-fast schemes, miracle cures, hot sex sites or whatever. Junk e-mail must have a lower hit rate than junk postal mail – and that is low enough – but because the cost of sending it is so slight, this is not a problem. It costs no more to send the same e-mail to 1,000 addresses than it does to send it to one. So if the junk mailer hooks only one mug out of 10,000, the mailshot was worth the effort.

Outlook's junk e-mail facilities will help you to control them. You can set up rules to spot junk or 'adult content' e-mail as it arrives and either colour it, for easy identification, or move it to another folder – including 'Deleted items'.

You can also take other steps to help yourself.

- Be wary of giving out your e-mail address when on-line.
- If there is an option to be removed from the mailing list, only use it if you know the senders, otherwise you may just prove that your address is live – and get even more junk mail!
- Forward a copy of the message to your ISP – who may be able to block similar messages in future – or to the sender's ISP, who may take action against junk e-mailers.
- Junk is normally easy to identify from the subject lines – delete the messages without reading them.

Basic steps

1 Click [Organize].

❑ Automatic marking

2 Switch to the Junk E-Mail tab.

3 For Junk, select *Color* or *Move* from the drop-down list.

4 Pick the colour or the target folder and click [Turn on].

5 Repeat steps 3 and 4 for Adult Content messages.

❑ Creating sender lists

6 Right-click on a junk message.

7 Point to Junk E-Mail and select Add to Junk (or Adult Content) Senders List.

8 Click on the click here link at the bottom of the Junk E-Mail tab.

9 Follow the links to view or edit the lists, or go to the Outlook Web Site to download the latest filters.

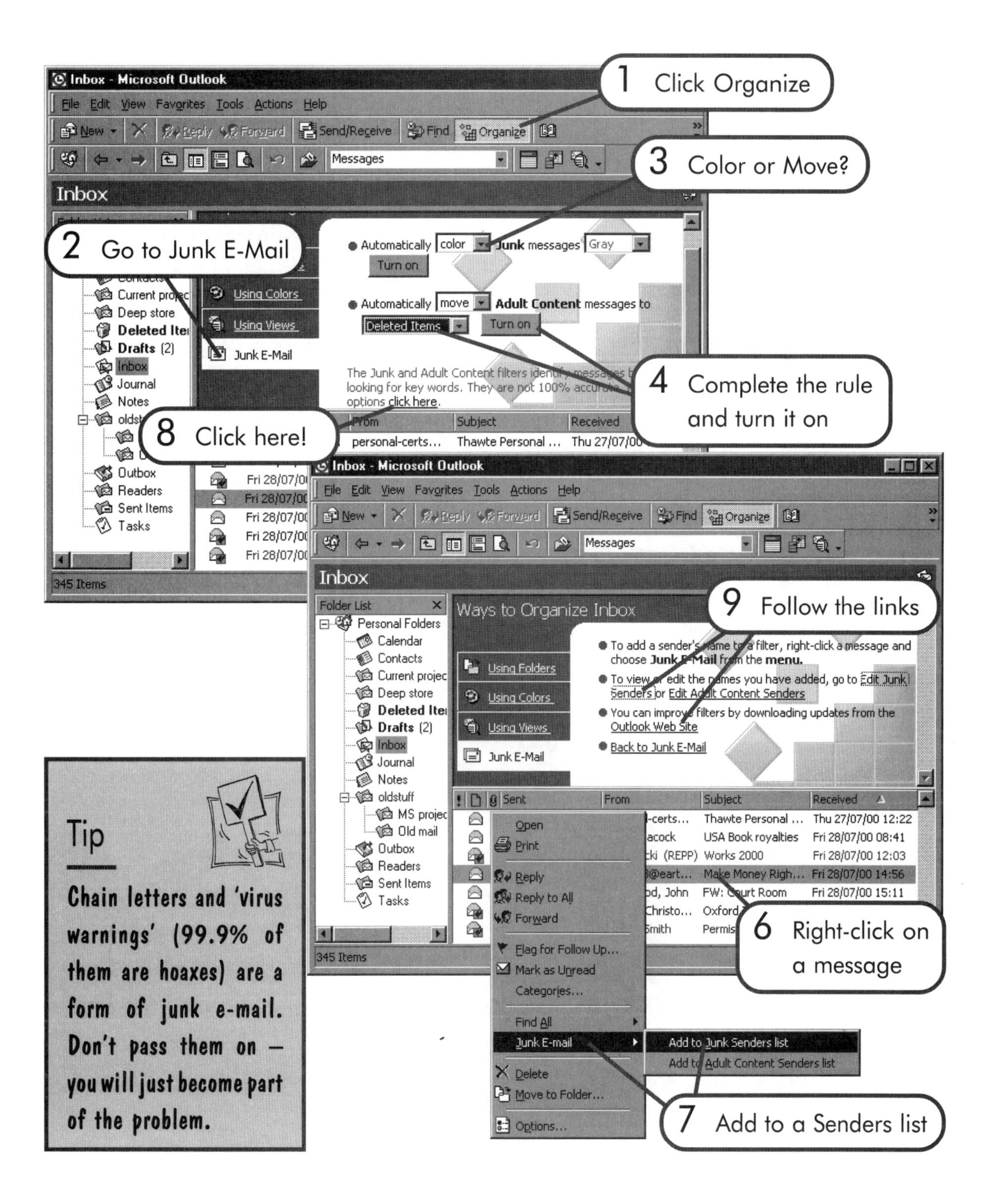

Tip

Chain letters and 'virus warnings' (99.9% of them are hoaxes) are a form of junk e-mail. Don't pass them on – you will just become part of the problem.

Files by mail

Basic steps

Files of any type – graphics, word-processor and spreadsheet documents, audio and video clips, Web pages (or links to them), can be attached to messages and sent by e-mail. Compared to sending them printed or on disk in the post, e-mail is almost always quicker, cheaper and often more reliable. The larger the file, the longer it takes to get through, and the greater the chance of errors – increasing transmission time even more. Somewhere over 2Mb, the time you and your recipient spend on-line will start to outweight the postage costs.

You can type an URL into a message at any time, but if you are on a page and want to send its URL (or the whole page!) to someone, there is a routine that will make it simple.

1 Compose the message as normal.

2 Open the Insert menu and select File...

3 Browse through your folders and locate the file.

4 Click Insert.

- The file will be shown in a panel at the bottom of your message.

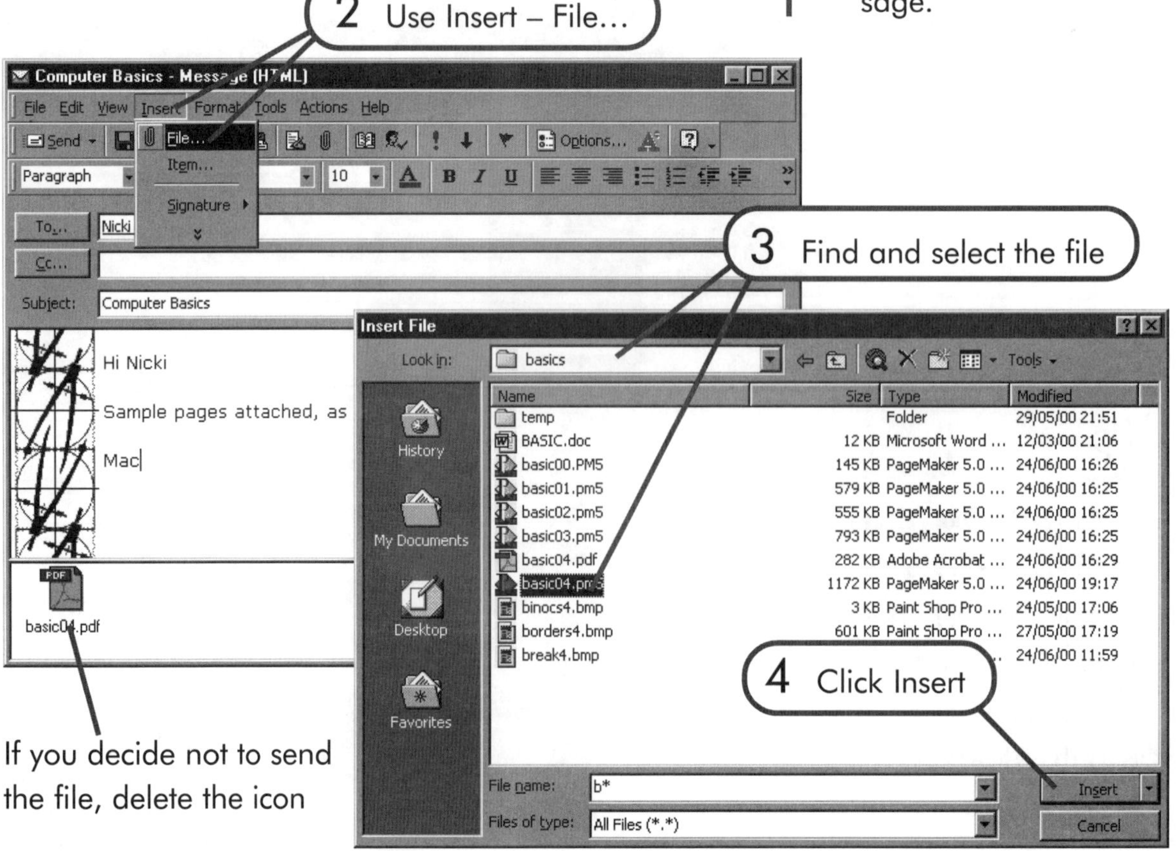

- To send a page or an URL from IE

5 Go to the page.

6 Open the File menu, point at Send and select either Page by E-mail… or Link by E-mail….

7 The page title will be in the Subject line and the URL given as a link in the bottom panel. Enter your recipient and a message.

- To insert an URL into the message text

8 Open the Insert menu and select Hyperlink…

9 Enter the URL and click OK.

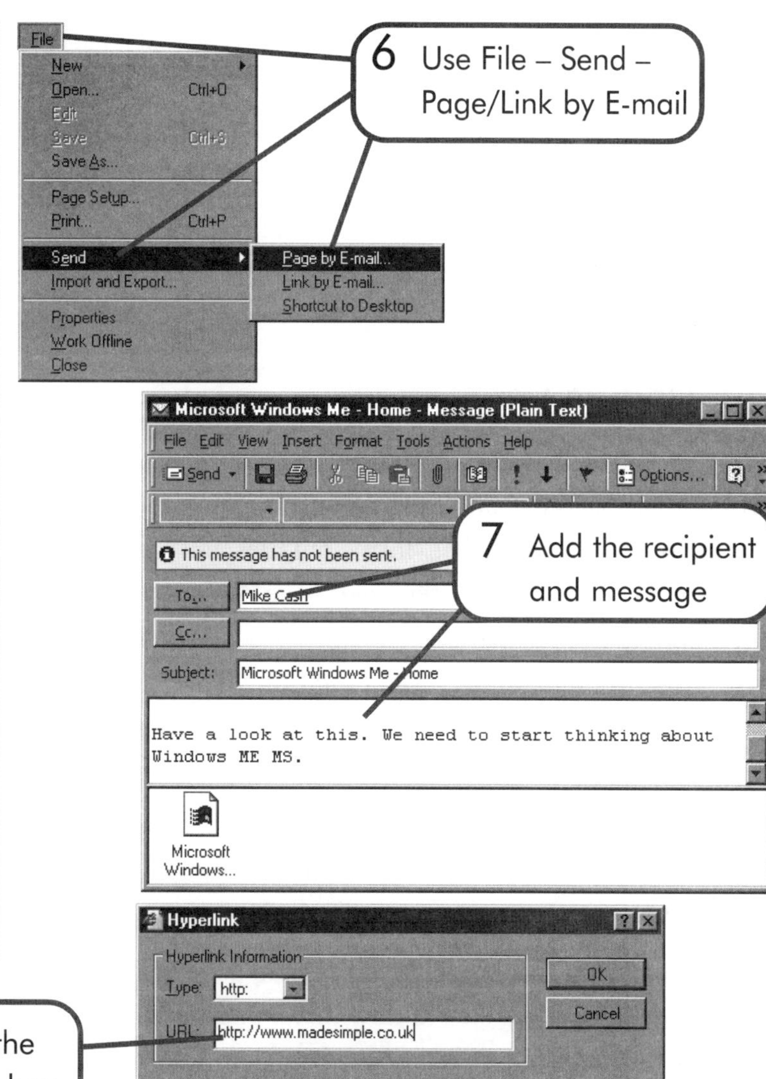

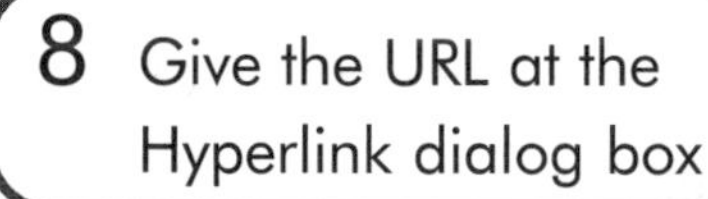

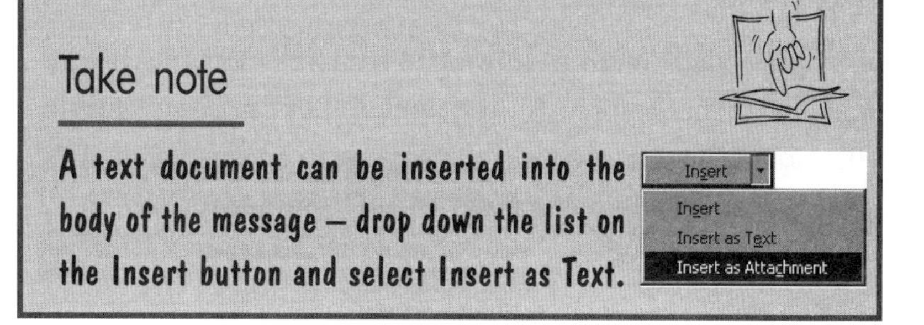

Take note

A text document can be inserted into the body of the message – drop down the list on the Insert button and select Insert as Text.

E-mail etiquette

When you send someone a paper letter, you know that what they receive will be the same as you send, and if you enclose lots of material, you will pay the extra postage.

E-mail is different. Your recipients actively download your messages, which takes time and can cost money. Further, if they are using non-HTML mail software, it can affect the appearance of your messages.

Text and data files

A lot of business users, and some individuals, have e-mail systems that can only handle plain text. There is, of course, no point in sending them HTML-formatted files, but plain text has other implications. These users may have difficulty removing attached files from your messages. Always test with a small file first! There is no point in wasting their download time.

Size

Some e-mail systems set a limit to the size of messages. 1,000 lines (roughly 60Kb) is a typical maximum. An attached file can easily push the message size over the limit.

Even where there is no limit, file size is still a factor. The larger the file, the longer it takes to download, and the higher your recipients' phone bills.With a good modem and a standard phone line, e-mail usually comes in at around 3Kb per second, or 1Mb in 6–7 minutes.

Use the standard WinZip software to compress data files before attaching them. Graphics and document files can be reduced to 10% or less of their original size this way. Even executable files – the most difficult to compress – show some reduction.

Tip

Treat all attached files with caution – this was how the Love Bug virus spread!

Graphics, audio and video files can usually be opened safely, but documents are only safe if you have macro-execution turned off – a Word macro can be very destructive – and executable files (programs or scripts with .EXE, .BAT and .VBE extensions) should never be opened unless you are absolutely sure about their origin.

If a friend sends you a file unexpectedly and it may be damaging, check with them before opening it – someone may be misusing their name.

Subject lines

A clear Subject line identifies a message. Your recipients need this when the mail arrives, to see which to deal with first – and which to ignore completely! They also need it when organising old mail, so that they know which to delete and which to place in what folder.

> **Take note**
>
> **If you want to add a signature to messages, create the file in NotePad or a word-processor, saving it as plain text. Go to the Mail Format tab in the Options dialog box and link it in there.**

Signatures

A signature file can be added to the end of every message. This is a plain text file, usually saved as *personal.sig* or something similar, containing your name, e-mail address and any other contact details you want to give. People's signatures often also contain a favourite quote, advert, or a picture or name created from ASCII characters. e.g.

Example 1

```
-------------
P.K.McBride     |macbride@tcp.co.uk

Computing's Made Simple at http://www.madesimple.co.uk
--------------
```

Example 2

```
------------------------
Gary
           _                                     __/ /__ .
ThE ______/ \ ____    _____ _____ ___ ___    _____  /_ ____/_____   _____
   /  ______// __ \  /  __ \ _ \/ / \ \  / __ \ / /   / __ \  / _  \
  /  \_____/ \_\ \/  \\_/ \\_/  \__\ \/  \_\ \/ \/\/  \_\ \/  \\_/
  \          \  // /    \    \ \    // /    // /    \   // /    \
   \   _____/\____/_____/____/  \_____/  _____/_______/\____/_____/96
  --\_/==============================/   /=========================---
                                    /  \
                                    \___/
```

Summary

- ❑ You can choose which panes to include in the screen display and adjust the layout.
- ❑ When sending a messages, start by selecting who it will go to and write the subject of the message.
- ❑ Messages can be plain text or HTML formatted.
- ❑ You can easily reply to incoming mail, or forward it to a third person.
- ❑ You can specify recipients by giving their nicknames or part of their real names.
- ❑ New mail folders can be created to store old mail. Messages can be easily moved between folders.
- ❑ The Find routines will track down lost messages.
- ❑ The Organize routines make it simpler to manage your mail – the good stuff and the junk!
- ❑ Documents and other files can be sent by mail.
- ❑ E-mail etiquette is based on not wasting other people's time (and phone bills).
- ❑ Signatures can add something extra to your mail – and long ones can add far too much!

5 Inbox options

View options

Basic steps

The **View** menu offers you a range of options for displaying message headers. 'Messages' is the default. Dip in and try the others – some of them can be useful at times.

- The Advanced toolbar is handy for this. If it is not present, go to **View – Toolbars** and turn it on.

1 Open the View menu, point to Current View and select a style.

Or

2 Select from the list in the Advanced toolbar.

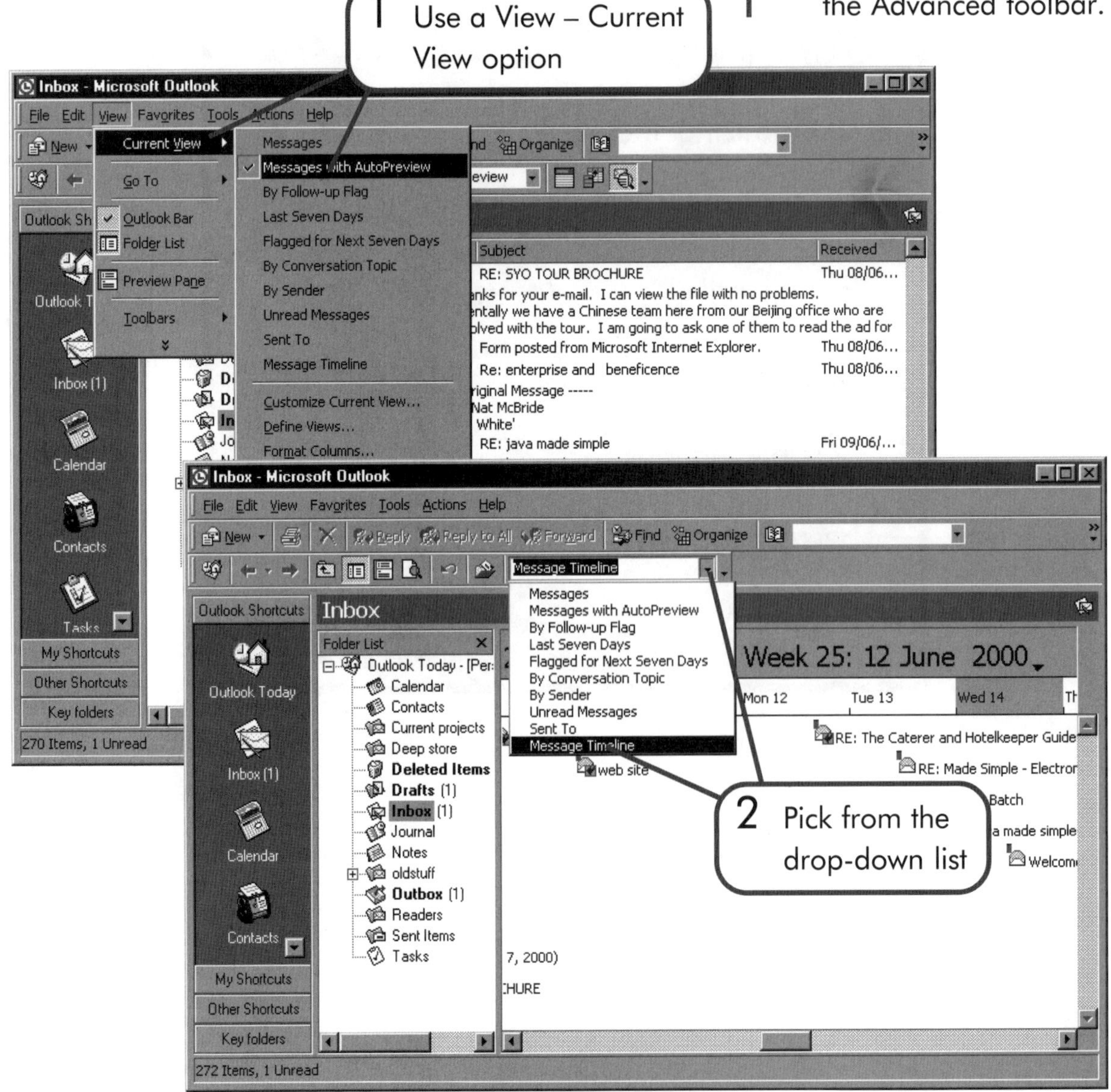

Basic steps

1. In the View menu point to Current View and select Format Columns...
2. Select a Field.
3. Pick a Format from the drop-down list.
4. Edit the column Label if required.
5. Enter a Specific width, or select Best fit to let Outlook set it.
6. Set the Alignment to suit – in general use *Left* for text, *Center* for icons and *Right* for numbers.
7. Click OK.

2 Select a field

Take note

'Field' and 'column' can be used interchangeably, but strictly speaking the field is the data; the column is the space it is displayed in.

Formatting the columns

The Format Columns option allows you to set the style, width and headings of the columns.

- The **Format** options vary according to the nature of the material in the column.
- The **Width** and **Alignment** options are only available with text and date fields.

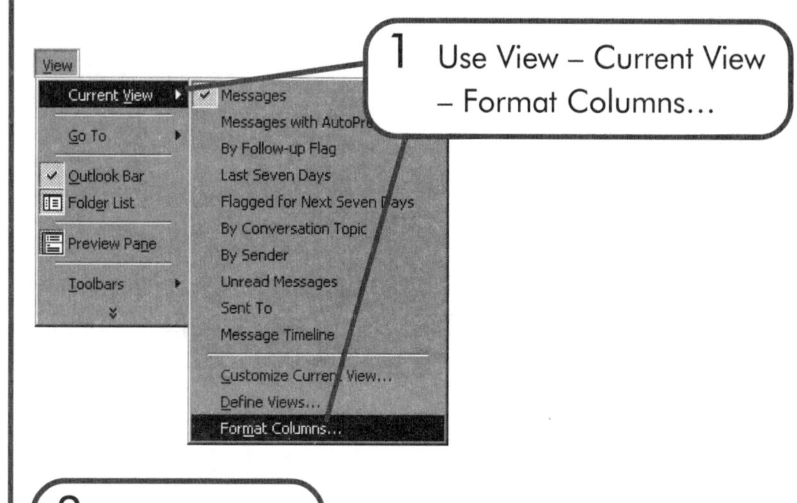

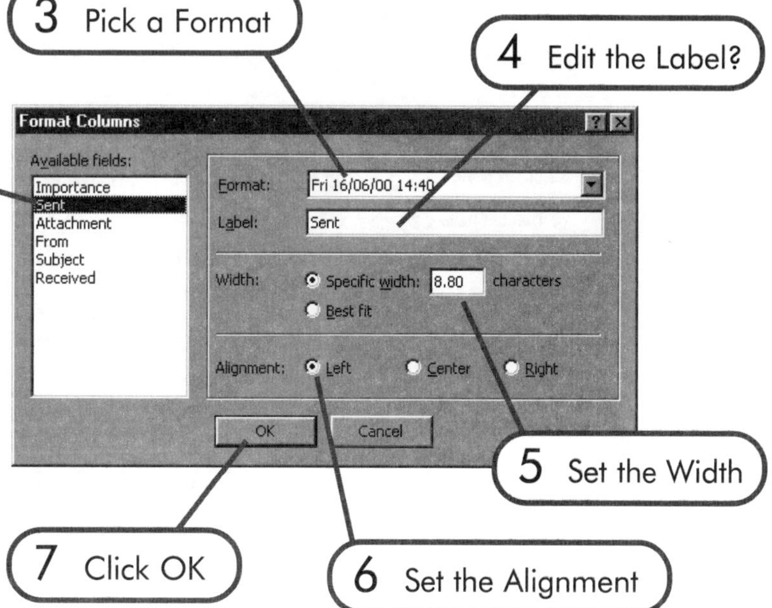

Adding Fields

The standard set of columns will suit most people most of the time, however, other fields can be added easily if required.

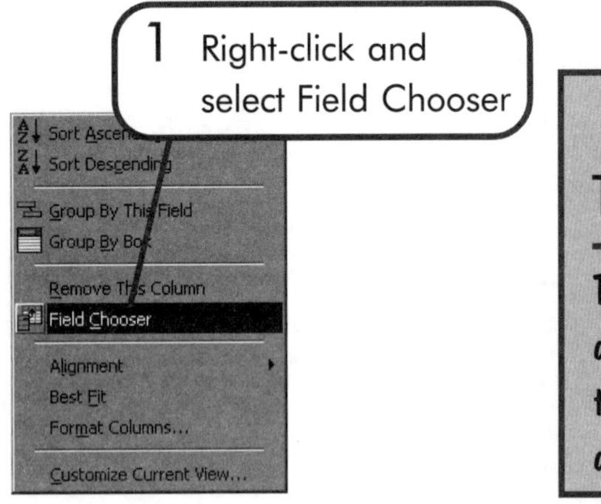

Basic steps

1. Right-click on any column label and select Field Chooser.
2. If you cannot see the field that you want, open the drop-down list and select a different set of fields.
3. Drag the label off the Field Chooser list and drop it between the column labels where you want it to go.

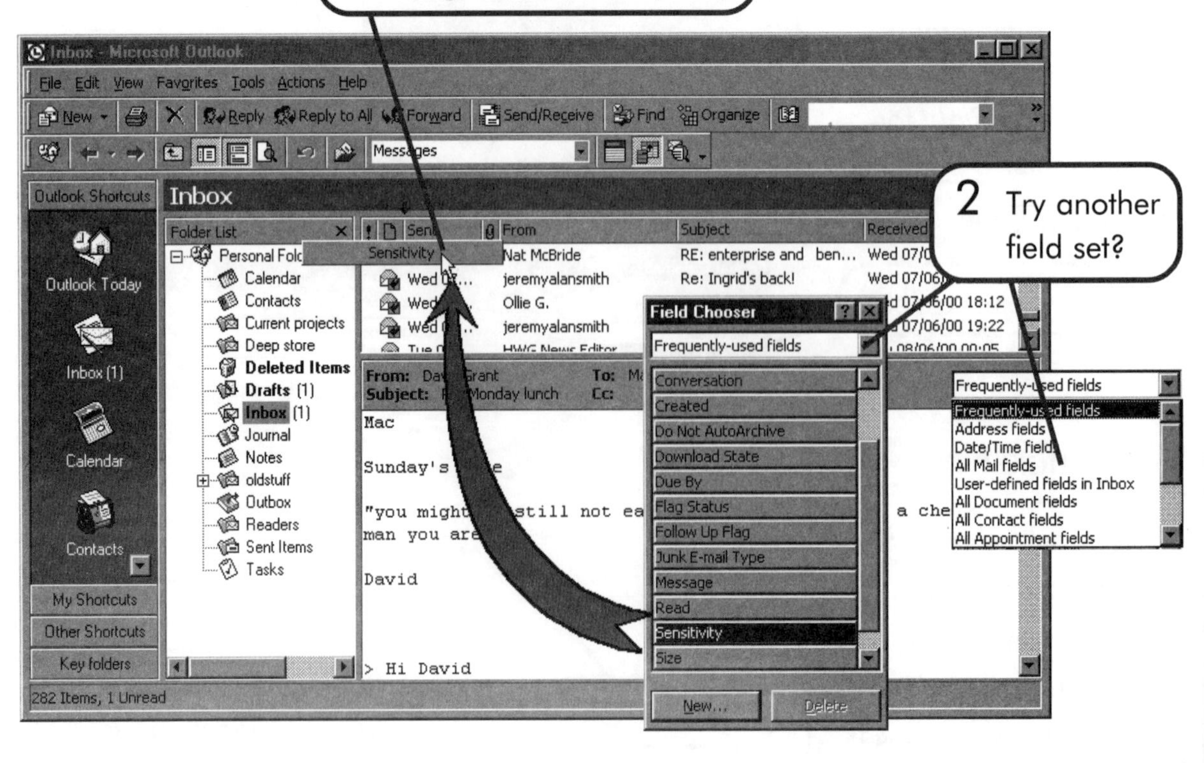

Basic steps

1. Open the View menu, point to Current View and select Customize Current View...
2. At the View Summary panel, check the existing settings.

❑ Adjusting the fields

3. Click [Fields...].
4. If the field that you want is not in the list, pick a new set from the drop-down list.
5. Select a field from the Available list and click [Add ->].
6. Select an item from the Displayed list and click [<- Remove].
7. Adjust the position of a selected field with the Move buttons.
8. Click [OK] to return to the View Summary panel.

Customizing the View

It is important to realise that any changes you make through the Customize Current View routine only apply to that view – and not to any others. So, don't spend a long time fine-tuning a view unless it is one that you will be using regularly, or unless you have a lot of messages and need to get them grouped or filtered so that you can do some serious work on them.

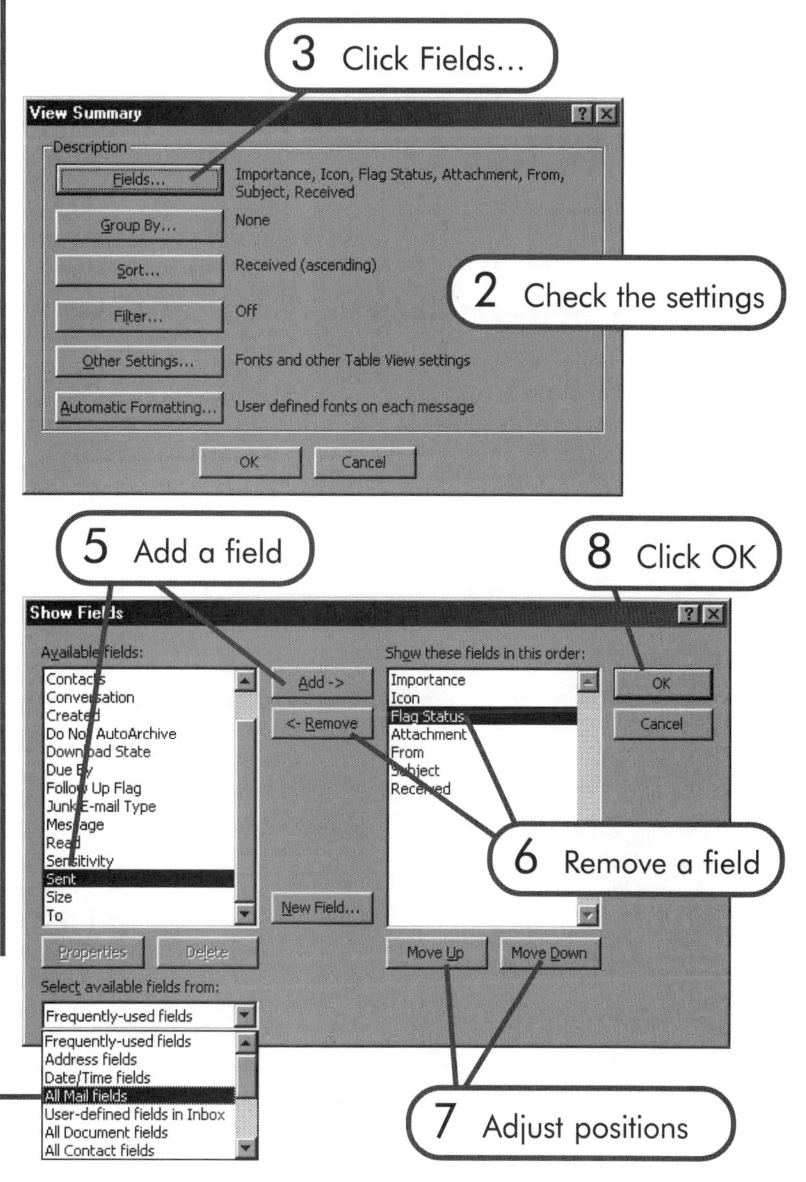

Grouping and sorting

These two view options may be more useful for organising the messages in your long-term storage folders. As both have the same effect of bringing related messages together, you would normally use either one or the other, or perhaps group on one field and sort on another.

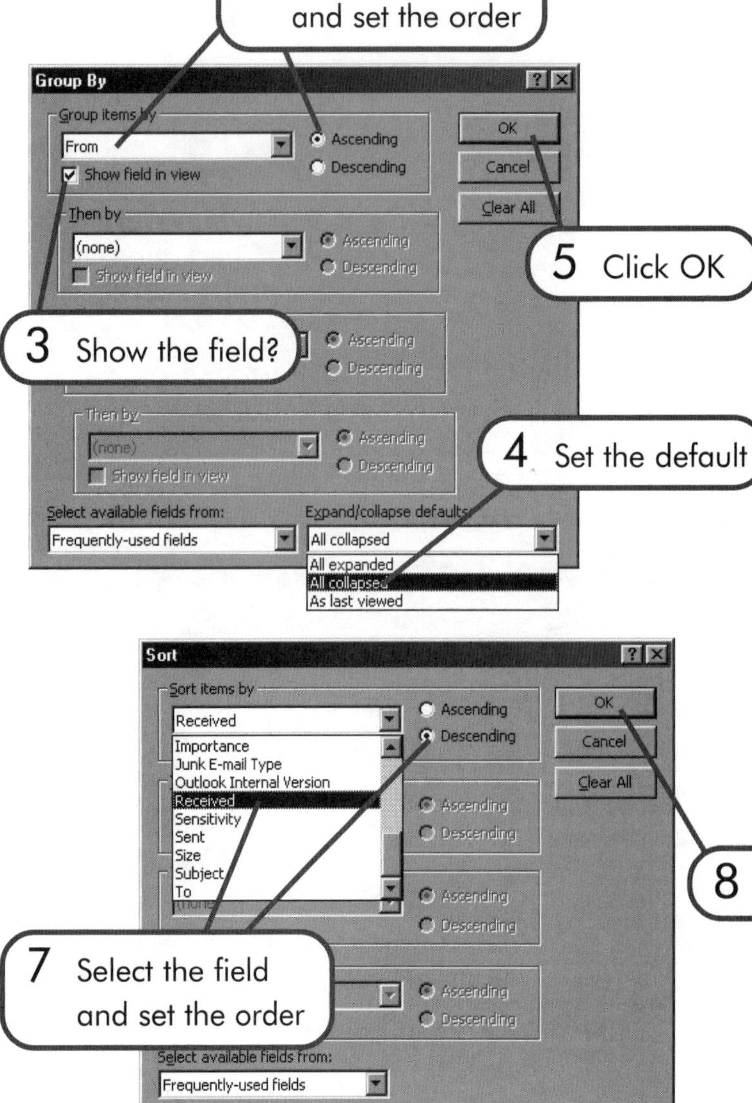

Basic steps

❑ Grouping

1 Click [Group By...].

2 Select the field to Group by, and set *Ascending* or *Descending* order.

3 Clear the Show field in view if it is not wanted.

Repeat steps 2 and 3 for other fields if required.

4 Select the Expand/ collapse default from the drop-down list.

5 Click [OK].

❑ Grouping

6 Click [Sort...].

7 Select the field to Sort by and set the order.

8 Repeat for other fields if required then click [OK].

Basic steps

1. Click Filter... .
2. Click Clear All to clear any existing settings.
3. On the Messages tab, enter the text to find and where to find it; define the sender or recipients; and/or set the time frame.
4. On the More Choices tab, select a Category and/or define one of the other features.
5. On the Advanced tab, define criteria on selected fields.
6. Click OK .

Filters

A filter is set up in almost the same way as an Advanced Find (see page 64). This is not surprising, as both are concerned with defining which messages to display.

Define as many or as few aspects as you need to be able to focus on the messages that you want to access.

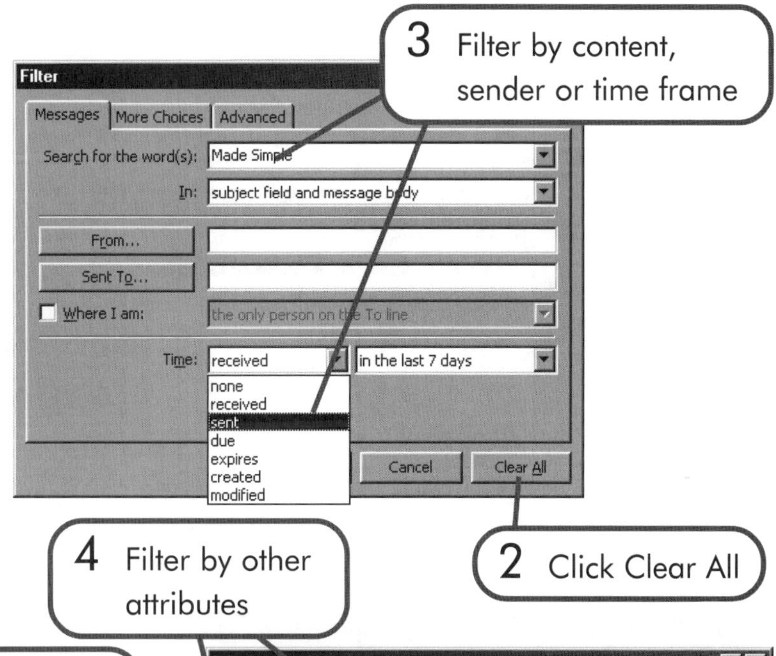

4 Filter by other attributes

5 Define specific criteria

Filter
Messages | More Choices | Advanced
Find items that match these criteria:
Junk E-mail Type equals Junk E-mail
Remove
Define more criteria:
Field
Condition:
Value:
Received
on or before
last week
this week
next week
last month
this month
next month
Add to List
More Advanced...
Cancel
Clear All

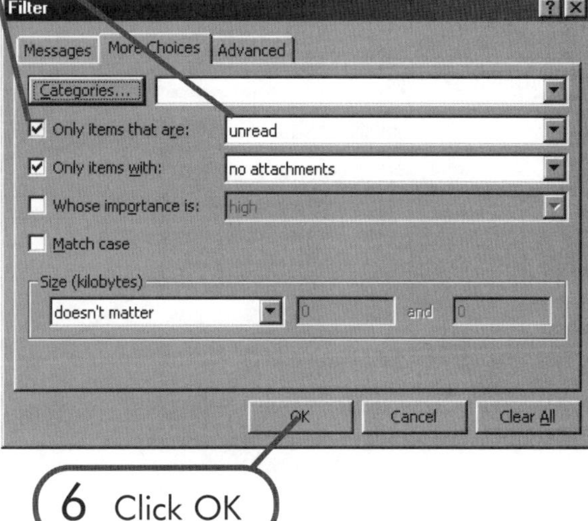

6 Click OK

Using the Rules

Rules are instructions to Outlook to perform actions on messages when specified conditions are met. We met them briefly when looking at junk e-mail, but rules can be applied to any types of messages and can be set up easily using the Wizard.

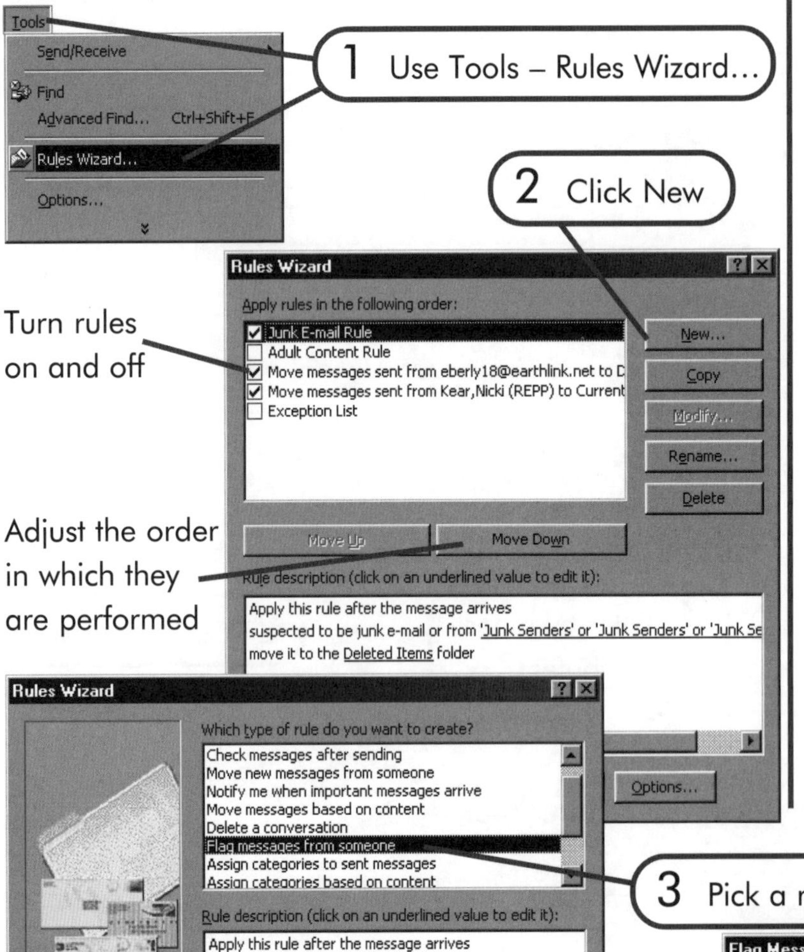

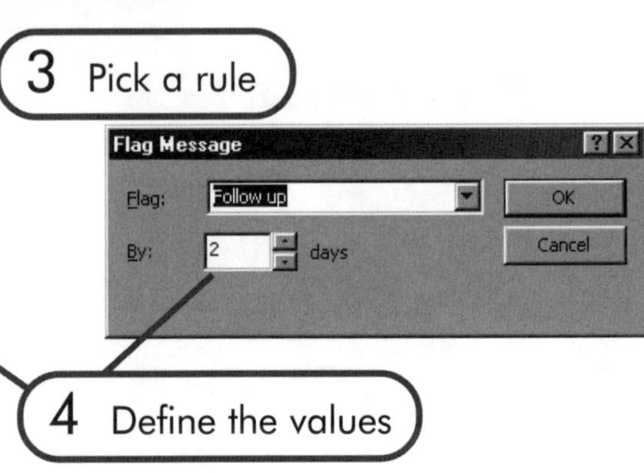

Basic steps

1. From the Tools menu select Rules Wizard...
2. Click New...
3. Select the rule that is closest to what you want to do.
4. Click on the underlined condition and action values to define them properly – e.g. specifying names and actions.
5. Click Next >
6. Work through the Wizard, setting other conditions, actions or exceptions as needed.
7. Give the rule a name and turn it on.
8. Click Finish.

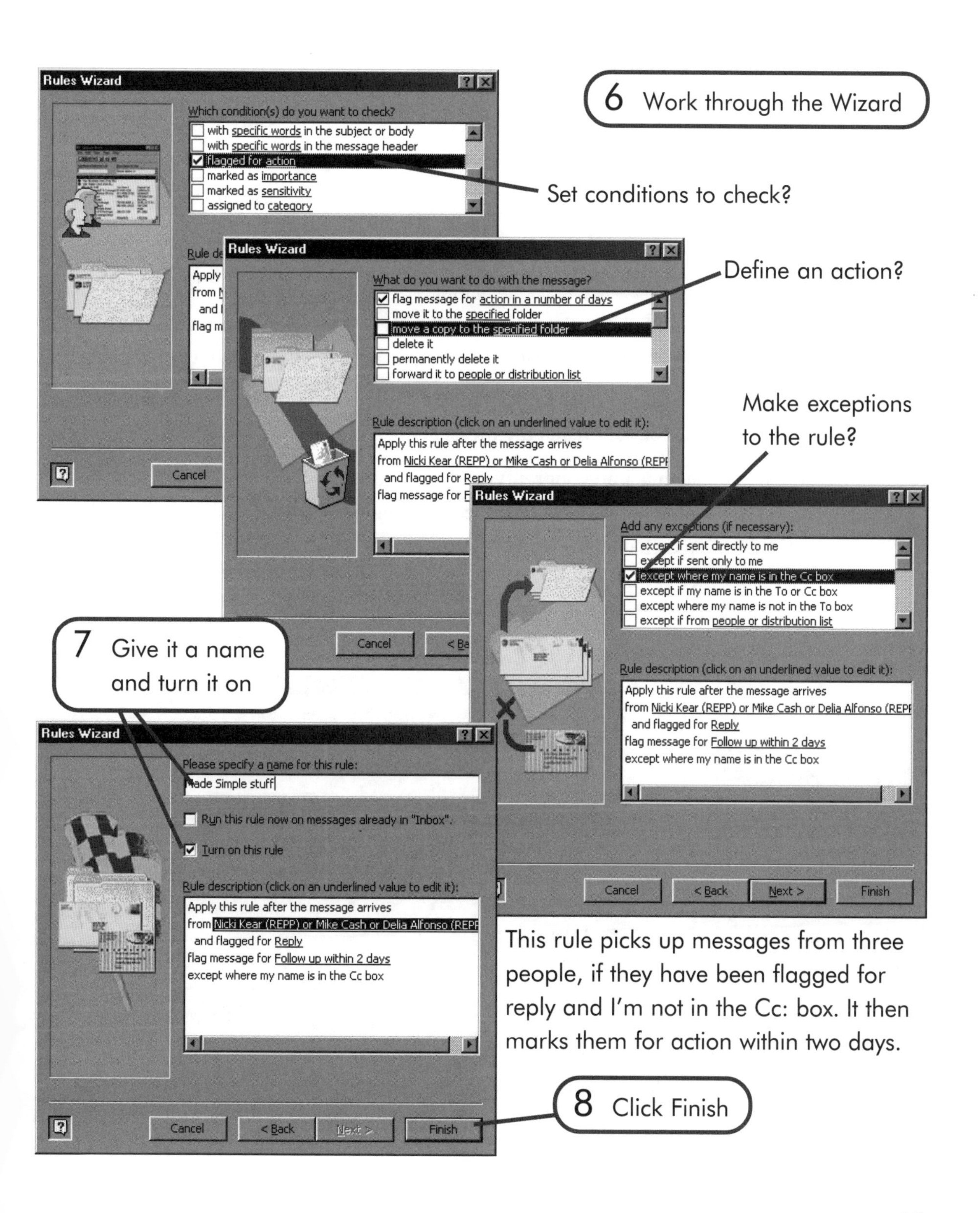

This rule picks up messages from three people, if they have been flagged for reply and I'm not in the Cc: box. It then marks them for action within two days.

E-mail options

Some of the more significant options are in the **E-mail options** panel that opens from the Preferences tab. Do you want to:

- save copies of sent and of forwarded messages?
- save part-written (unsent) messages automatically? This is handy if you often break off while writing messages.
- be notified when new mail arrives? This is only useful if you are in an organisation with a permanent connection to the Internet or tend to be on-line for long sessions.
- use read receipts? These are little messages sent back to the sender when the recipient reads the message.
- copy the original message into your reply, and if so, how? The text can be ignored, attached or included with either an indent or a prefixed character. With business mail, it's often useful to include a copy of the message when replying – but less useful with personal mail.

Basic steps

1. Open the Tools menu and select Options...
2. On the Preferences tab click [E-mail Options...].
3. Set your Message handling options.
4. Drop down the On replies and forwards lists and select your copy options.
5. Click [Advanced E-mail Options...].
6. On the Advanced panel, set the options for saving messages and for alerting you to new mail.

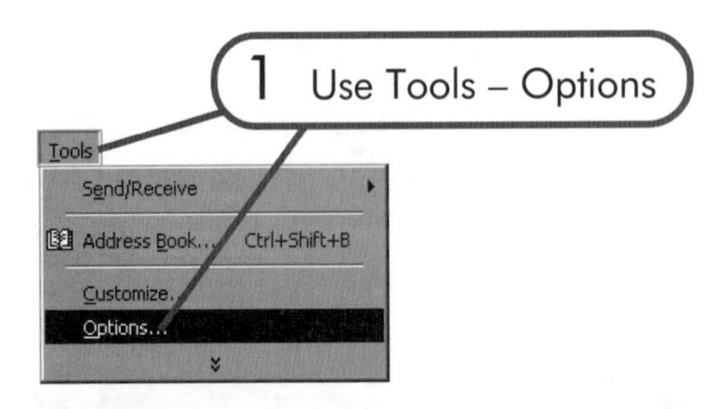

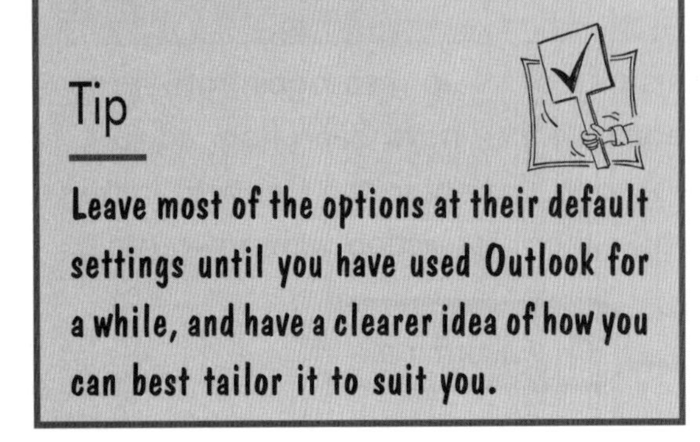

Leave most of the options at their default settings until you have used Outlook for a while, and have a clearer idea of how you can best tailor it to suit you.

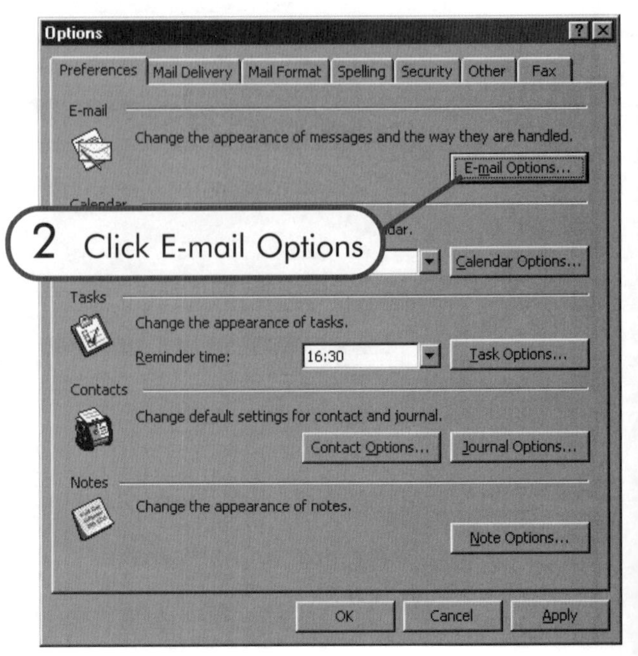

7 Back at the E-mail options dialog box, click Tracking Options... .

8 At the Tracking panel, set how to process read receipts on incoming mail, and turn on Request a read receipt... if required.

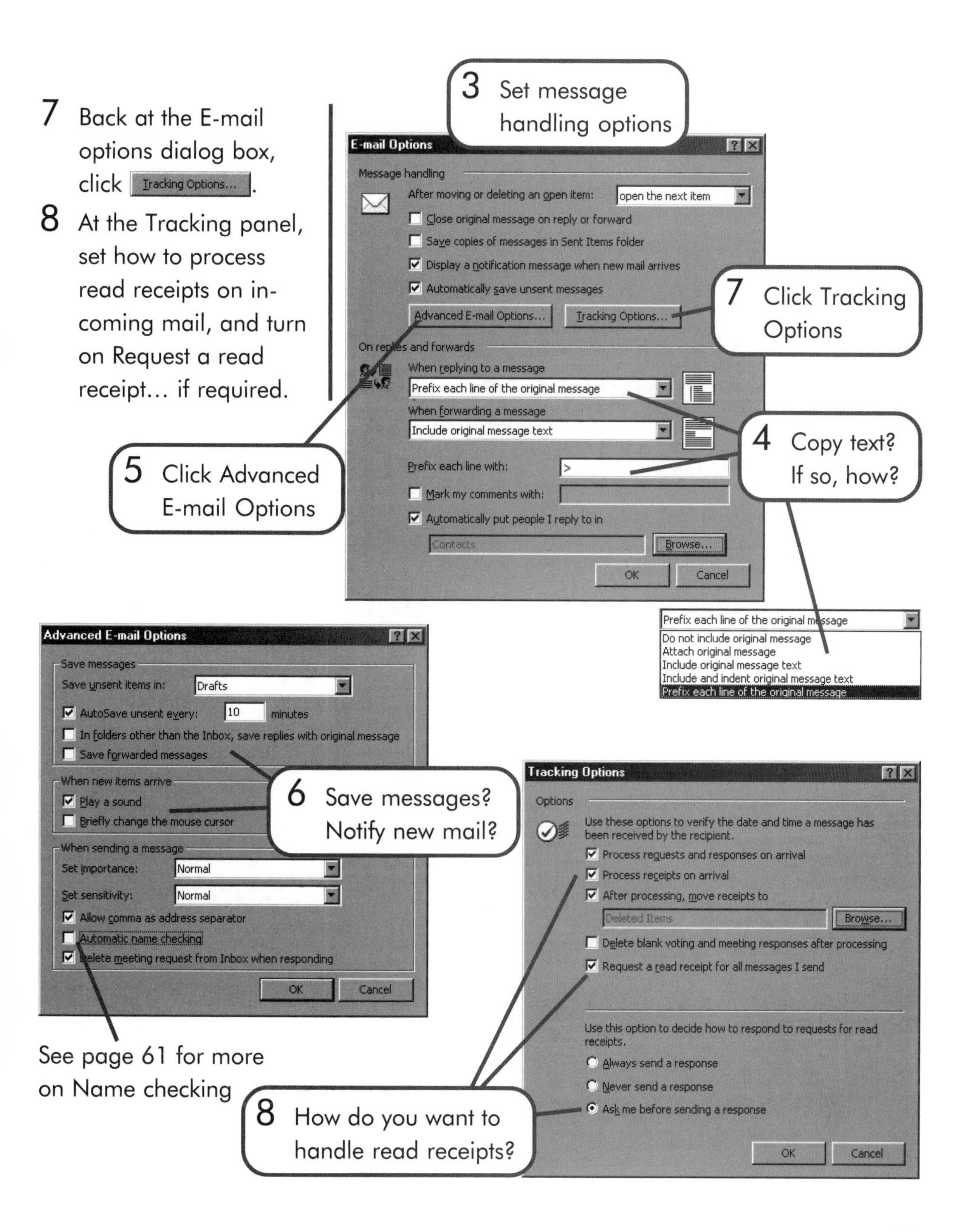

Other mail options

These are scattered over the other tabs in the Options dialog box. Have a look through. You may want to change some settings now; others you may prefer to leave for a while.

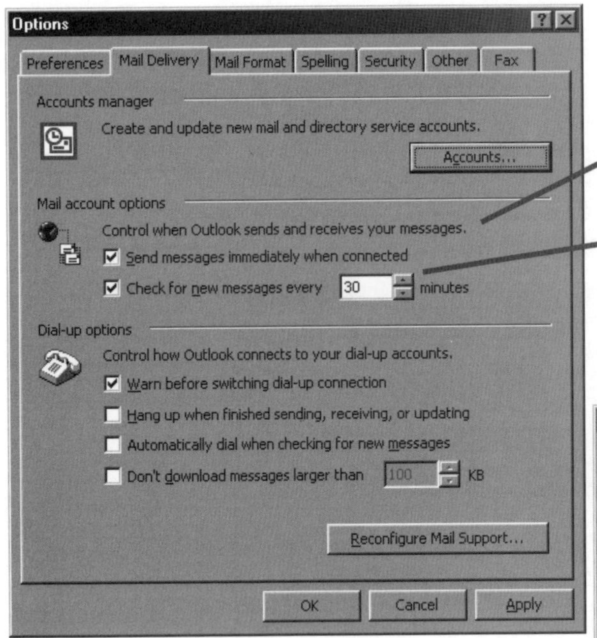

On the Mail Delivery tab, choose how to send and receive messages

Turn this on if you are on-line for long sessions

On the Mail Format tab, set the defaults format (HTML or Plain text) for messages

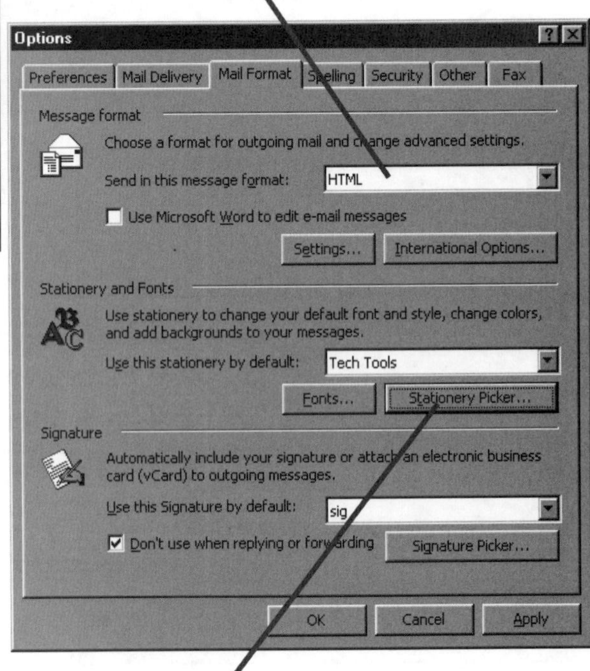

If you want decorated stationery, open the Stationery Picker and choose one – some are only suitable for special events

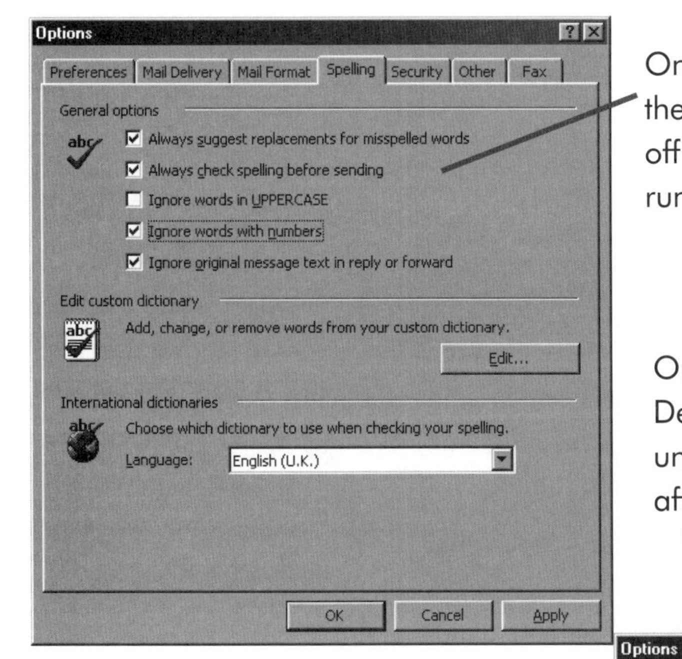

On the Spelling tab, you can control the way the Spellcheck works, or turn off automatic checking and then just run it when you feel the need

On the Other tab, turn on Empty the Deleted Items folder upon exiting, unless you regularly change your mind after deleting stuff

Click AutoArchive to set its options – archiving transfers old items to a backup folder. They can still be retrieved if necessary, archiving merely stores them more compactly

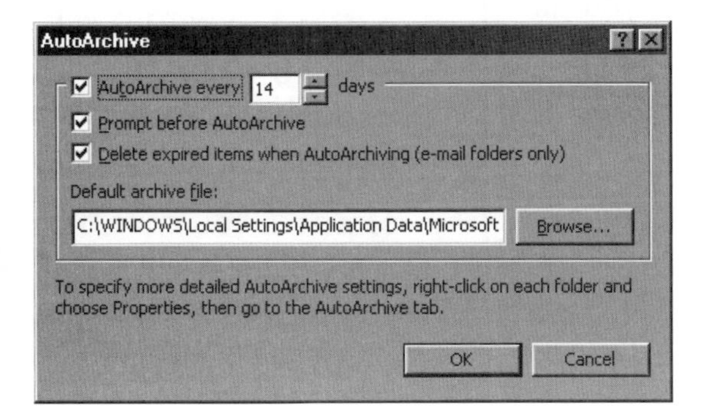

Preview Pane options are mainly concerned with when an item is marked as read

Security

Basic steps

There are two distinct aspects to security: protecting the privacy of your communications, and protecting your PC from e-mail-borne viruses.

Secure e-mail

There is no such thing as totally private e-mail. Every message that you send will leave a copy on your disk, your recipient's, your ISP's server, their ISP's server and every server between the two. If they want to, the server administrators can get into your mail; hackers may be able to find their way in; and in the UK, the government can read your mail any time it likes.

If there is anything confidential about your business or personal e-mail, you can give it a measure of protection by getting a digital ID and encrypting your messages before sending them. It's fiddly to set up, and only works with people who also have digital IDs but if your data is valuable – or your personal life is complicated – you should think about it.

To set up secure e-mail, you must first sign up for a digital ID – allow yourself half an hour for this, as you will have to go on-line to get the ID, then copy it out of the browser (the steps are based on IE5) and into Outlook.

Thawte will provide a limited one for free, but a good secure digital ID is a service you should expect to pay for. Attaching a digital ID to a message guarantees that it comes from you, and if you go a step further and exchange IDs with your contacts, you can then send encrypted mail.

- In Outlook

1 Open the Tools menu and select Options...

2 On the Security tab click [Get a Digital ID...].

- IE will start up and go on-line to Microsoft's site where you will be given a choice of links to digital ID providers. Follow a link and sign up for an ID.

- In Internet Explorer

3 When you have your ID, open the Tools menu and select Internet Options.

4 On the Content tab, click [Certificates...].

5 At the Certificate Manager dialog box, select the ID and click [Export...]. A wizard will run to guide you through the export process – make a note of where you save the exported data.

cont...

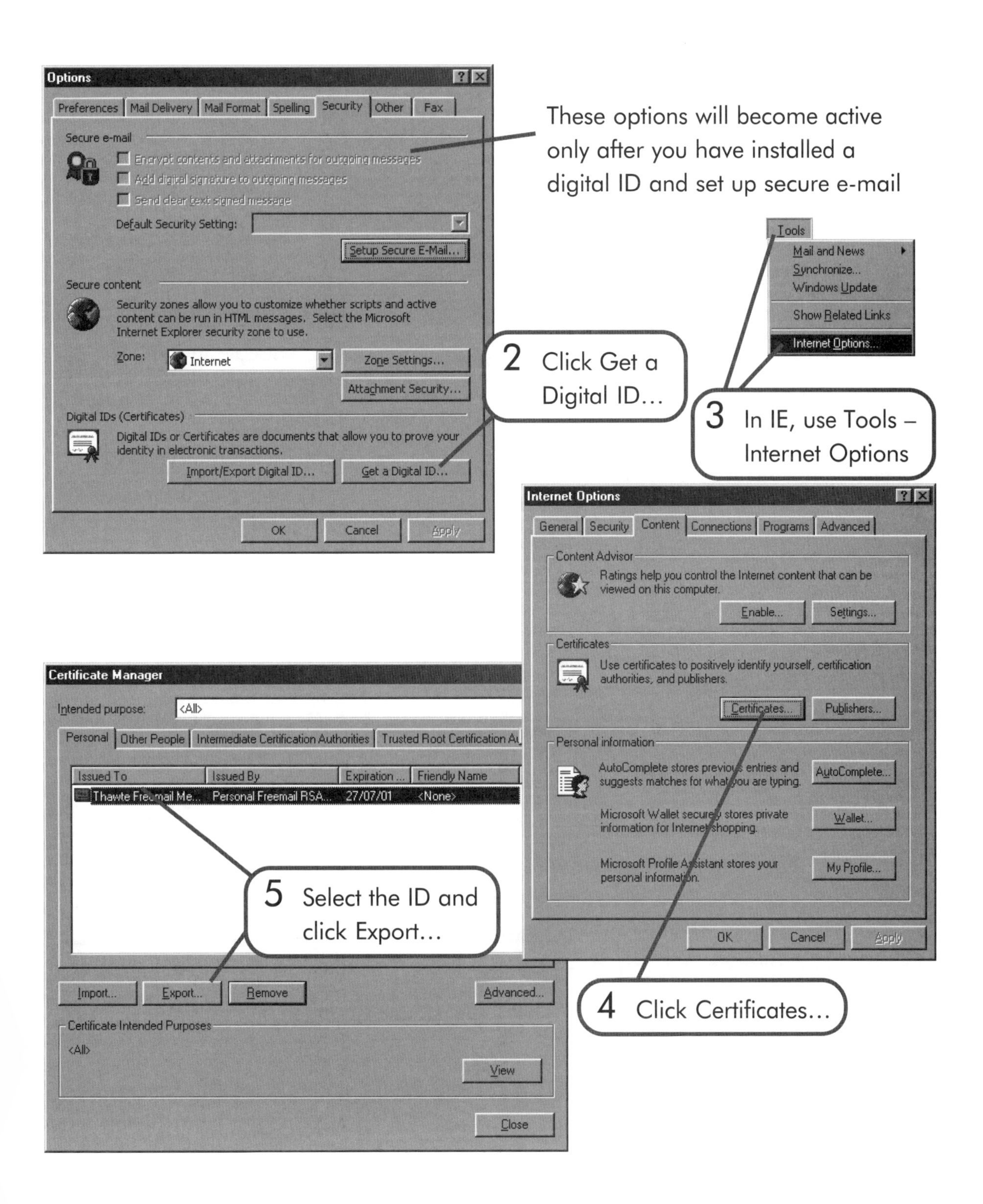
These options will become active only after you have installed a digital ID and set up secure e-mail
2 Click Get a Digital ID...
3 In IE, use Tools – Internet Options
4 Click Certificates...
5 Select the ID and click Export...
Options
Preferences
Mail Delivery
Mail Format
Spelling
Security
Other
Fax
Secure e-mail
Encrypt contents and attachments for outgoing messages
Add digital signature to outgoing messages
Send clear text signed message
Default Security Setting:
Setup Secure E-Mail...
Secure content
Security zones allow you to customize whether scripts and active content can be run in HTML messages. Select the Microsoft Internet Explorer security zone to use.
Zone:
Internet
Zone Settings...
Attachment Security...
Digital IDs (Certificates)
Digital IDs or Certificates are documents that allow you to prove your identity in electronic transactions.
Import/Export Digital ID...
Get a Digital ID...
OK
Cancel
Apply
Tools
Mail and News
Synchronize...
Windows Update
Show Related Links
Internet Options...
Internet Options
General
Security
Content
Connections
Programs
Advanced
Content Advisor
Ratings help you control the Internet content that can be viewed on this computer.
Enable...
Settings...
Certificates
Use certificates to positively identify yourself, certification authorities, and publishers.
Certificates...
Publishers...
Personal information
AutoComplete stores previous entries and suggests matches for what you are typing.
AutoComplete...
Microsoft Wallet securely stores private information for Internet shopping.
Wallet...
Microsoft Profile Assistant stores your personal information.
My Profile...
Certificate Manager
Intended purpose:
<All>
Personal
Other People
Intermediate Certification Authorities
Trusted Root Certification Au
Issued To
Issued By
Expiration ...
Friendly Name
Thawte Freemail Me...
Personal Freemail RSA...
27/07/01
<None>
Import...
Export...
Remove
Advanced...
Certificate Intended Purposes
View
Close

Basic steps

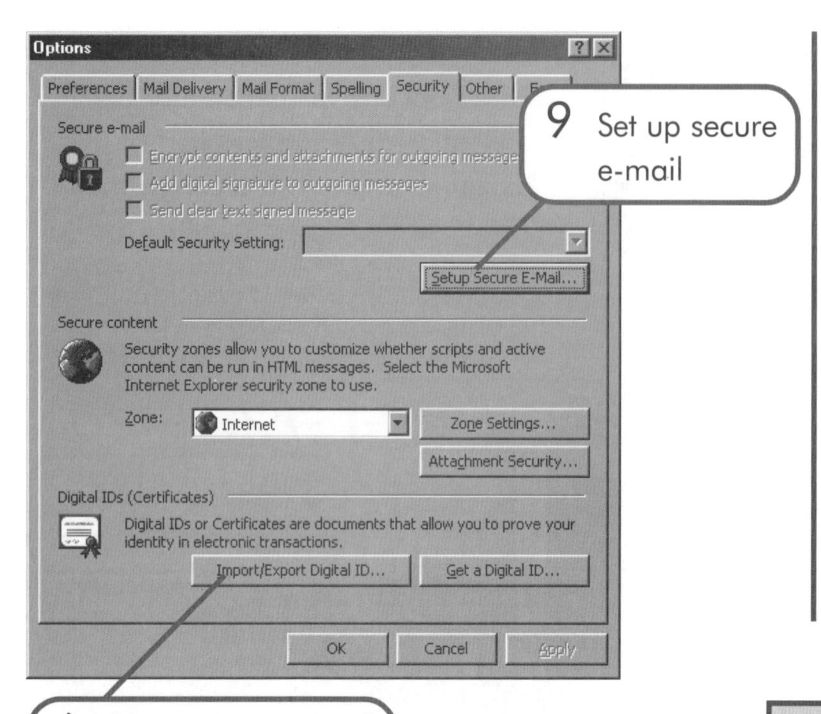

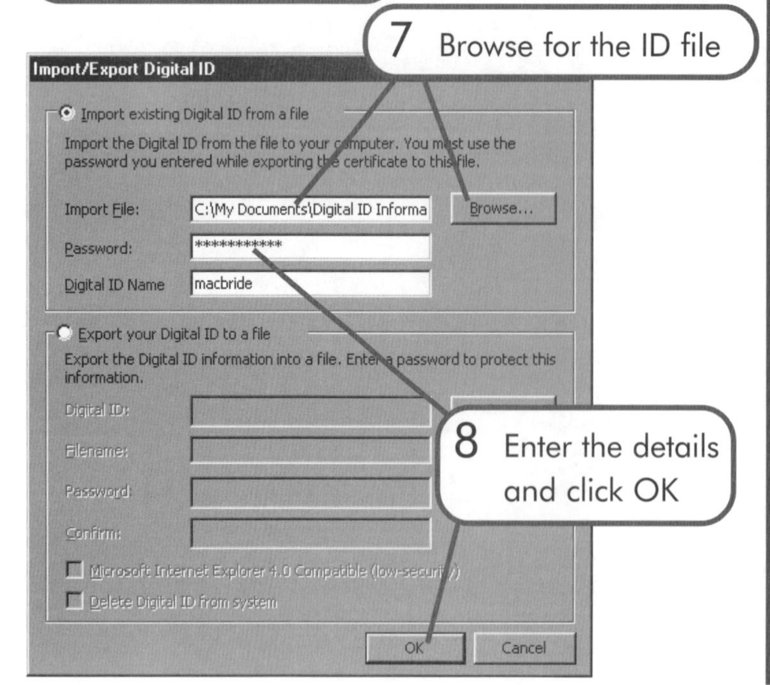

cont...

- Back in Outlook

6 Return to the Security tab in the Options dialog box and click [Import/Export Digital ID...].

7 Click [Browse...] and locate the ID file.

8 Enter the ID's password and user name and click [OK].

9 Click [Setup Secure E-Mail...].

Take note

Encrypting your e-mail will not protect you from government snooping, and could make matters worse. Under the Regulation of Investigatory Powers Act, if you cannot supply, on request, the password for any encrypted material on your PC, you can be sent to jail. Big brother really is watching you, and if you don't like it he assumes that you have something criminal to hide.

10 At the Change Security Settings dialog box, enter a new name – if you like – but leave the other settings at their defaults.

11 Click OK.

12 Back at the Options dialog box, set the Secure e-mail options. Do not turn encryption on at first – you can only use this after you have exchanged digital signatures with people.

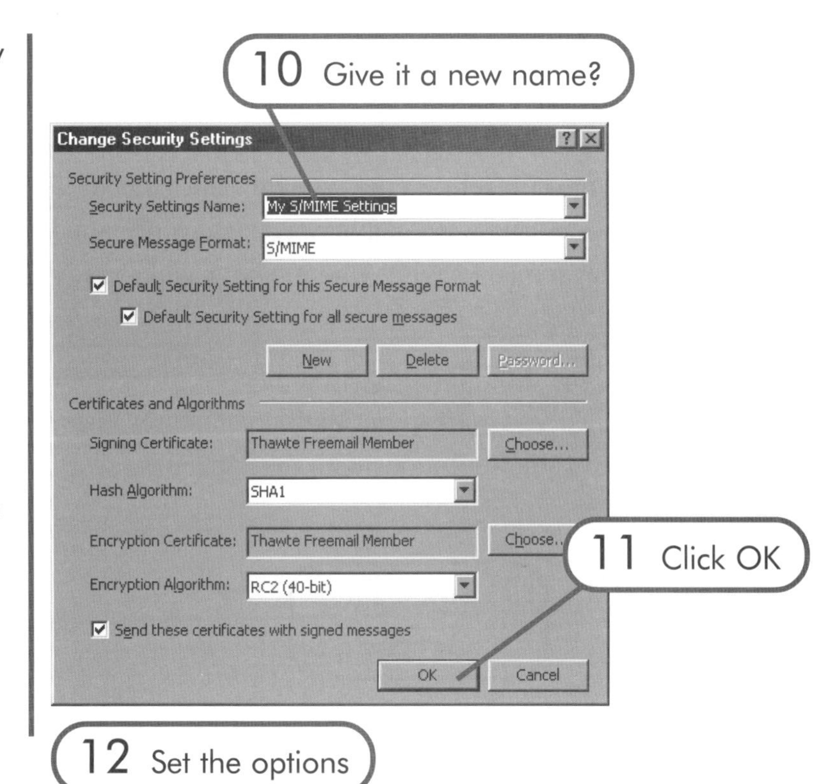

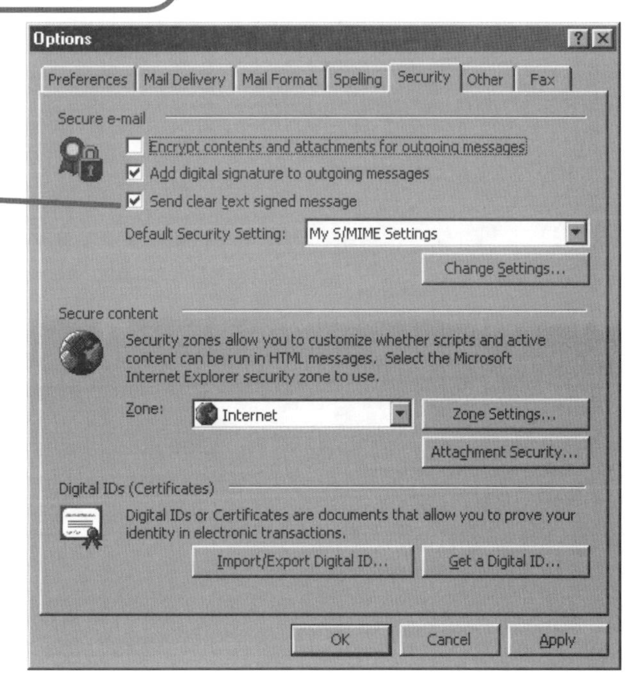

If you send messages to people whose e-mail software can't read digital signatures, you must turn this on so that they can still read your messages

Take note

These secure e-mail settings are only defaults – you can change them for individual messages (see next page).

Security options

Basic steps

The security settings are among the options that can be set for individual messages before sending them. This is just as well, because until everyone that you write to has a digital ID – and we are a long, long way from there – you will not be able to encrypt all your messages. Remember, you can only send encrypted mail to someone with whom you have already exchanged digital IDs.

Start the ball rolling. Add your digital signature to all your messages, and when you start to get digital signatures back, move to encrypted communications with those people.

1 When composing a new message, open the View menu and select Options... or click Options... .

2 If you have exchanged IDs with the recipient, tick Encrypt message contents and attachments.

3 Click Close .

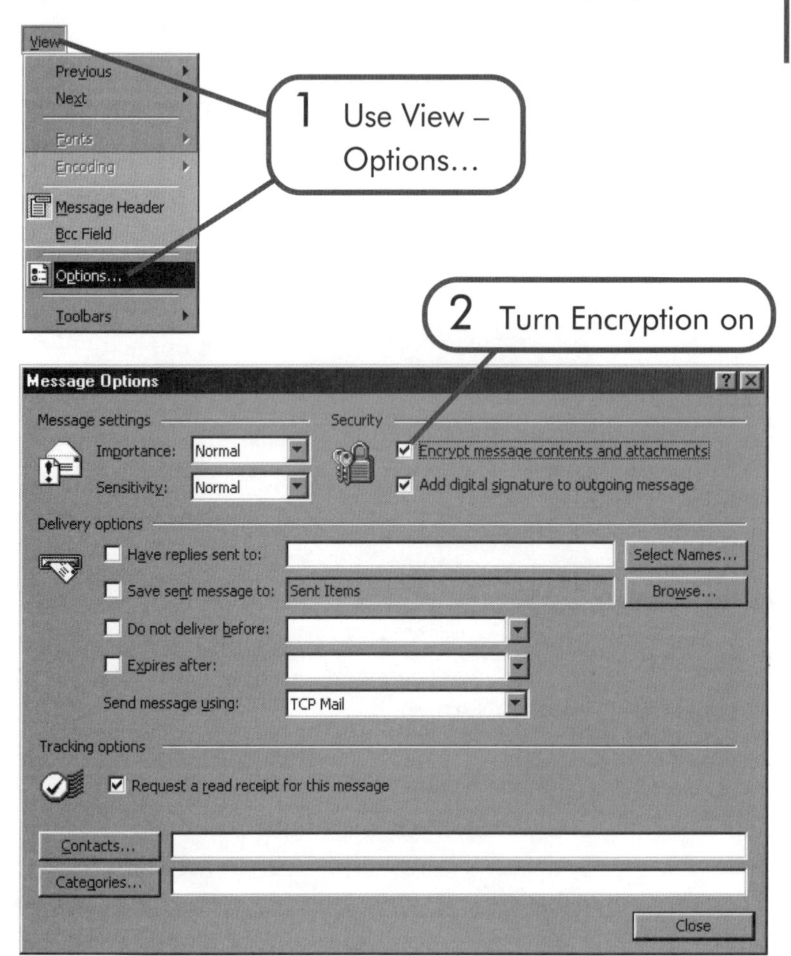

Tip

If you want to make your your mail more secure, get the PGP (Pretty Good Privacy) freeware. You can pick up a copy at any good shareware site, or find out more about it at the PGP site, http://www.pgp.com

Secure content

1 On the Security tab of the Options panel (see page 89), click Zone Settings... .

2 Set the security level the Internet zone is to Medium or High, if possible, and click OK .

3 At the Security tab of the Options panel, click Attachment Security... .

4 Make sure that this is set to High.

A message in HTML format can have the same kind of active contents – ActiveX controls, Java applets or JavaScript code – that you find on Web pages. Attachments to any message – plain text or HTML – can be executable programs or documents containing macros. Viruses can lurk in any of these. Play safe. Make sure that no code can run in your Inbox without your permission – and don't give that permission unless the program is one that you are expecting and from a trusted source.

The behaviour of active content in message is controlled by the **Zone Settings**. These are the same ones that apply in IE, so if you change them within one, they are changed for the other. If your Internet connection is mainly used for e-mail, then these can be set to the highest level – stopping all but the very safest active content from working. If you make much use of the Web, you will find this very restricting – many pages will simply not work! – and you will have to settle for the medium setting.

The **Attachment Security** should always be turned on so that you are always asked before an attachment is opened.

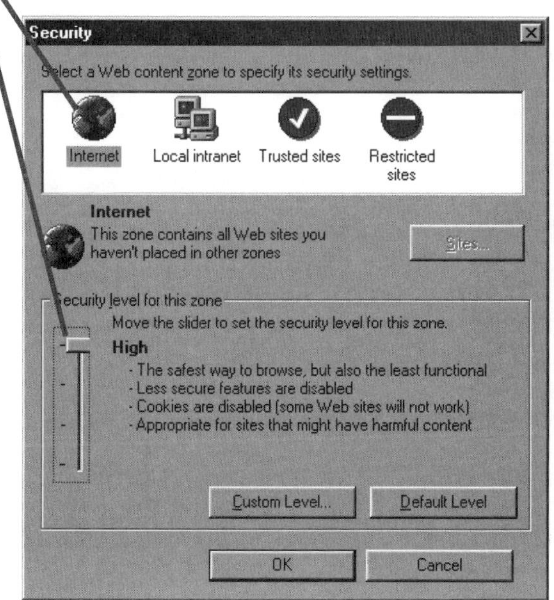

Summary

- The View Options let you define just about all the aspects of the display.
- You can add fields to the display, and format the appearance of the columns.
- Messages can be grouped, sorted and/or filtered by the contents of selected fields.
- You can create rules to automate mail handling.
- There is an extensive set of e-mail options that control the way messages appear and are treated.
- You can improve the security of your e-mail if you get a digital ID and use encryption.
- The Internet zone security setting should be set as high as is practicable and the Attachment Security turned on for greatest protection against viruses.

6 Calendar

Views

Calendar offers two basic ways of looking at the data, with several variations on each.

You can view your data:

- As a calendar, viewed by day, work week, week or month. In the day and work week view, the days are divided into time slots, and any notes are shown if AutoPreview is on.
- As a list of appointments and/or all-day events, which can be grouped by recurrence pattern or category.

You can switch between these views, and turn the screen components on and off, using the toolbar buttons or the options on the View menu.

Take note

The TaskPad, listing any current tasks, is present in most Day/Week/Month views. We'll come back to this in the next chapter.

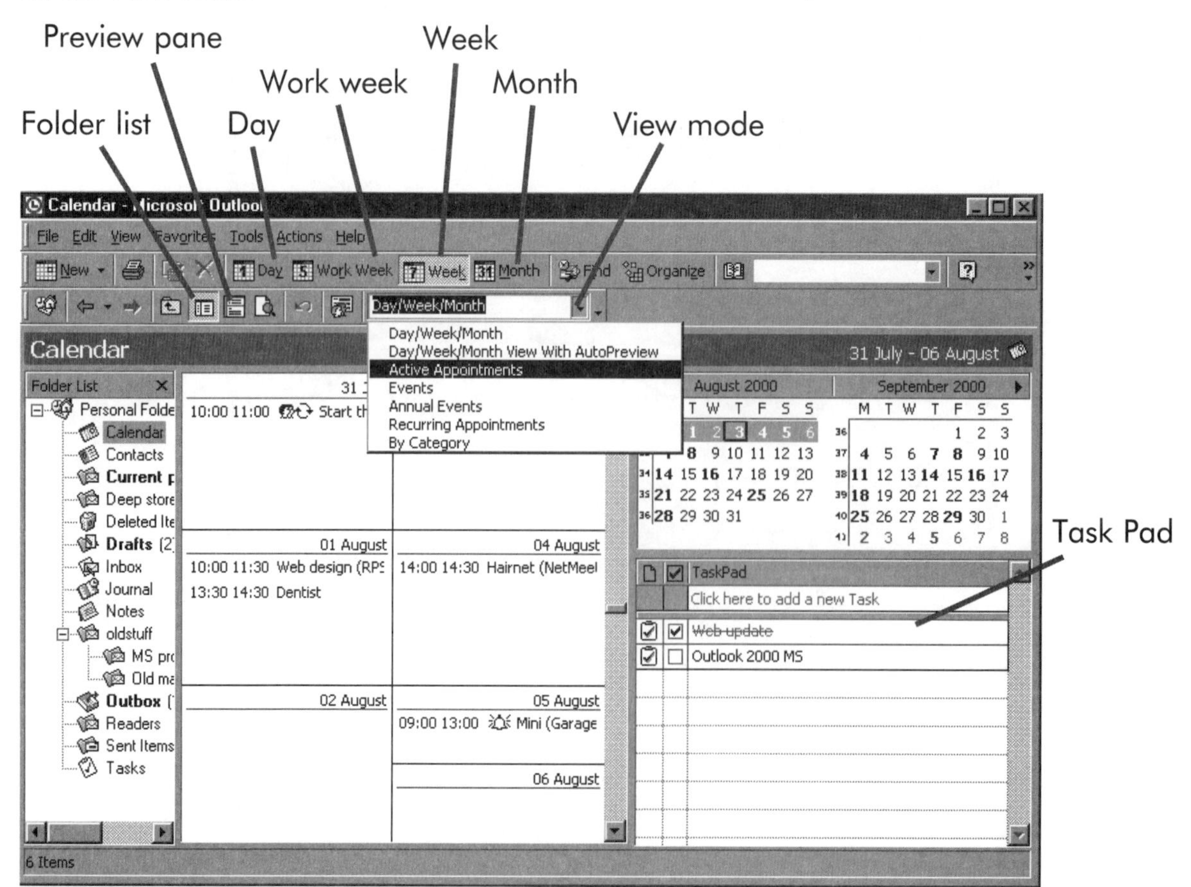

Day View with AutoPreview – the TaskPad and 2-month calendars are shown in the day and weeks views

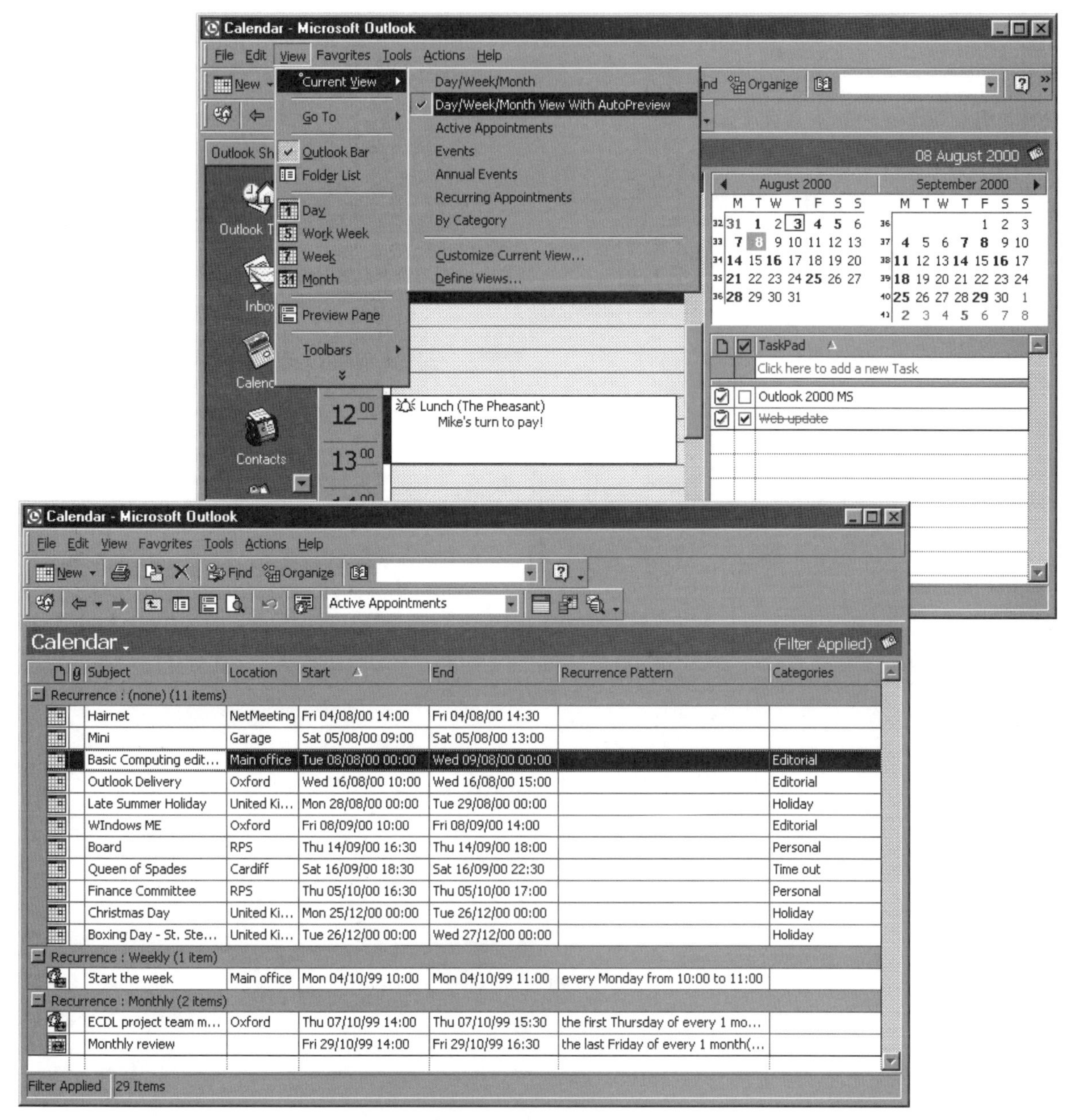

Subject	Location	Start	End	Recurrence Pattern	Categories
Recurrence : (none) (11 items)					
Hairnet	NetMeeting	Fri 04/08/00 14:00	Fri 04/08/00 14:30		
Mini	Garage	Sat 05/08/00 09:00	Sat 05/08/00 13:00		
Basic Computing edit...	Main office	Tue 08/08/00 00:00	Wed 09/08/00 00:00		Editorial
Outlook Delivery	Oxford	Wed 16/08/00 10:00	Wed 16/08/00 15:00		Editorial
Late Summer Holiday	United Ki...	Mon 28/08/00 00:00	Tue 29/08/00 00:00		Holiday
WIndows ME	Oxford	Fri 08/09/00 10:00	Fri 08/09/00 14:00		Editorial
Board	RPS	Thu 14/09/00 16:30	Thu 14/09/00 18:00		Personal
Queen of Spades	Cardiff	Sat 16/09/00 18:30	Sat 16/09/00 22:30		Time out
Finance Committee	RPS	Thu 05/10/00 16:30	Thu 05/10/00 17:00		Personal
Christmas Day	United Ki...	Mon 25/12/00 00:00	Tue 26/12/00 00:00		Holiday
Boxing Day - St. Ste...	United Ki...	Tue 26/12/00 00:00	Wed 27/12/00 00:00		Holiday
Recurrence : Weekly (1 item)					
Start the week	Main office	Mon 04/10/99 10:00	Mon 04/10/99 11:00	every Monday from 10:00 to 11:00	
Recurrence : Monthly (2 items)					
ECDL project team m...	Oxford	Thu 07/10/99 14:00	Thu 07/10/99 15:30	the first Thursday of every 1 mo...	
Monthly review		Fri 29/10/99 14:00	Fri 29/10/99 16:30	the last Friday of every 1 month(...	

The Active Appointments view – items can be sorted and grouped in these table-based displays

Calendar options

Some of these may not apply in your situation, but others will need early attention. Set your defaults for:

- how long before a meeting you receive a reminder;
- the pattern of your working week, and working day;
- the public holidays for your country and for those with which you work closely.

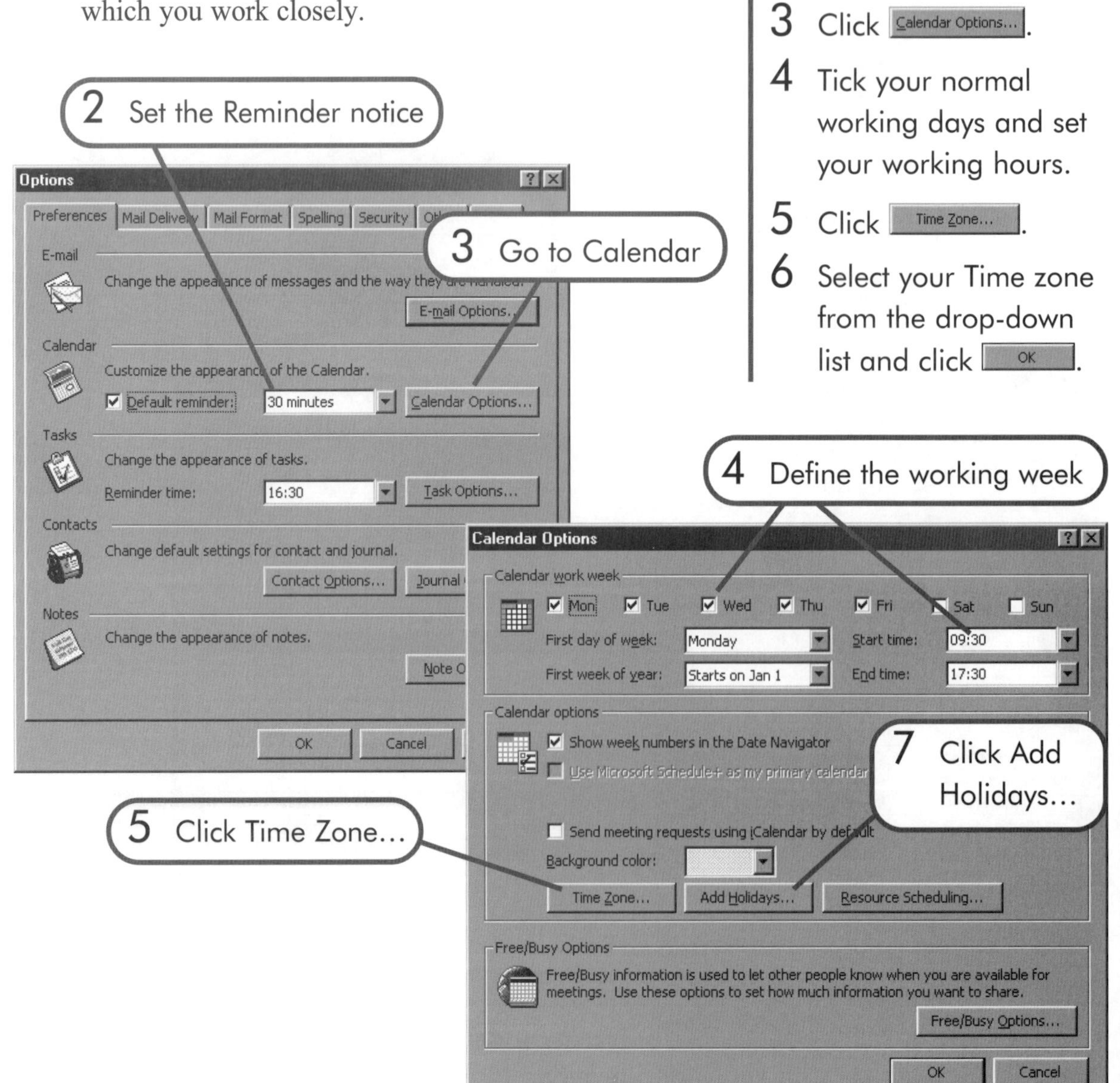

Basic steps

1. Open Tools menu and select Options...
2. On the Preferences tab, set length of the Reminder notice.
3. Click [Calendar Options...].
4. Tick your normal working days and set your working hours.
5. Click [Time Zone...].
6. Select your Time zone from the drop-down list and click [OK].

7 Click [Add Holidays...].

8 Select the countries and click [OK].

9 If you are responsible for booking resources, click [Resource Scheduling...] and set the default responses to requests.

10 If you want to make your calendar data available to others, click [Free/Busy Options...] and give the URL where it will be stored.

If you work closely with people in another country, you can add its time zone to the display

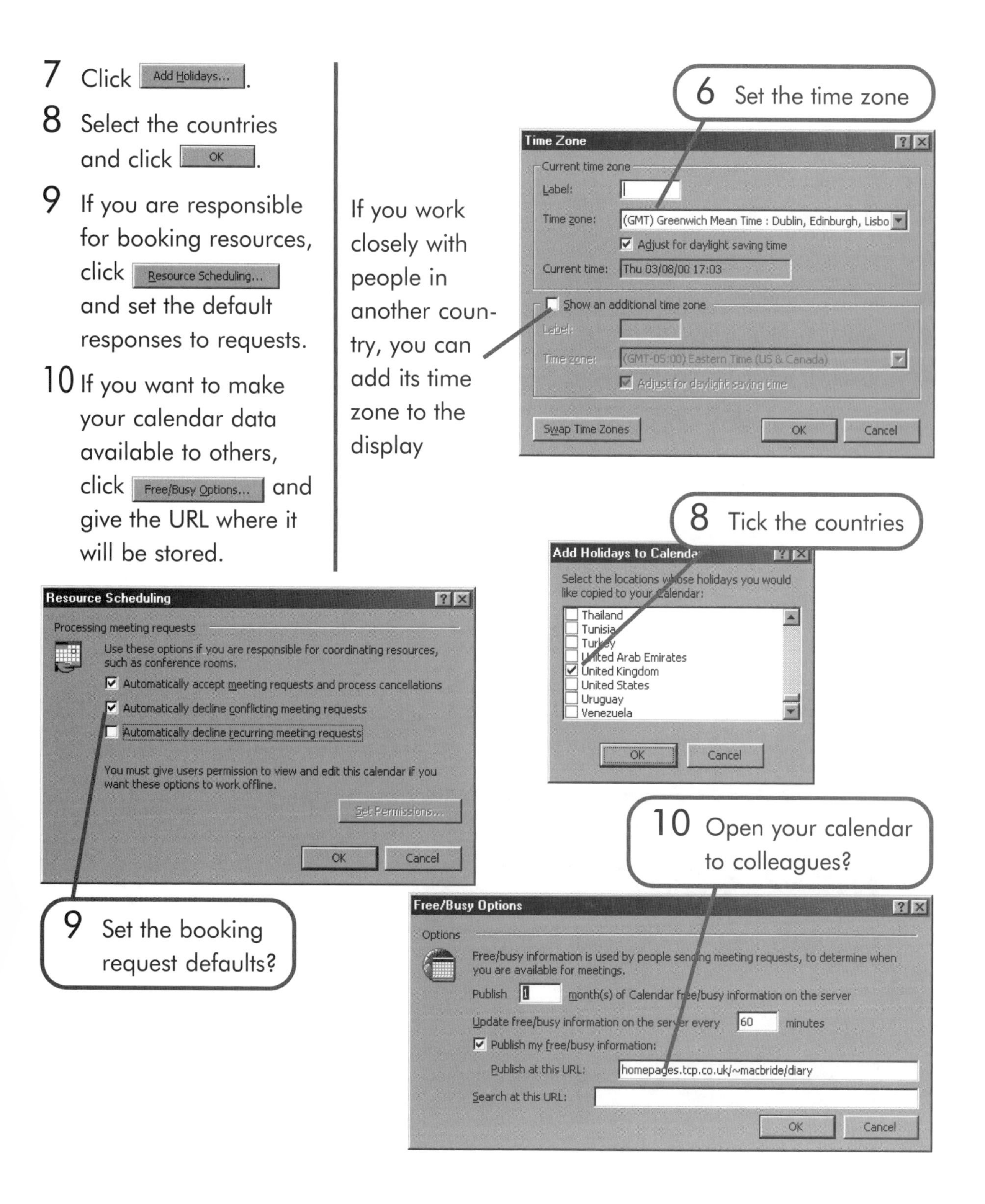

Making a date

A simple appointment can be set up in seconds – all you have to do is select the time and type in a subject. But the appointment cards have space for other information which you may find it useful to enter. You can:

- store the location;
- add notes;
- set a reminder;
- link to people in your Contacts;
- assign it to one or more categories.

Basic steps

1. Switch to 1 Day or Work Week view.
2. Select the day.
3. Point to the start time and drag highlight to the planned end time.
4. Click New or select Appointment from the drop-down menu of the New button.

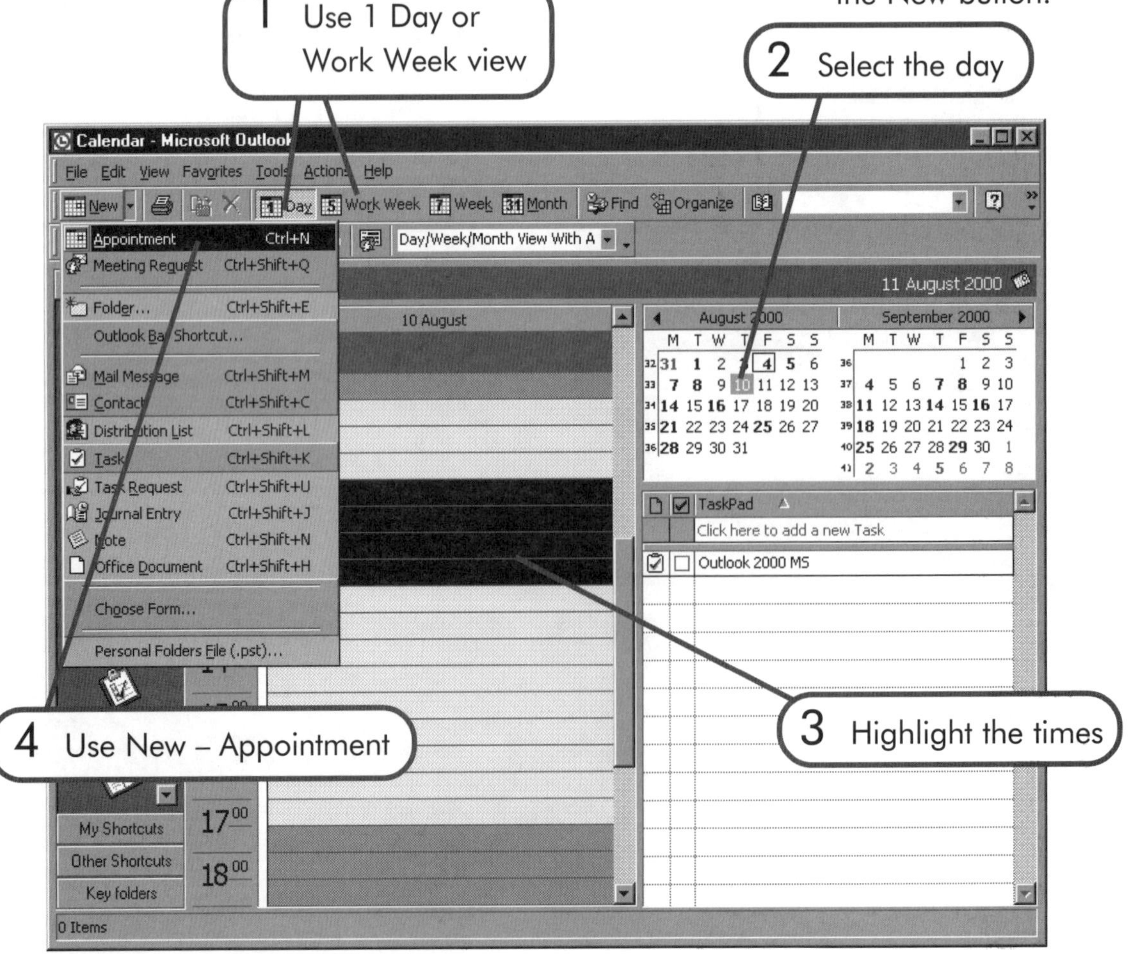

5 Enter a Subject.

6 Enter the Location if you need to.

7 Type any notes as required.

8 Click [Categories...].

9 Tick the categories and click [OK].

10 Click [Save and Close].

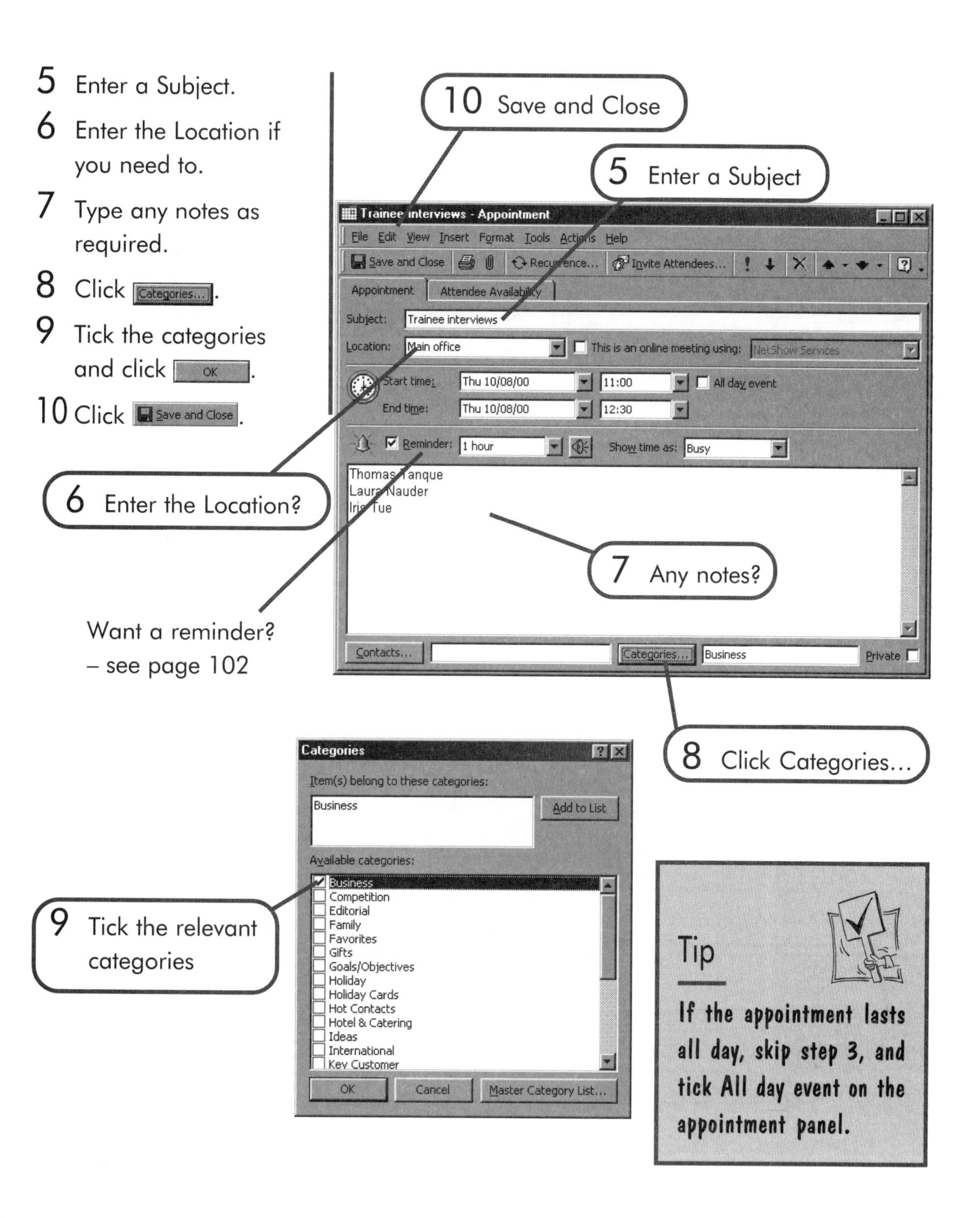

Tip

If the appointment lasts all day, skip step 3, and tick All day event on the appointment panel.

Reminders

Basic steps

If you get Outlook to give you a reminder of the appointment at a chosen time beforehand. A message box will pop up on screen, accompanied – if wanted – by a sound alert.

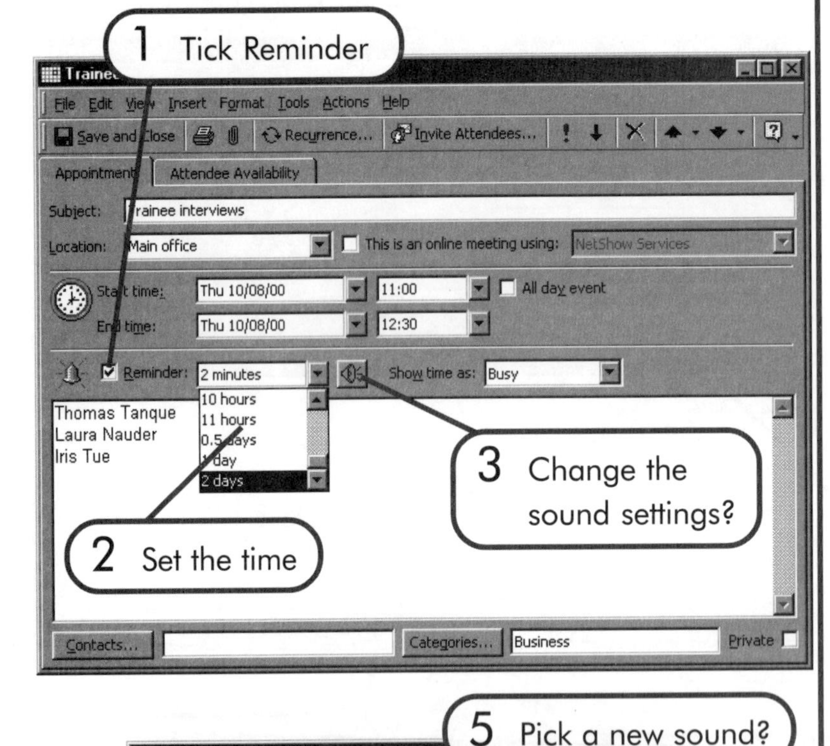

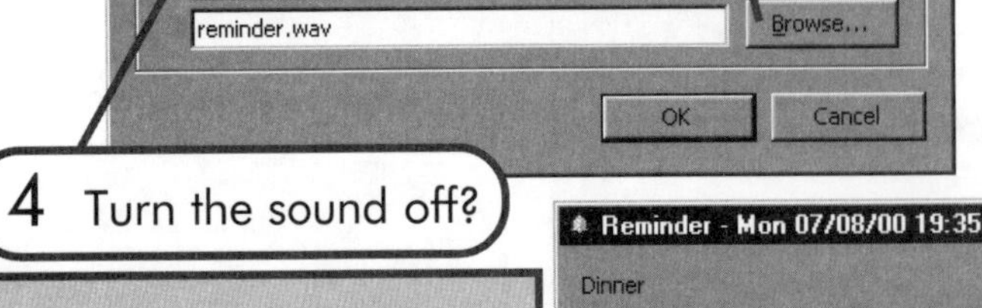

Reminder - Mon 07/08/00 19:35

Dinner

Location: (The Club)

Dismiss

Snooze

Open Item

Click Snooze to be reminded again: 5 minutes before start

6 Turn it off

7 Remind me later!

Tip

There are sound files in the C:\Windows\Media folder.

1 Tick the Reminder checkbox.

2 Open the list and set the time – anything from 0 minutes to 2 days.

3 If you want to change the sound settings click [sound button].

4 Clear the Play this sound checkbox if an alert is not wanted.

5 Click [Browse...] if you want to change the sound.

❑ When the reminder appears...

6 Click [Dismiss] to remove it.

Or

7 Click [Snooze] to be reminded again later.

Basic steps

Recurring appointments

1. Follow the steps on page 100 to set the day and time of the first appointment of the series.
2. Click Recurrence... .
3. Check the times.
4. In Recurrence pattern, set the frequency.
5. Set the Day (of the week, month or year).
6. Check the Start date.
7. Select No end date, or End after or End by and set the limit.
8. Click OK.
9. Click Save and Close.

If you have a series of regular appointments, you can set them all up in one operation.

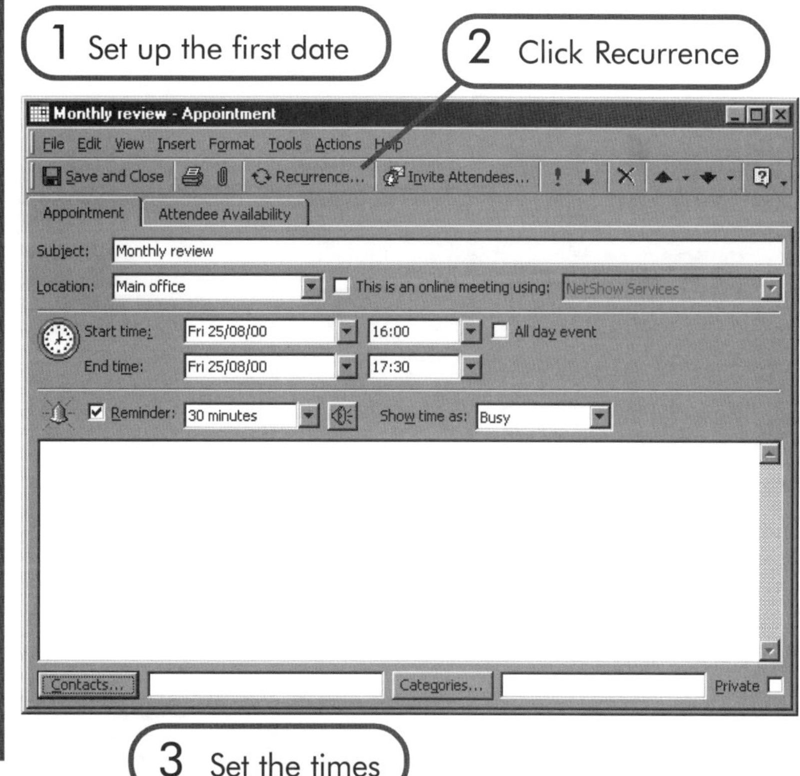

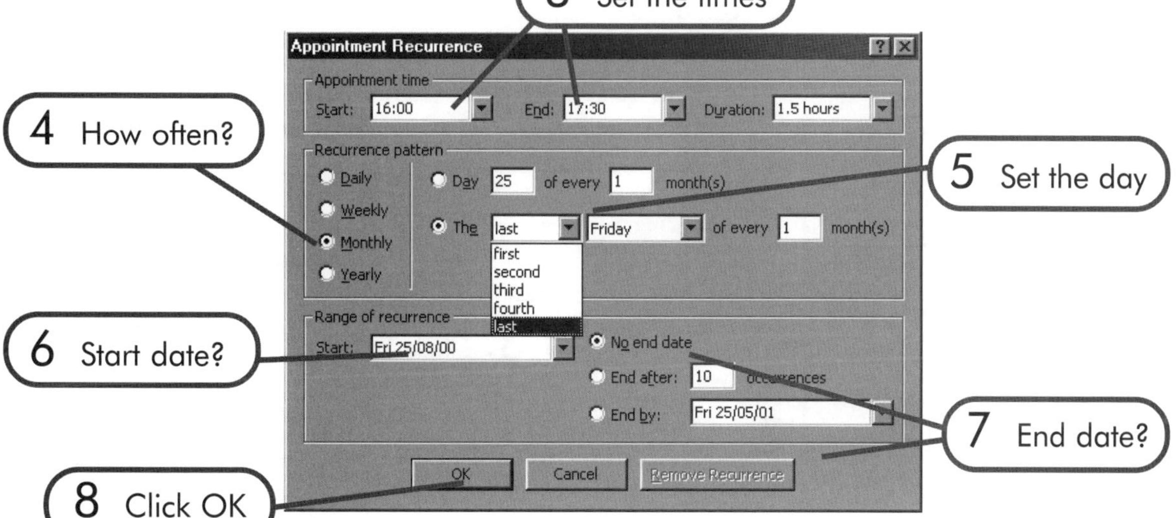

Arranging meetings

Basic steps

This is probably of most use to people working on a local area network, where each has access to the (public) diary of the others. But, it is also a convenient way to call a meeting with those whom you can contact by fax or e-mail.

1. Select the day and time as for an appointment.
2. Select New – Meeting Request from the Calendar menu.
3. Click the To... button.
4. Select the source for the names – normally Contacts for external mail/fax and Post Office Address book for people on your local area network.

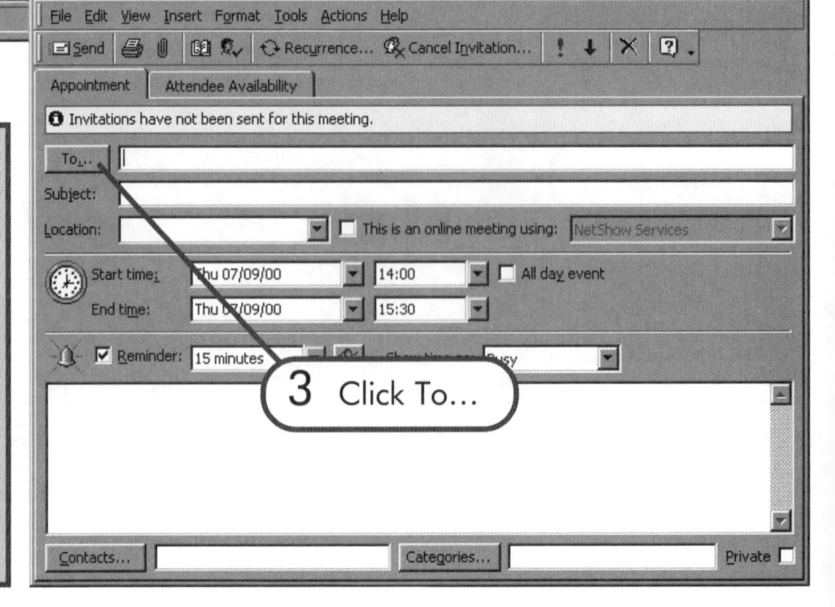

Take note

When you have set up the meeting, Outlook will send faxes and e-mails containing the details and notes you have typed into the Appointment panel.

5 Select the attendees who are Required or Optional, or will supply Resources, and click the buttons to copy them to the appropriate panes.

6 Click OK.

7 Back at the Appointment panel, type the Subject and Location.

8 Type any message that you want to add to the meeting notice.

9 Click Send.

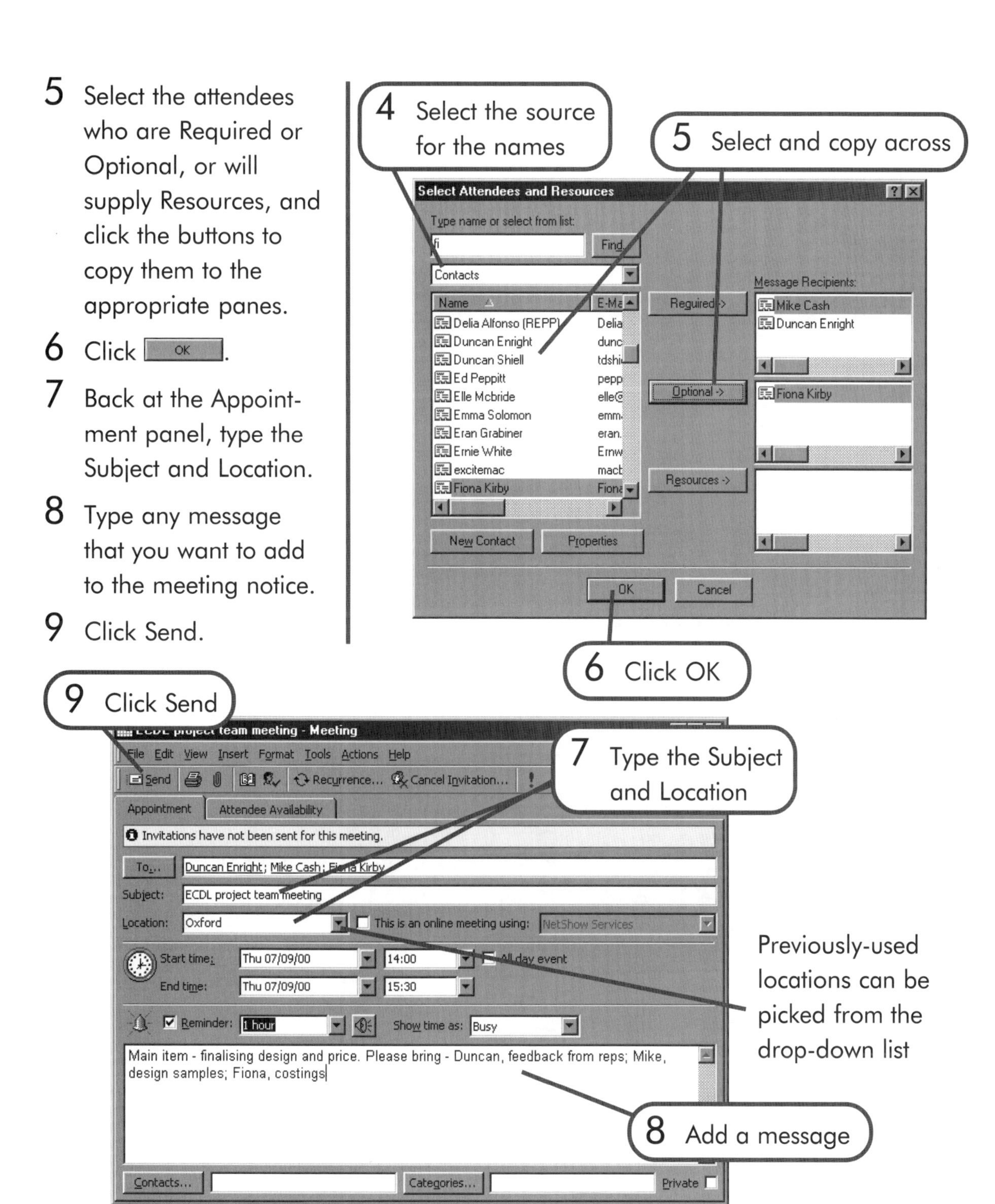

Previously-used locations can be picked from the drop-down list

Checking availability

Where the other attendees are on your local area network – and are all using Outlook's Calendar to plan their time – you can check their availability. On the Attendee Availability tab, you can see who is busy when, and can rearrange your meeting time if necessary.

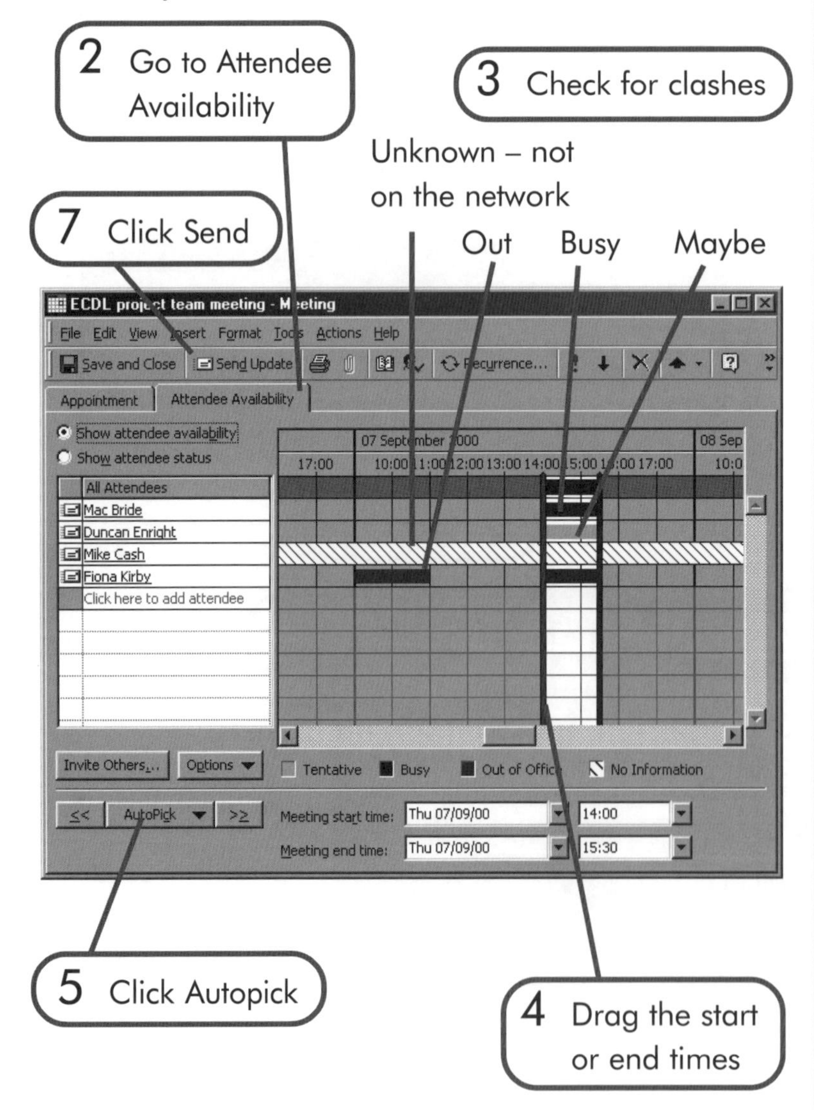

Basic steps

1. If you have closed the Appointment window, double-click on the time to re-open it.
2. Switch to the Attendee Availability tab.
3. Check for clashes – you can only do this for people on your local network.

❑ To adjust the time

4. Drag the start or end line for minor adjustments.

Or

5. Click [<< AutoPick >>] heading backwards and forwards to let Outlook find the next free time for all attendees.
6. Switch back to the Appointments tab, and type a message.
7. Click Send, or if you have already sent a request, click Send Update.

Basic steps

Organizing Calendar

1 Click [Organize].

❑ To add a category

2 Switch to the Using Categories tab.

3 Select the appointment.

4 Pick a category from the drop-down list and click [Add].

❑ To change the view

5 Switch to the Using Views tab.

6 Select a view.

Compared to the Inbox, there's not a lot to the Organize routine here. There are only two modes:

- **Using Categories** lets you assign categories to appointments, if you did not do so when creating them;
- **Using Views** offers yet another way to change views, but does no more than the View menu or the drop-down list.

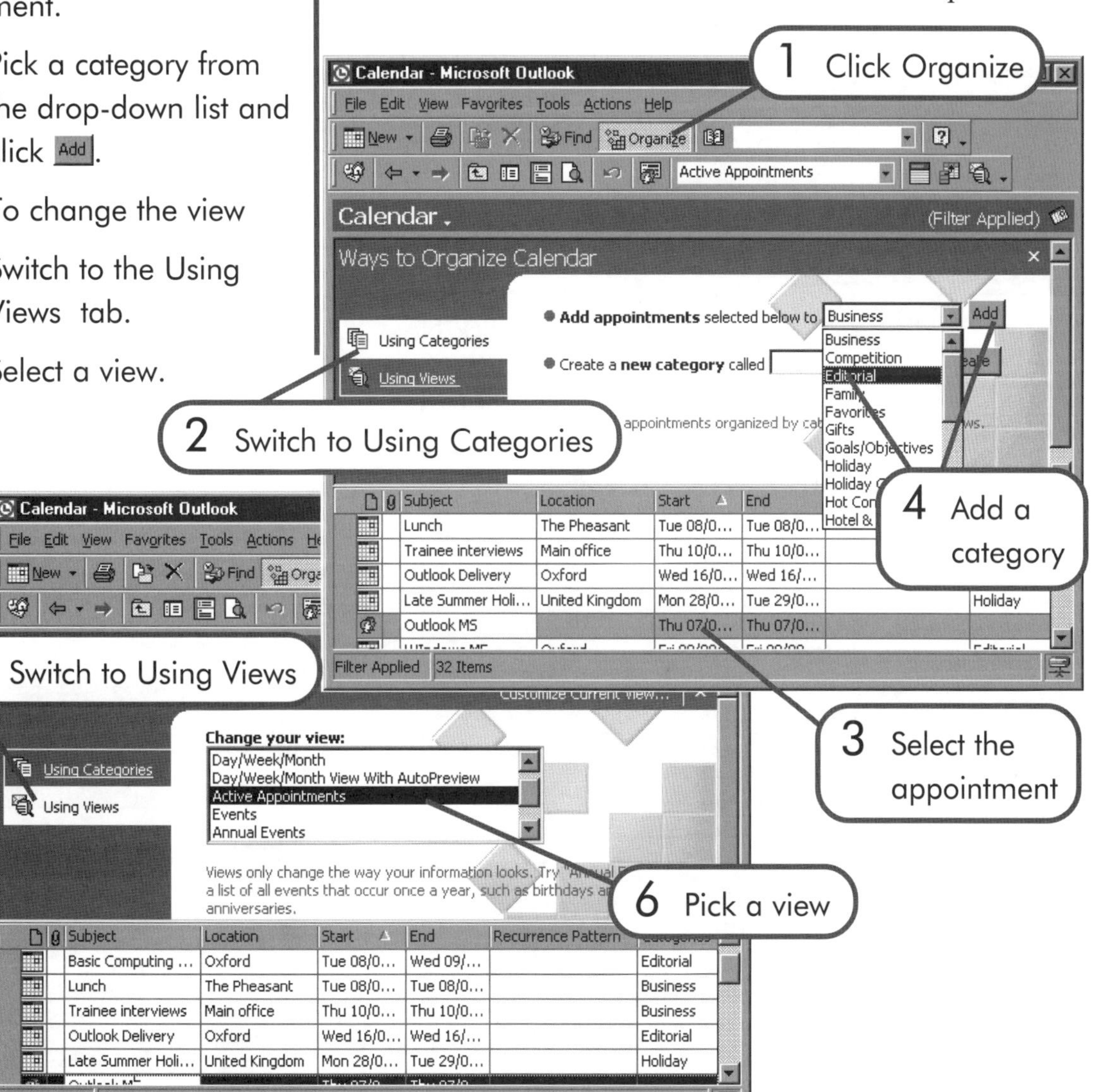

Defining Views

Here, as elsewhere in Outlook, you can customise views or define your own. I don't expect many readers will need their own views, but you may like to have a play just to see the possibilities and the limitations.

After you have created a new view by setting its name and type, it is defined in the same way as customising an existing view.

Basic steps

1. Open the View menu, point to Current View and select Define Views…
2. Click New... .
3. Give it a name.
4. Set the type – Day/Week/Month and Table work best.
5. Set where it can be used on and click OK .
6. At the View Settings dialog box, click on the buttons to adjust any settings and then click OK .

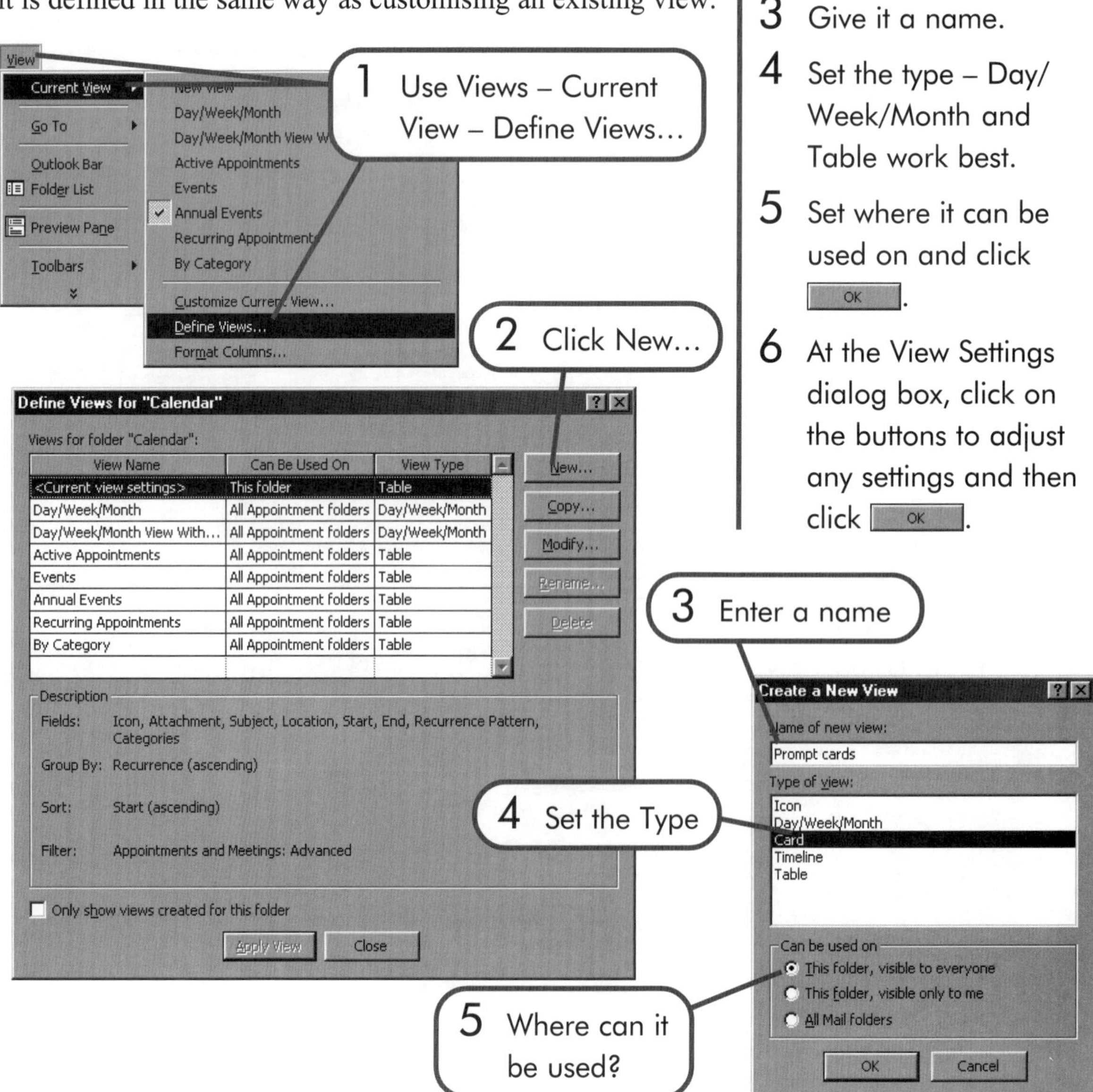

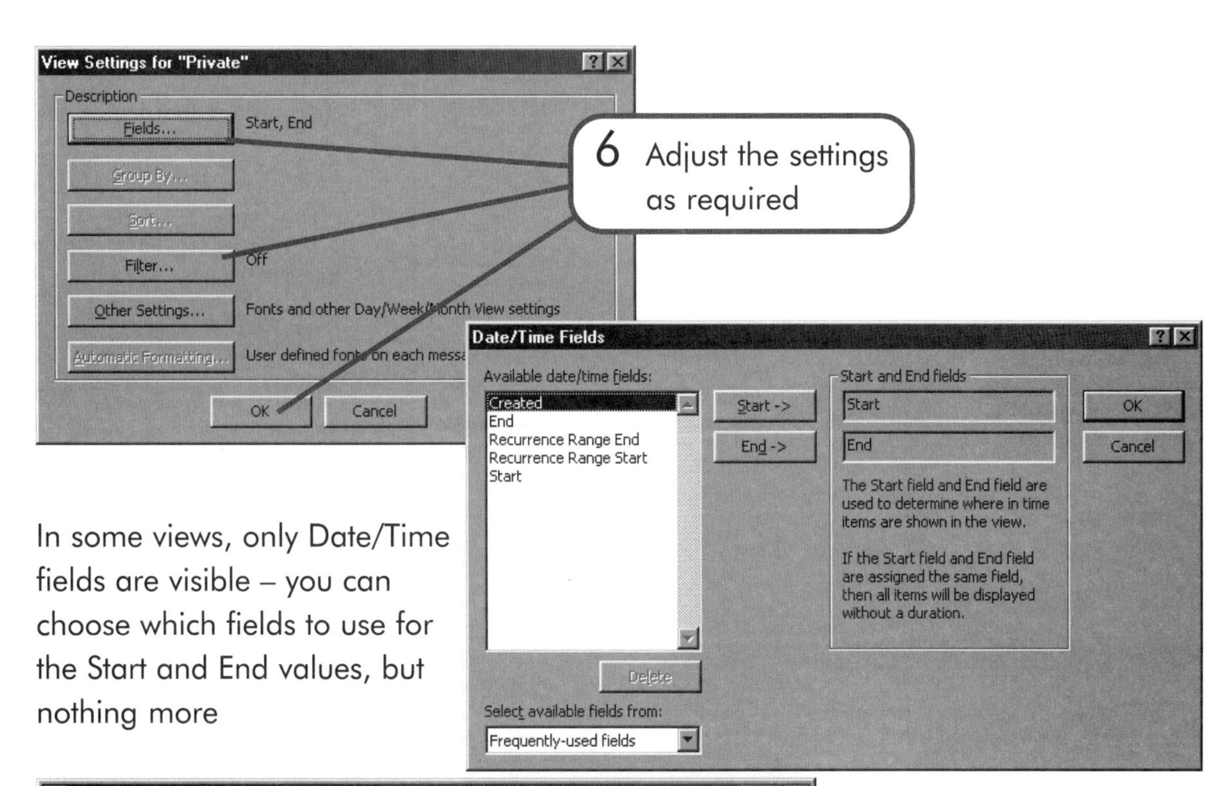

In some views, only Date/Time fields are visible – you can choose which fields to use for the Start and End values, but nothing more

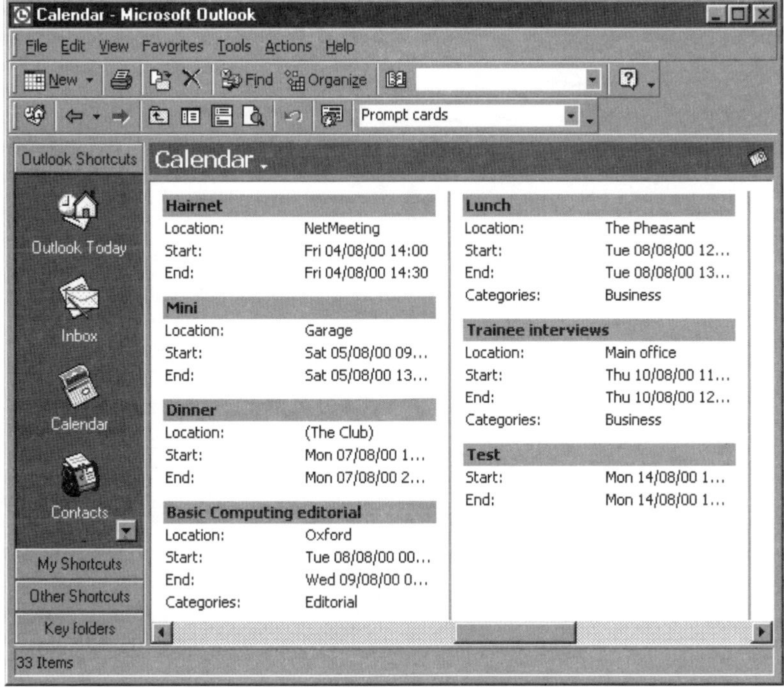

Card views are not an obvious choice for displaying date-based information, but they can work

Printing calendars

Basic steps

You can print any selected days, weeks or months from Calendar as a reminder to take with you away from your PC. There are several alternative formats, each of which can be tailored to your requirements.

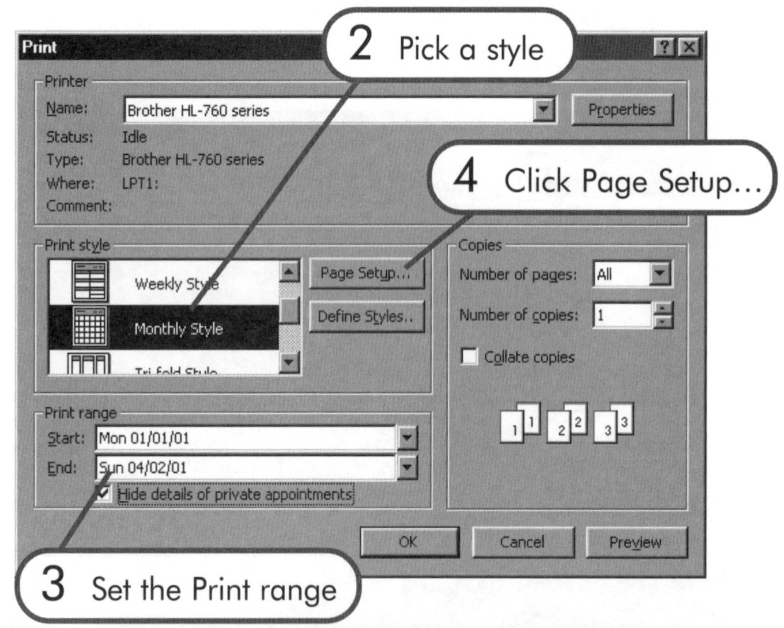

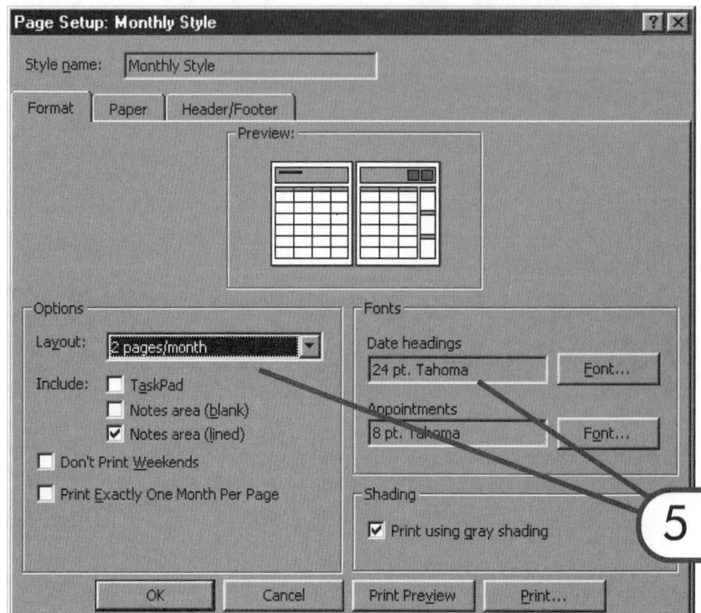

1. Open the File menu, and select Print.
2. Pick a Print style.
3. Set the dates for the Print range.
4. Click Page Setup... .
5. On the Format tab, set the Layout and Fonts options.
6. On the Paper tab, set the Margins and Orientation.
7. On the Header/Footer tab add headers and footers if wanted.
8. Click Print Preview .
9. If the display suits, click Print... to print it immediately. If you don't like it, click Page Setup... and adjust the set up.

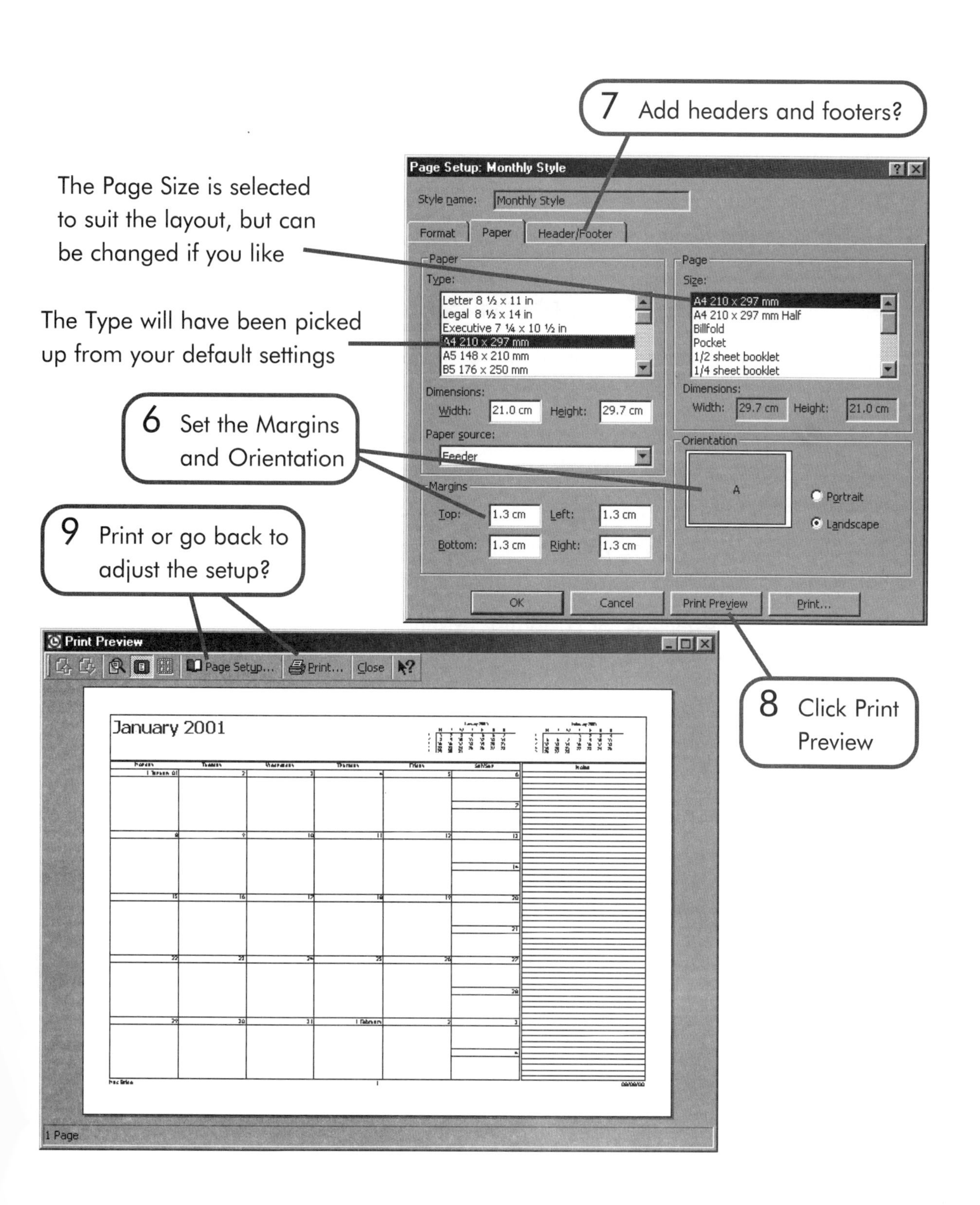
7 Add headers and footers?
The Page Size is selected to suit the layout, but can be changed if you like
The Type will have been picked up from your default settings
6 Set the Margins and Orientation
9 Print or go back to adjust the setup?
8 Click Print Preview
Page Setup: Monthly Style
Style name: Monthly Style
Format
Paper
Header/Footer
Paper
Type:
Letter 8 ½ x 11 in
Legal 8 ½ x 14 in
Executive 7 ¼ x 10 ½ in
A4 210 x 297 mm
A5 148 x 210 mm
B5 176 x 250 mm
Dimensions:
Width: 21.0 cm
Height: 29.7 cm
Paper source:
Feeder
Margins
Top: 1.3 cm
Left: 1.3 cm
Bottom: 1.3 cm
Right: 1.3 cm
Page
Size:
A4 210 x 297 mm
A4 210 x 297 mm Half
Billfold
Pocket
1/2 sheet booklet
1/4 sheet booklet
Dimensions:
Width: 29.7 cm
Height: 21.0 cm
Orientation
A
Portrait
Landscape
OK
Cancel
Print Preview
Print...
Print Preview
Page Setup...
Print...
Close
January 2001
1 Page

Summary

- Calendar has several ready-made Views, which can be selected from the View menu or the drop-down list in the toolbar.
- Go to the Options panel to define your working week and set the Reminder notice time.
- When adding appointments, you can set them to recur weekly, monthly or at any fixed interval.
- Reminders can be set for any time before an appointment.
- You can use Outlook to arrange meetings with other users on your local area network, or who are accessible by e-mail or fax.
- The Organize facility gives you another way to add categories to appointments and to change views.
- You can define new views, or customise existing ones, to suit your way of working.
- Selected days, weeks or months can be printed.

7 Tasks

Tasks

Basic steps

Use the Tasks module to keep track of your current and scheduled tasks. For each task you can record:

- The start and due dates;
- The percentage complete;
- The status and priority;
- The *Categories* – this can be just a way of keeping the same kinds of jobs together, or it can be a way of organising multi-part projects and monitoring the progress of the component tasks.

If all you need to record is the task, and perhaps its due date, you can type this directly into the Tasks display. If you want to enter more details than this, you will need to open the New Task dialog box.

❑ Quick and easy

1. Open the Tasks module.
2. Click into the 'Click here to add a new task' slot.
3. Type the Subject.
4. Click into the Due Date and set the date on the drop-down calendar.
5. Press [Enter]. The task will be added to the list.

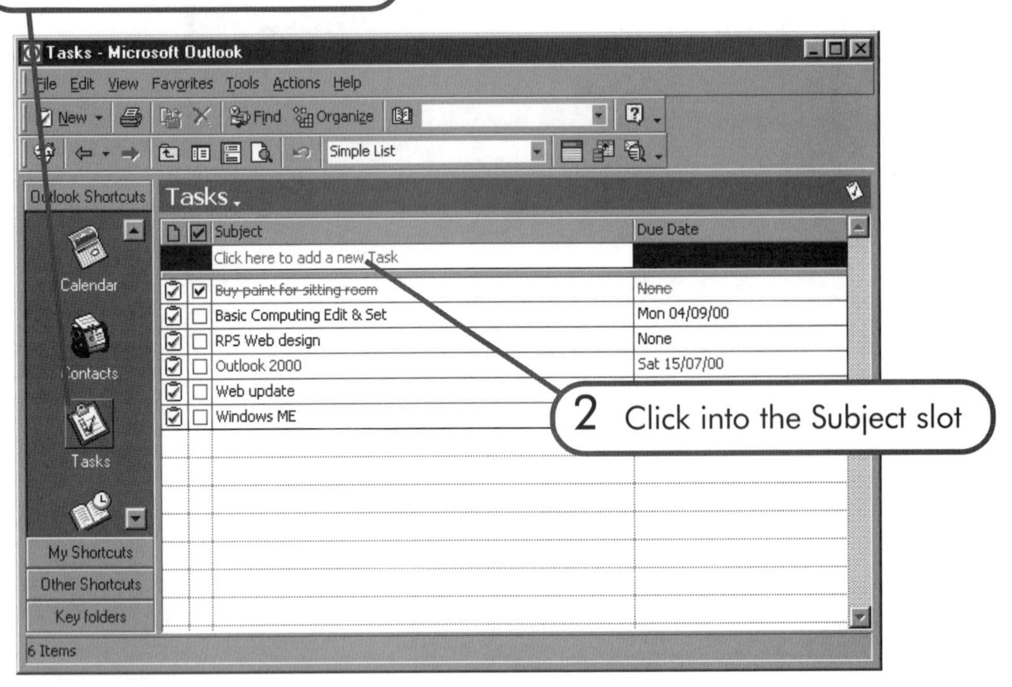

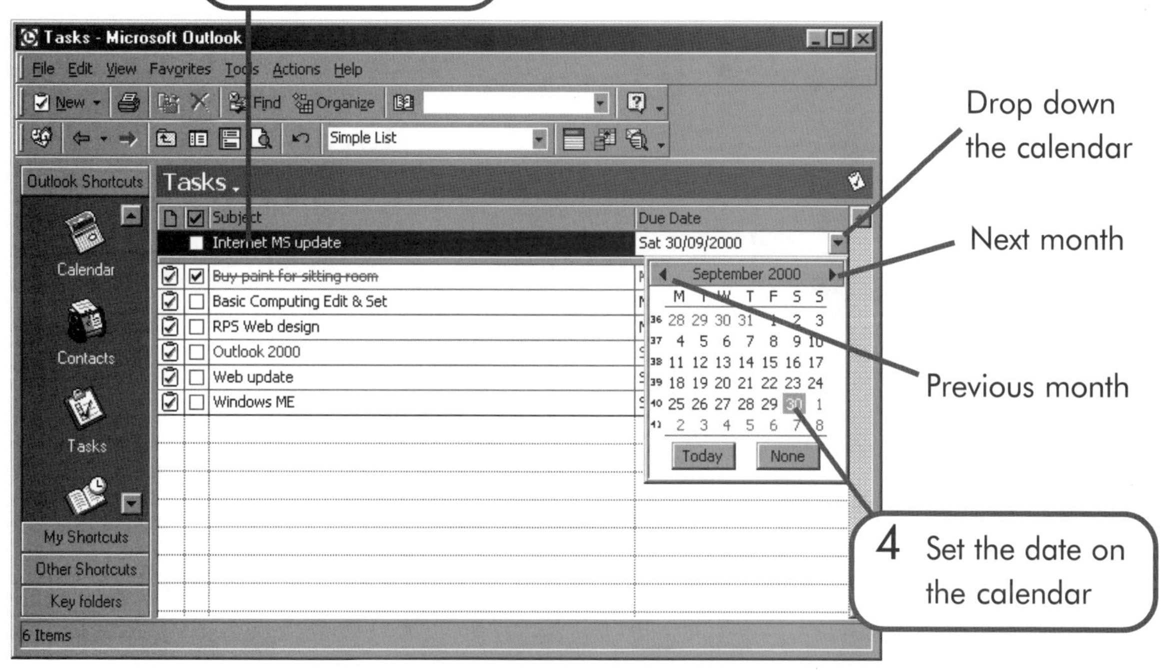
3 Type a Subject
Drop down the calendar
Next month
Previous month
4 Set the date on the calendar
Tasks - Microsoft Outlook
Tasks
Subject
Due Date
Internet MS update
Sat 30/09/2000
September 2000
Buy paint for sitting room
Basic Computing Edit & Set
RPS Web design
Outlook 2000
Web update
Windows ME
Today
None
6 Items

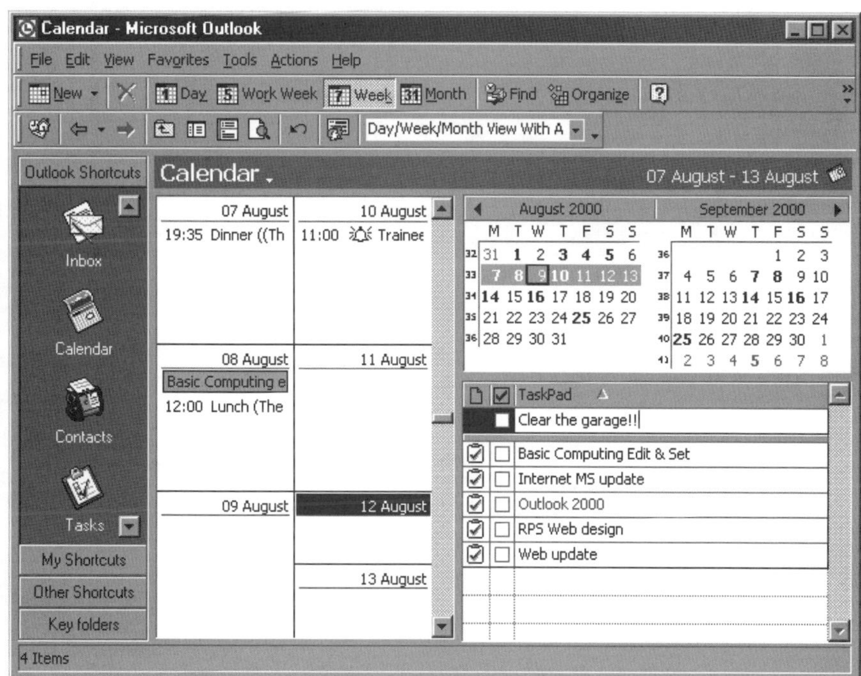
Calendar - Microsoft Outlook
Calendar
07 August - 13 August
August 2000
September 2000
TaskPad
Clear the garage!!
Basic Computing Edit & Set
Internet MS update
Outlook 2000
RPS Web design
Web update
4 Items

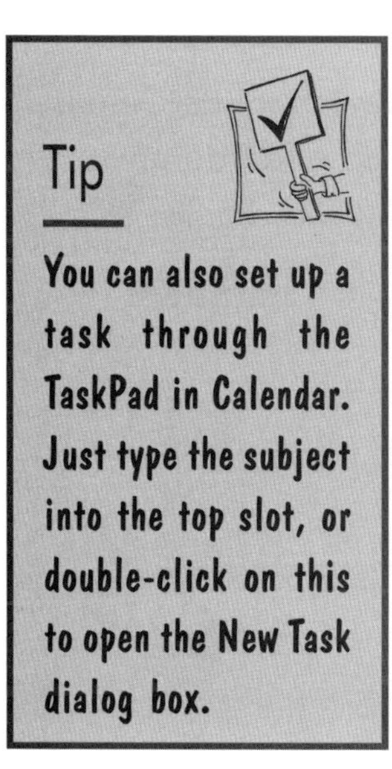
Tip
You can also set up a task through the TaskPad in Calendar. Just type the subject into the top slot, or double-click on this to open the New Task dialog box.

The New Task dialog box

Use this to enter details of a task when you first set it up, or to add or edit details of an existing task.

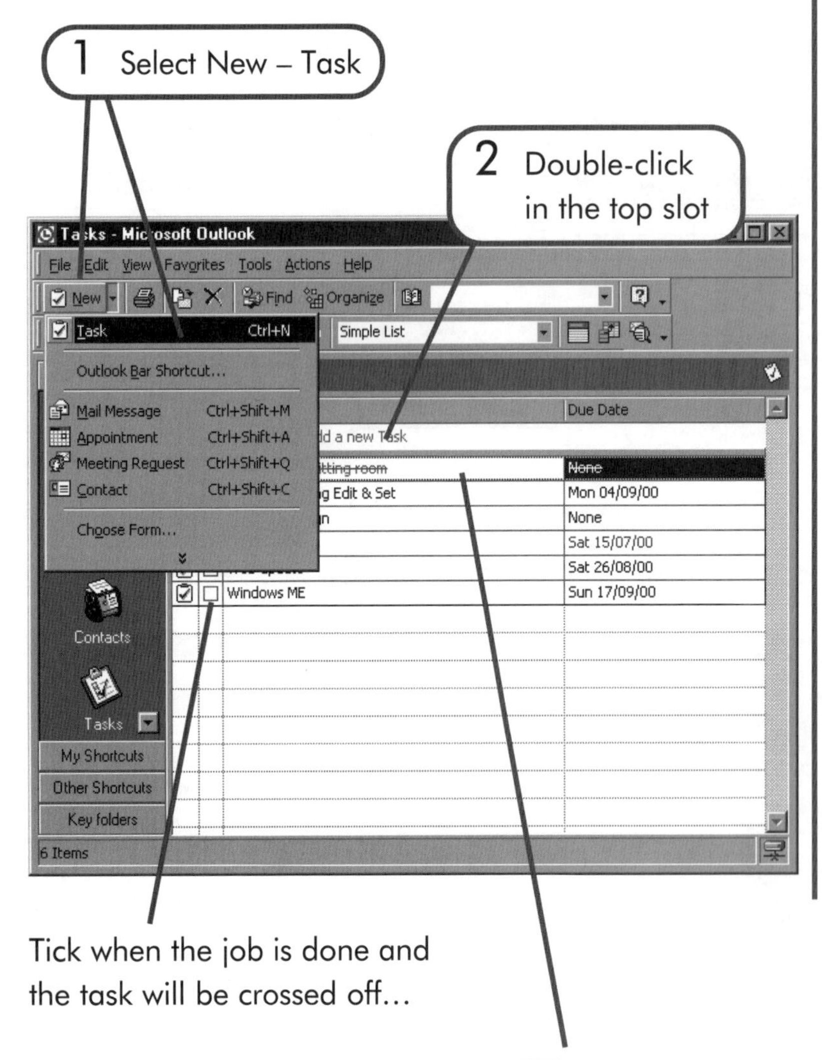

Tick when the job is done and the task will be crossed off...

... then use [X] to delete them when the records are no longer needed

Basic steps

1 Drop down the New list and select Task or click [New].

Or

2 Double-click on the 'Click here to add a new task' slot.

3 Type a Subject.

4 Set the Due date and Start date, if relevant.

5 Select the Status from the drop-down list.

6 Click [Categories...].

7 Select one or more Categories.

8 Click [OK].

9 Switch to the Details tab and add any known details.

10 Click [Save and Close].

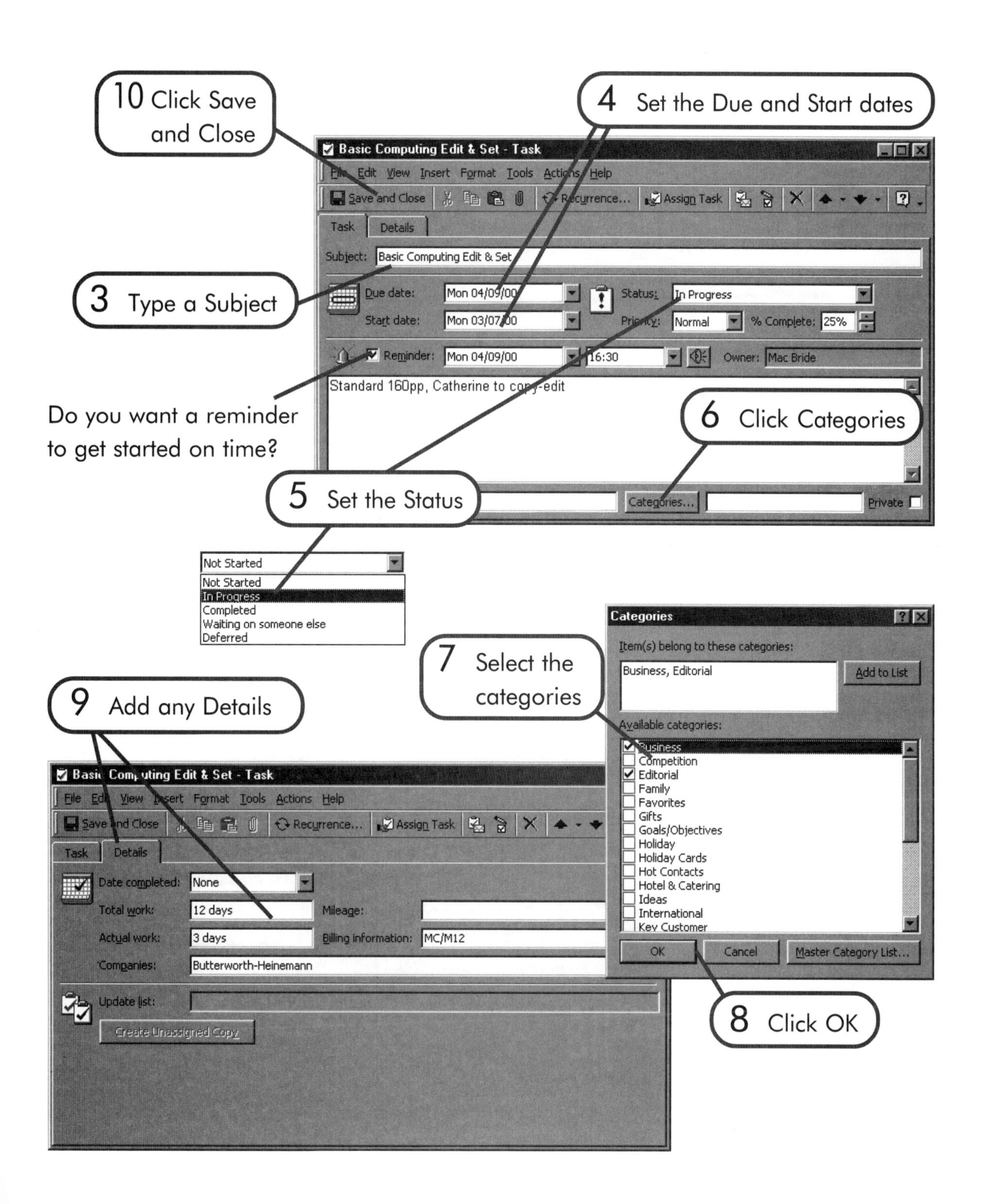
10 Click Save and Close
4 Set the Due and Start dates
Basic Computing Edit & Set - Task
File Edit View Insert Format Tools Actions Help
Save and Close
Recurrence...
Assign Task
Task
Details
Subject: Basic Computing Edit & Set
3 Type a Subject
Due date: Mon 04/09/00
Start date: Mon 03/07/00
Status: In Progress
Priority: Normal
% Complete: 25%
Reminder: Mon 04/09/00
16:30
Owner: Mac Bride
Standard 160pp, Catherine to copy-edit
Do you want a reminder to get started on time?
6 Click Categories
5 Set the Status
Categories...
Private
Not Started
Not Started
In Progress
Completed
Waiting on someone else
Deferred
Categories
Item(s) belong to these categories:
Business, Editorial
Add to List
7 Select the categories
Available categories:
Business
Competition
Editorial
Family
Favorites
Gifts
Goals/Objectives
Holiday
Holiday Cards
Hot Contacts
Hotel & Catering
Ideas
International
Key Customer
OK
Cancel
Master Category List...
9 Add any Details
Date completed: None
Total work: 12 days
Mileage:
Actual work: 3 days
Billing information: MC/M12
Companies: Butterworth-Heinemann
Update list:
Create Unassigned Copy
8 Click OK

Assigning Tasks

When Outlook talks of 'assigning tasks' it actually means setting up a task and sending the details to someone by e-mail.

If you are organising work in the Tasks area, then this offers a simple means of e-mailing, but if you are in the Inbox or Contacts, it may be just as simple to send them a message from there.

Basic steps

1. Set up the task as normal.
2. Click Assign Task.
3. Type the recipient's name or click To-> and select it from the Address Book.
4. Add a message if the Task notes alone will not be enough.
5. Click Send.

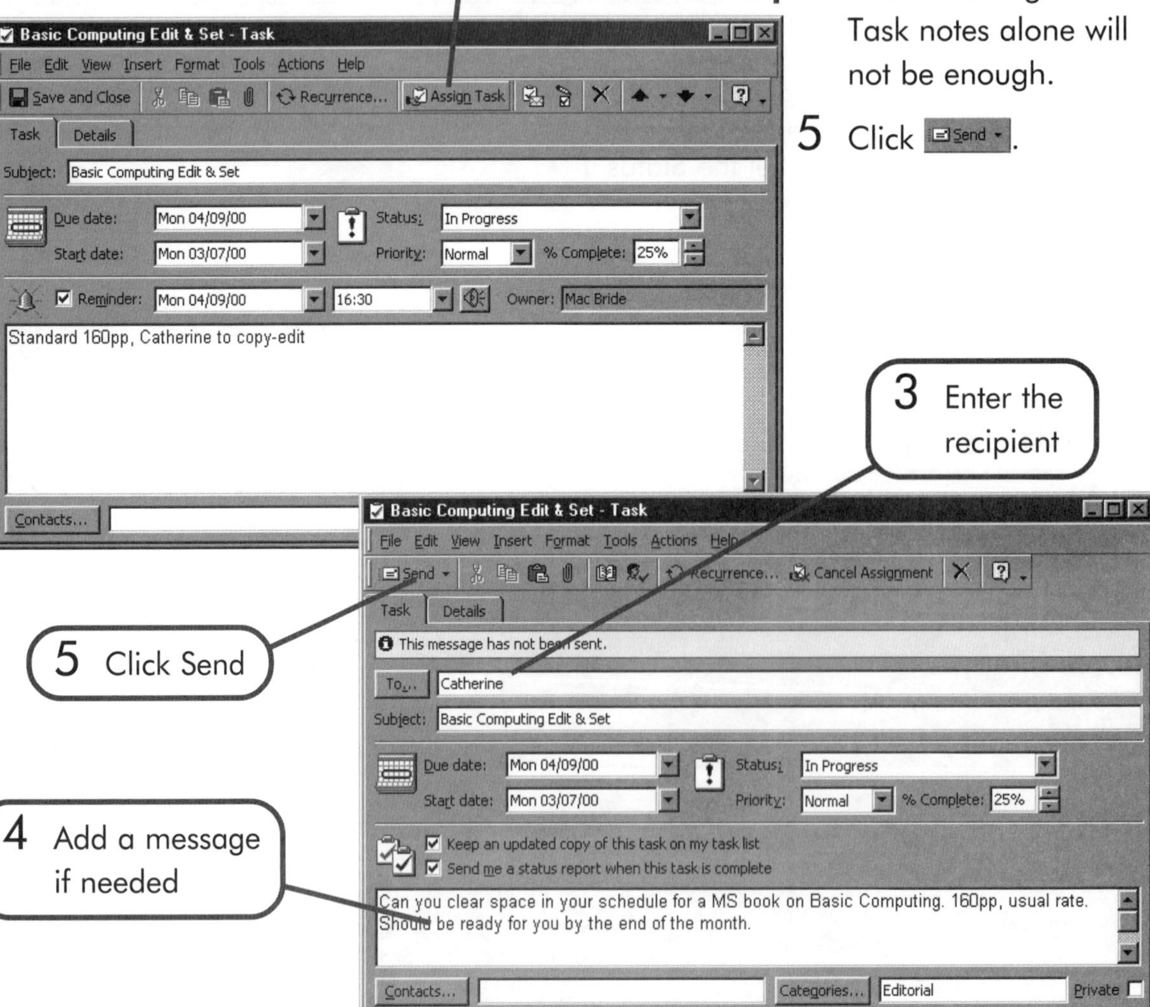

Basic steps

1. Double-click on the task to open it.
2. Open the Actions menu and select Send Status Report or click [icon].
3. Type the recipient's name or click To-> and select it from the Address Book.
4. Add a message or other notes if wanted.
5. Click Send.

Status reports

This also produces e-mail from within a Task, but in this case it sends the current details of the task to a recipient, while leaving the task itself unchanged.

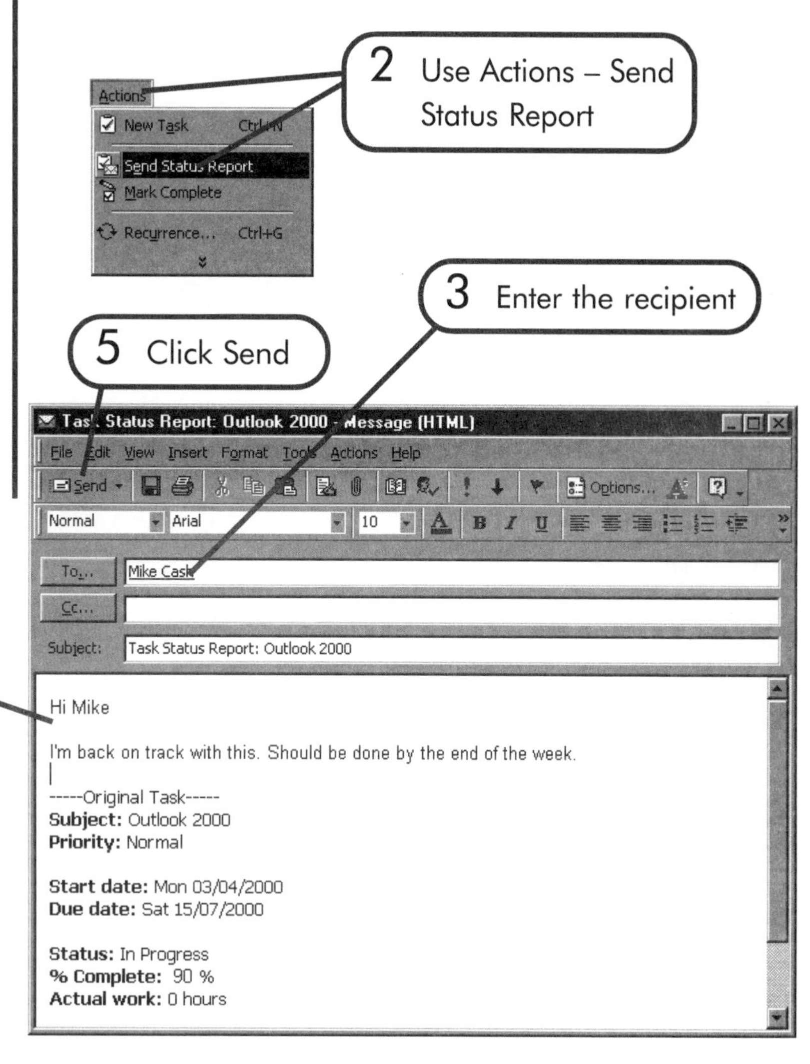

Tip

If you want to send a status report to someone who is not on e-mail, use the File – Print command – it produces a report in the same format.

Task Views...

Basic steps

Most of the pre-defined views display the same information about tasks. They vary mainly in the filters that they use to display a different selection – tasks due, overdue, done, etc.

The **By Category** view is one of the most useful – as long as you make a point of assigning tasks to categories – this is the only view with AutoPreview by default. It can be turned on for other views if required.

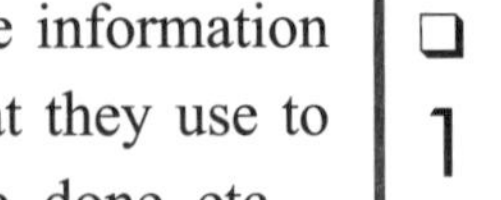

- ❑ To turn on AutoPreview

1. Select the view from the drop-down list or the View menu.
2. Open the View menu, point to Current View and select Customize Current View.
3. At the View Summary click [Other Settings...].
4. Turn on Preview all items.
5. Click [OK].

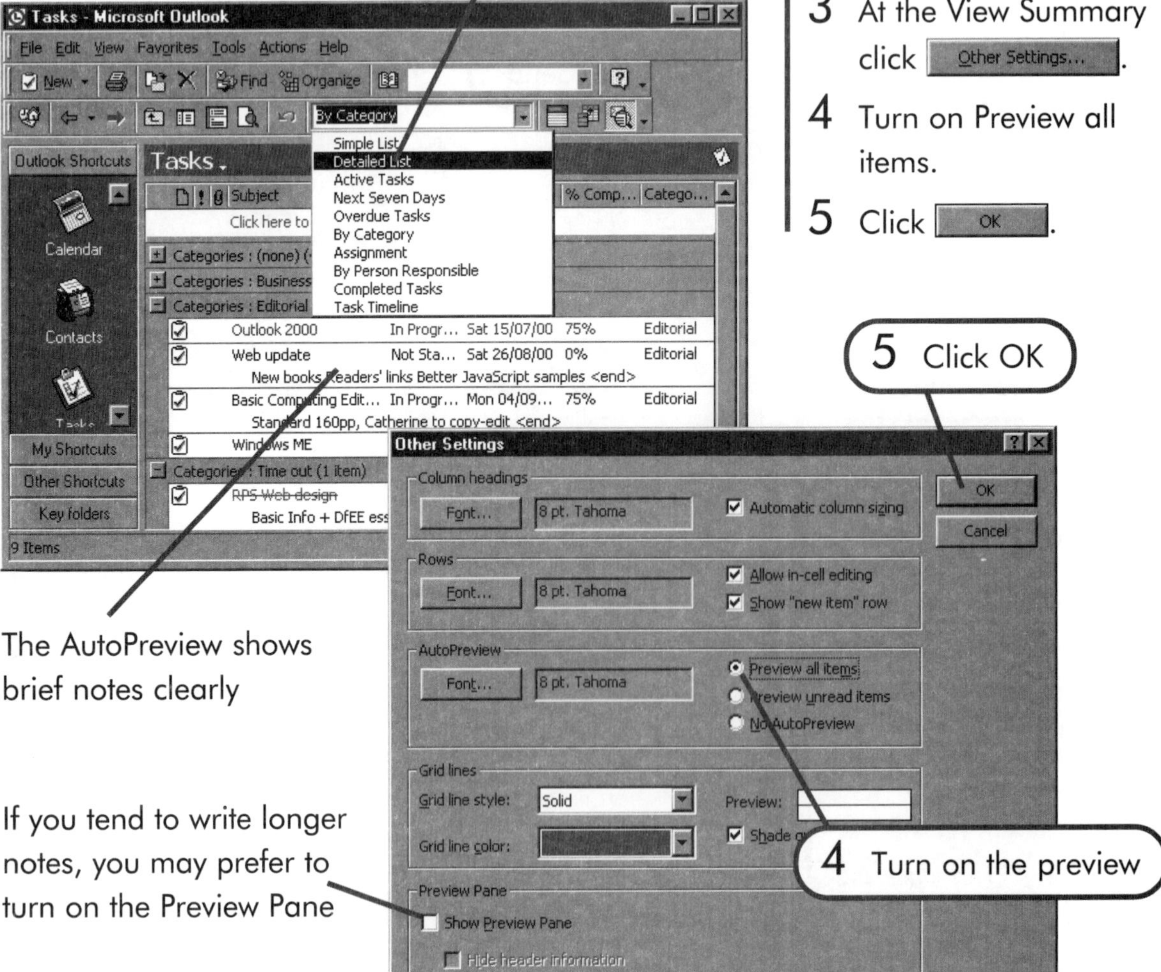

Basic steps

...and TaskPad Views

1 Go to Calendar.
2 Open the View menu, point to TaskPad View and select a view.

❑ Sorting into order

3 Click once on a heading to sort by order of that column.
4 Click again on the heading to sort into reverse order.

The TaskPad in Calendar also has a range of views – or rather, can apply a range of filters to the tasks. The filters all relate in various ways to the due date, but note that there is also an option to include undated tasks.

The tasks can be sorted into order by name or whether or not they are complete. Name order is good for finding tasks; completed/incomplete order is handy for seeing how far you have got through your chores.

1 Go to Calendar

2 Pick from the View – TaskPad View menu

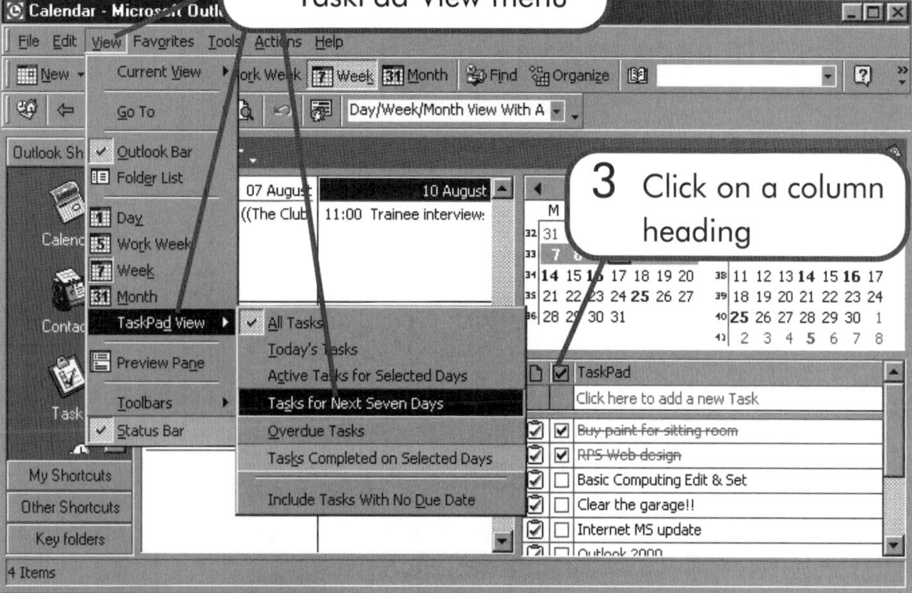

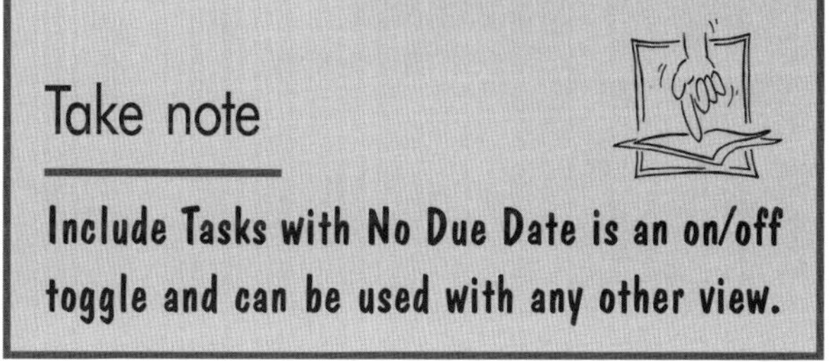

Take note

Include Tasks with No Due Date is an on/off toggle and can be used with any other view.

Summary

- ❑ The Task list can be used to schedule activities and to record progress on them. Reminders can be set for time-limited tasks.
- ❑ You can assign tasks and send Status reports to contacts by e-mail.
- ❑ The different views are mainly based on date-related filters.
- ❑ The TaskPad also has a variety of views available.
- ❑ You need never forget anything if you set Reminders for your appointments and tasks.

8 Journal and Notes

Logging activities

Basic steps

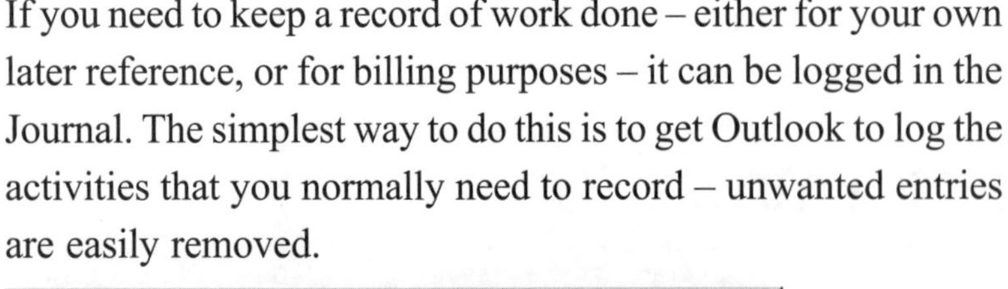

If you need to keep a record of work done – either for your own later reference, or for billing purposes – it can be logged in the Journal. The simplest way to do this is to get Outlook to log the activities that you normally need to record – unwanted entries are easily removed.

1 In any module, open the Tools menu and select Options.

2 Click Journal Options... .

3 Tick the items you want to log and the contacts you want to log them for.

4 Tick the applications for which you want to record all activity.

5 Choose what you want to happen when you double-click a journal entry.

6 Click .

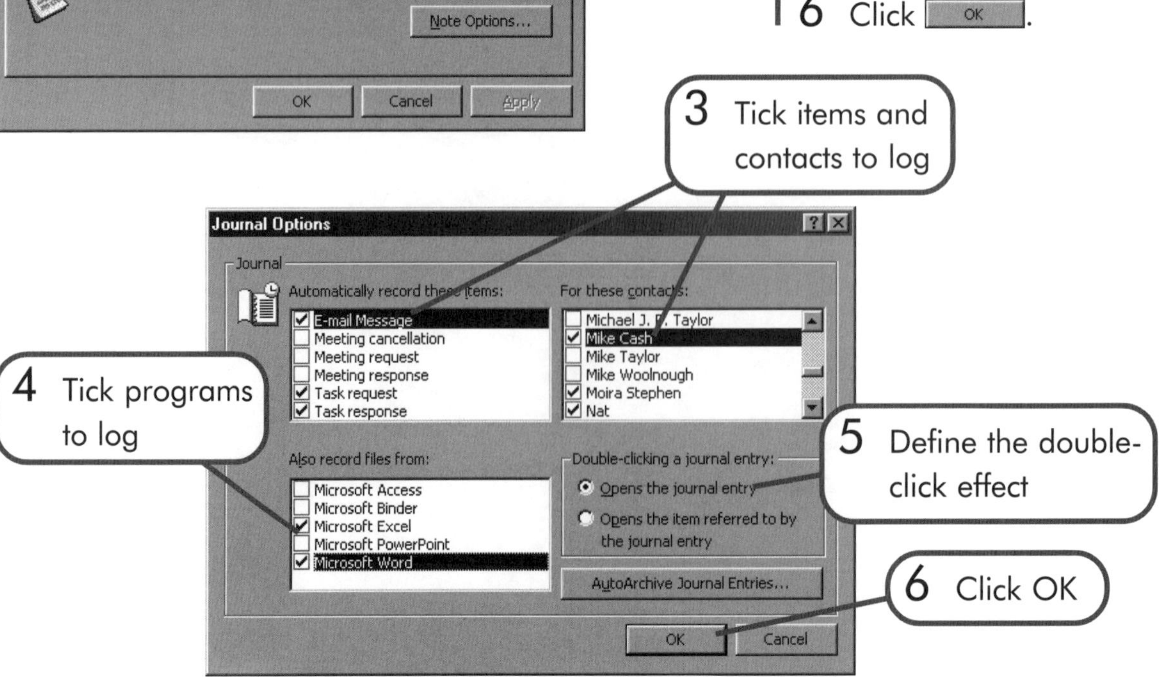

Basic steps

1. Open the Journal panel and click New.

Or

2. If you are working in any other module, use New – Journal Entry.
3. Type the Subject.
4. Select the Entry type.
5. Note the Start time and Duration.
6. Add a note if wanted.
7. Select a Category.
8. Click Save and Close.

Creating Journal entries

You can also log calls as you make them (see page 40), and, if necessary, create a Journal entry directly.

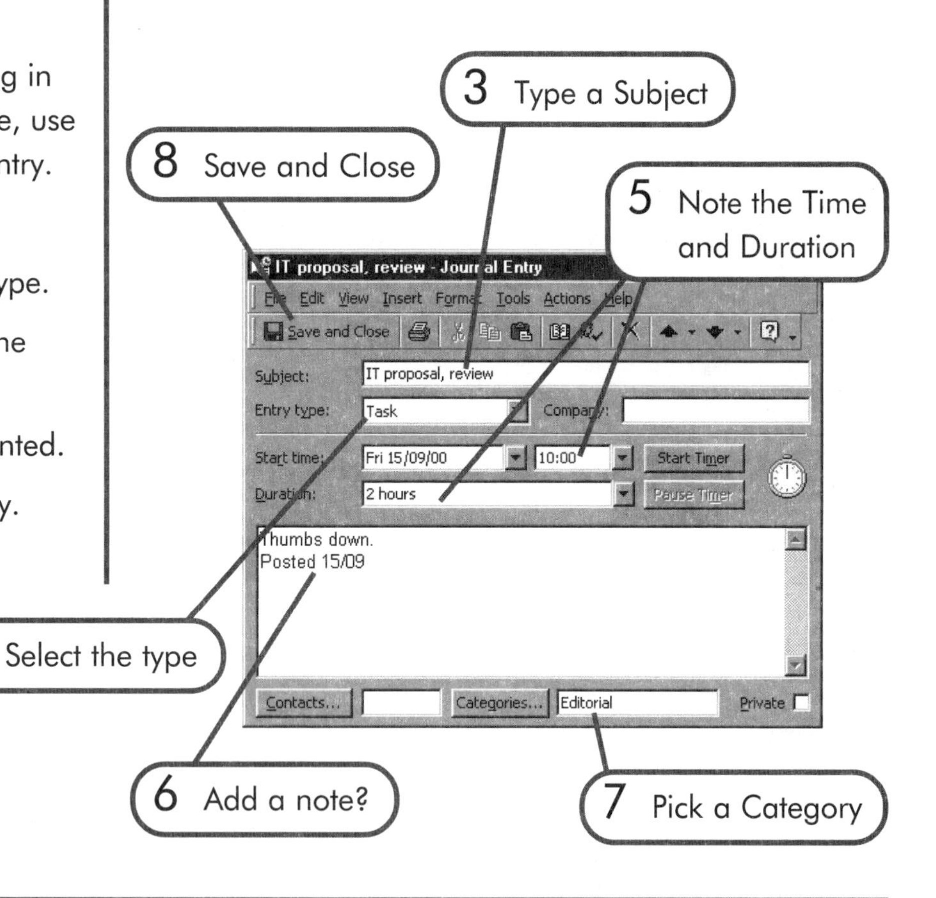

Take note

You can also log calls as you make them by ticking the Create new Journal Entry... option in the New Call dialog box. See page 40 for more on this.

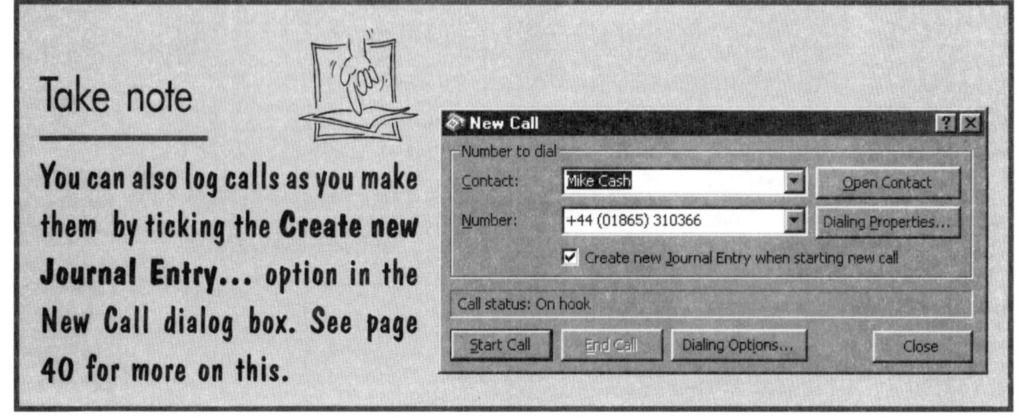

Viewing activities

Basic steps

If you want to view all your logged activities, the Journal panel is the place to do it. However, it may often be more useful to view the activities in relation to a contact, and this is best done through the Contacts panel.

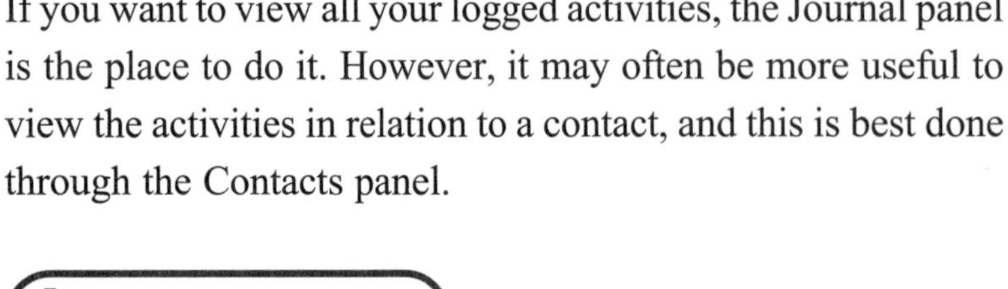

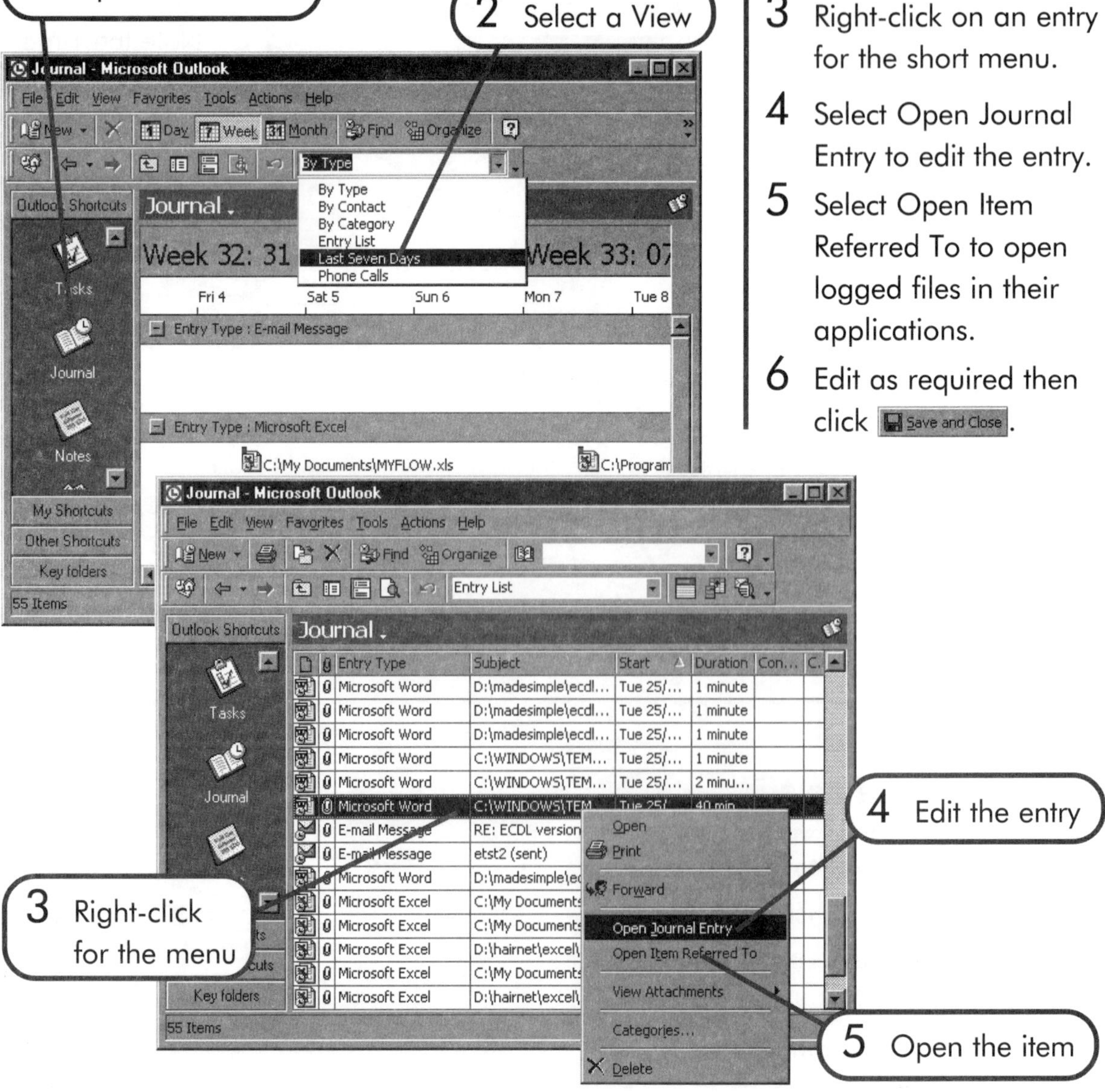

- ❑ Using the Journal

1. Open the Journal.
2. Select a View – the *Last Seven Days* view is probably the best.
3. Right-click on an entry for the short menu.
4. Select Open Journal Entry to edit the entry.
5. Select Open Item Referred To to open logged files in their applications.
6. Edit as required then click Save and Close.

❑ Contact Activities

7 Go to Contacts and select the person.

8 Switch to the Activities tab.

9 Select the type of items from the Show list.

10 Double-click on the item or right-click and select from the menu to open it – it may not have a Journal entry.

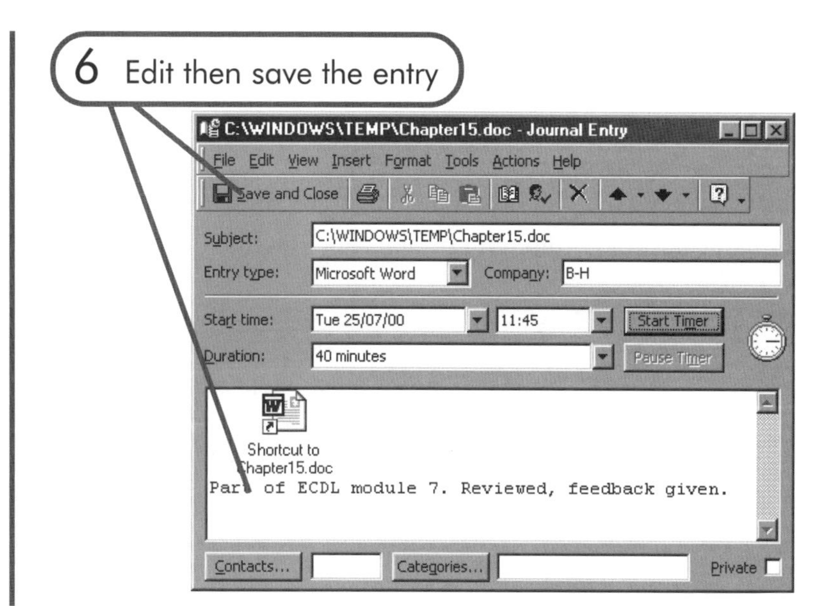

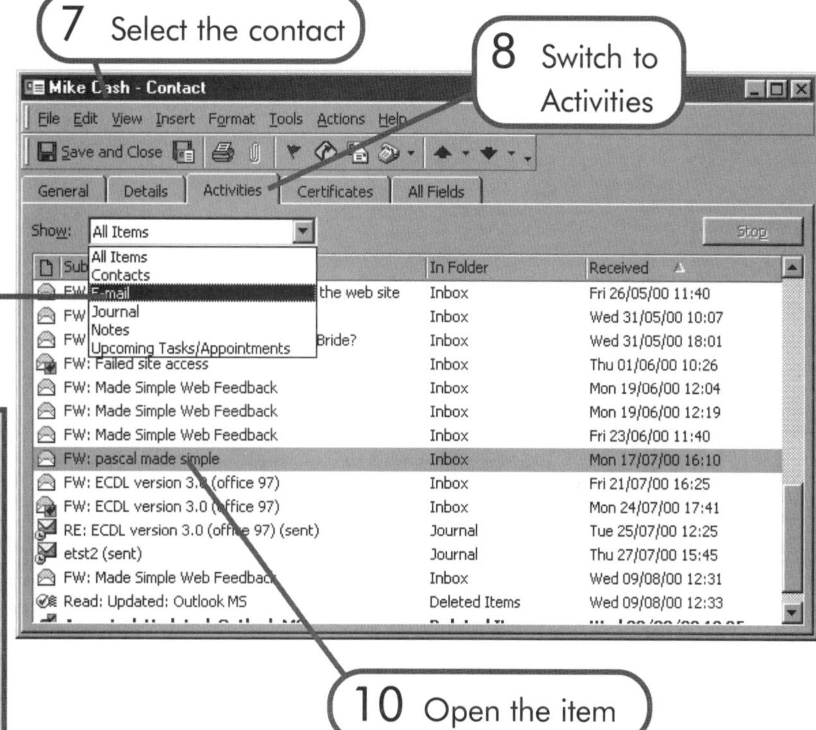

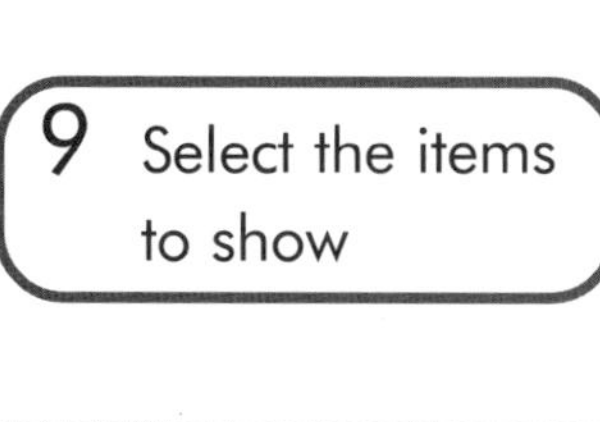

Take note

All relevant items are listed, not just the logged ones – to see just those, select Journal in the Show list.

Notes

Basic steps

If you are the sort of person who writes notes to yourself, here is an alternative to having Post-Its™ stuck to the side of your monitor. Outlook Notes save paper, and they don't drop off!

You can keep them in the Notes folder, or stick them anywhere on your desktop – though not onto documents.

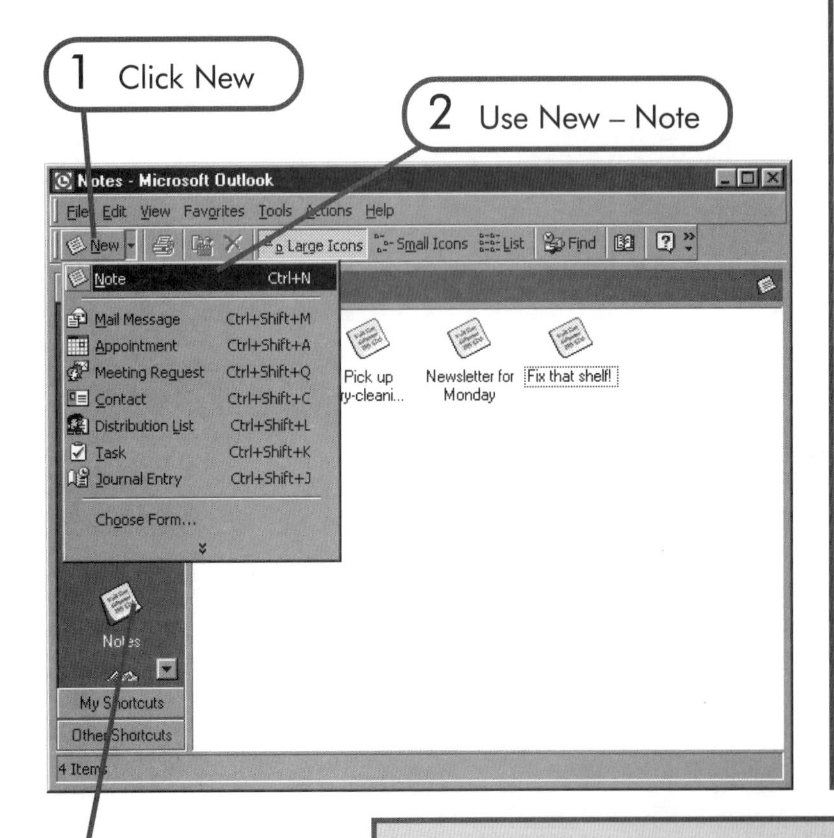

Notes shortcut

1 Open the Notes panel and click New.

Or

2 In any module, open the New menu and select Note.

3 Type your note – if you put a title in the top line, it will stand out more in the folder.

4 Drag the note onto the Desktop, if wanted.

5 Click X to close the note – it will be saved.

- To recolour a note

6 Right-click on the note, point to Color and pick a new colour.

- To delete a note

7 Select the note, and click X.

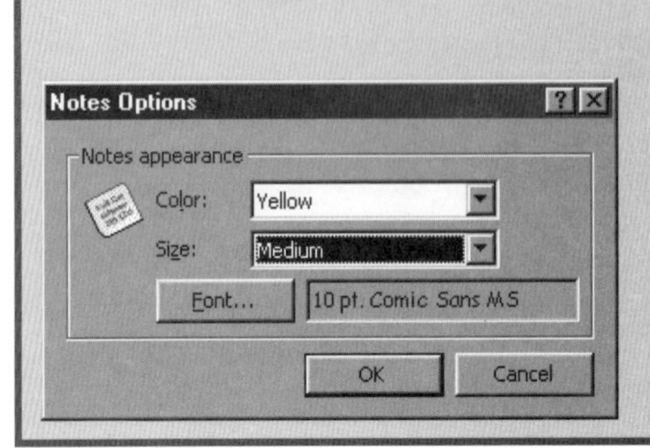

Tip

You can redefine the appearance in the Notes Options dialog box – reach it from the Preferences panel.

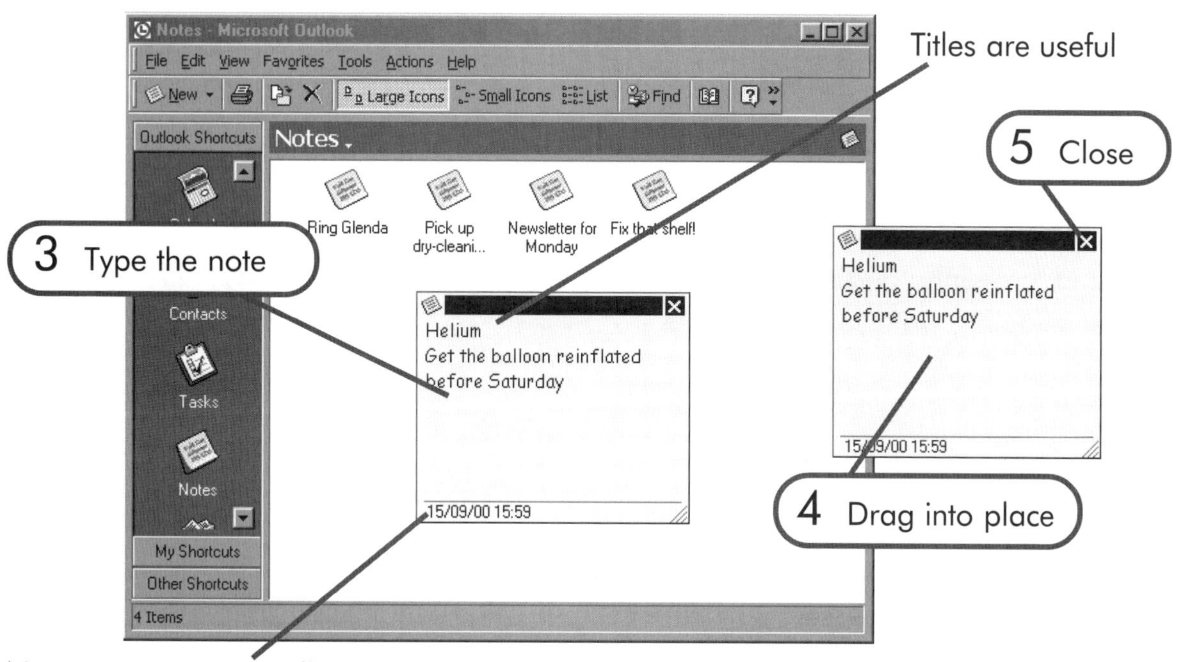

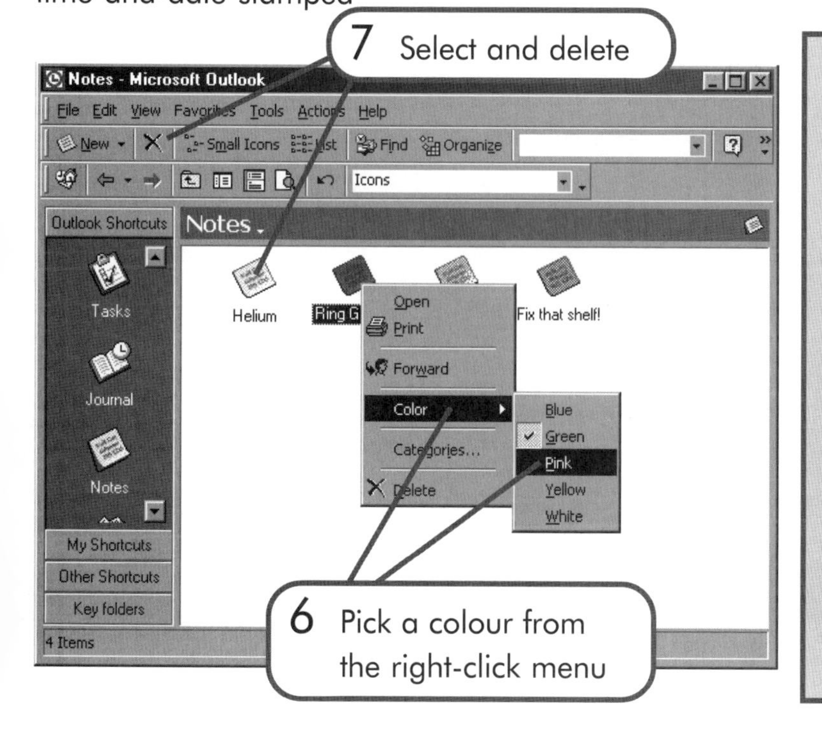

Take note

If you drag an open note onto the Desktop, it behaves like an application window, but cannot be minimised. When you close it, it disappears back into Outlook.

If you drag a notes icon onto the Desktop, it can be opened and closed as required, but stays there until deleted.

Summary

- The Journal can log your activities automatically, and entries can also be made at any time.
- Logged activities can be viewed through the Journal or through the Activity panels in Contacts.
- If you need to keep a bit of information close at hand, or want a persistent reminder of a chore that needs doing, write yourself a Note.

Index